Differential Diagnosis
in Pediatric Neurology

JORGE C. LAGOS, M.D.

Associate Professor of Pediatrics and Neurology, University of Oklahoma School of Medicine; Pediatric Neurologist, Children's Memorial Hospital, Oklahoma City

LITTLE, BROWN AND COMPANY · BOSTON

Differential Diagnosis
in Pediatric Neurology

To

Heidi, Christine, and David

Preface

IN ADDITION to the classic neurologic disorders of infancy and childhood such as cerebral palsy, seizures, and degenerative diseases of the nervous system, the field of pediatric neurology has expanded in recent years to include a large number of uncommon inborn errors of metabolism that may affect the nervous system, a growing number of rare chromosomal abnormalities, and the many problems relating to specific learning disabilities and other disorders.

Instead of the traditional textbook sections describing diseases by systems or etiology, the chapters in this book individually discuss 19 of the most common neurologic presenting complaints or clinical situations encountered in the practice of pediatrics. Since many diseases of the central and peripheral nervous systems may initially manifest in a similar manner, it is quite obvious that this type of approach to differential diagnosis presents a formidable problem of repetition and overlapping. An attempt has been made to keep this difficulty to a minimum.

The main purpose of this book is to provide medical students and physicians with a simple classification, as well as a concise description, of the main diagnostic possibilities that should come to mind when confronting a child with a specific complaint. Several appendixes at the end of the book deal with such additional subjects as the emergency treatment of cerebral edema, status epilepticus, the drugs most commonly used in pediatric neurology, and the milestones of psychomotor development.

Differential Diagnosis in Pediatric Neurology is not intended to be a reference textbook and therefore is not recommended for the neurologist or pediatric neurologist who, of necessity, is well acquainted with the large number of diseases of the nervous system of infancy and childhood. It is meant for medical students, residents in pediatrics, pediatric neurology, neurology, and neurosurgery, as well as for pediatricians and the busy family physician whose practice deals in great part with children.

Because of the practical nature of this book most of the references are either to comprehensive clinical reviews of selected topics or to the original description of a particular clinicopathologic entity.

I am indebted to J. R. Seely, M.D., Director of the Children's Memorial Hospital Clinical Research Center (supported by a grant from the National Institutes of Health), for most of the case material included in the chapter on chromosomal abnormalities and to H. D. Riley, Jr., M.D., Director of the Clinical Study for Birth Defects (supported by a grant from the National Foundation) where some of the photographs of patients with congenital malformations were taken.

I wish to express my appreciation to Miss Rebecca Corvin for her unlimited patience in the typing of the manuscript.

J. C. L.

Oklahoma City

Contents

Differential Diagnosis
in Pediatric Neurology

1
Flaccid Weakness of Sudden Onset

THE ACUTE ONSET of flaccid paralysis in a previously healthy child is a dramatic and not unusual occurrence. The clinical picture is one of a rapidly evolving disturbance, completely incapacitating the child. It is imperative that the physician evaluate the situation rapidly and take appropriate measures, being fully aware that fatal complications, especially respiratory paralysis, may occur. Death may ensue, the illness may be prolonged, or the patient may be left with neurologic sequelae if the correct diagnosis is not made initially.

POLYRADICULONEUROPATHY (GUILLAIN-BARRÉ SYNDROME)

The most common form of neuropathy affecting children is polyradiculoneuropathy. It is characterized by the acute onset of flaccid paralysis, absence of muscle stretch reflexes, variable sensory changes, and elevation of the protein of the cerebrospinal fluid (CSF) without pleocytosis. Pathologically, there is edema and cellular infiltration of the nerve roots, sensory ganglia, and peripheral nerves, with a variable degree of degeneration of the nerve fibers. The incidence of polyradiculoneuropathy appears to be increasing, and it is now recognized to be more common in childhood than was originally thought. The disease occurs in all age groups, with a peak in the first and the sixth decade. In childhood it is most common in the age group 5 to 9 but has been reported as early as 6 months of age.

A frequent finding is a history of an acute illness preceding the onset of neurologic symptoms by several days to three or four weeks. Some of the diseases which have been associated or followed by polyradiculoneuropathy are listed below. In children the preceding illness is usually

Parts of this chapter are reprinted from *Southern Medical Journal* with permission of the Southern Medical Association.

a mild to moderately severe respiratory infection, gastroenteritis, or one of the common exanthems. After complete recovery from that illness,

PRECEDING AND CONCOMITANT ILLNESSES IN POLYRADICULONEUROPATHY
(Guillain-Barré Syndrome)

Upper respiratory tract infections (50–60 percent)
Gastroenteritis
Smallpox vaccination
Japanese B vaccine
Tetanus toxoid immunization
Rabies immunization
Measles

Hepatitis
Infectious mononucleosis
Diphtheria
Diabetes
Certain surgical procedures
Inflamed skin ulcers
Uveoparotid fever
Rheumatic endocarditis, etc.

the child develops signs of disease of the peripheral nervous system (Fig. 1-1). These frequently are paresthesias and numbness or pain in the distal parts of the extremities. Weakness soon becomes a prominent feature and may progress in a matter of hours to complete flaccid paralysis. The paralysis is almost always symmetrical, bilateral, and ascending. However, in some instances the process may be reversed, with the upper extremities being involved first. Sensory loss is quite variable and has been a source of much discussion. It is well known that an accurate

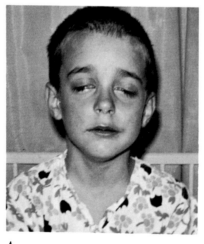 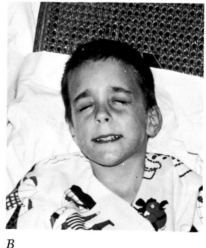

A   B

Fig. 1-1.   A, 4-year-old boy with polyradiculoneuropathy. Physical findings were moderate weakness of the muscles of the extremities, paresthesias, and loss of vibration and position sense in the lower extremities. Expressionless face and inability to close eyes well at onset of disease. B, 3 weeks later there is marked improvement of facial diplegia.

sensory examination is difficult to perform and not always reliable in younger children. It is probable that because of these factors the degree of sensory loss has been underestimated. Muscle stretch reflexes are always decreased or absent according to the degree of muscle weakness.

The cranial nerves are involved in about 40 percent of the cases. The glossopharyngeal, vagus, and facial nerves are the most commonly affected; there are difficulties in swallowing, slurred speech, and facial diplegia. In 25 percent of the cases the muscles of respiration are involved. An elevated blood pressure is not unusual and is probably due to involvement of the autonomic nervous system.

Examination of the CSF usually shows the classic albuminocytologic dissociation with an elevation of protein without pleocytosis. The CSF findings depend to a great extent on the time in the course of the illness at which the examination is performed. In most cases only a few cells are found, all of which are lymphocytes. The protein levels may often be within normal limits during the first week of the disease but afterward are usually elevated above 100 mg./100 ml.

Stabilization in the degree of muscle weakness appears after a few hours or days. Complete recovery occurs in about 75 percent of patients within a few months up to 2 or 3 years. It has been estimated that the regeneration of nerve fibers proceeds at a rate of 1 mm. per day. With good nursing care, antibiotics, and modern methods of assisted respiration, the mortality rate of polyradiculoneuropathy has decreased from 30 percent to about 5 percent. Steroid therapy does not appear to influence the length or severity of the disease, and severe intestinal hemorrhage, osteoporosis, and other problems may represent serious complications of this form of therapy. Passive exercises as well as the maintenance of physiologic positioning of joints are indicated during the initial stages of the disease. When muscle strength begins to return, a more active program of physiotherapy should be instituted.

POLIOMYELITIS

Poliomyelitis formerly was the most important cause of flaccid paralysis of acute onset in children. Although it has disappeared as an epidemic disease, occasional cases still occur, particularly in infants and young children.

Prodromal symptoms are seen in the majority of cases of poliomyelitis. These symptoms—fever, headache, vomiting, and diarrhea—are followed in 1 to 3 days by symptoms related to the central nervous system. Headache, back pain, muscle tenderness, irritability or drowsiness, and a temperature of 100° to 103°F are usually present. A stiff neck, head drop, and positive Kernig and Brudzinski signs are common. Transient twitchings of muscles and hyperreflexia may be encountered initially, followed by weakness and loss of muscle stretch reflexes. The paralysis is characteristically asymmetrical in distribution, with some groups of muscles more involved than others. Sensory examination is normal.

The CSF in poliomyelitis is clear, with a small percentage of instances having a slight increase in pressure. There is usually an increase in the number of cells from 25 to 1000, with an average of about 100/cu. mm. When the paralysis appears, which is usually at the time the diagnosis is made, the predominant cells are lymphocytes. The sugar and chlorides are usually normal and the protein is either normal or moderately elevated.

TICK PARALYSIS

Certain ticks of the species *Dermacentor andersoni* and *D. variabilis* elaborate a toxin that can produce an acute ascending flaccid paralysis that can end fatally if the tick is not removed before involvement of the muscles of respiration occurs. The disease is worldwide and is endemic in the northwestern part of the United States. *D. andersoni* is found primarily in the Rocky Mountain states and north into Canada, and *D. variabilis* in the southeastern United States. However, every physician should be aware of its manifestations, since symptoms usually do not begin until 5 to 10 days after the female tick attaches itself, by which time a traveler could be far away from an endemic area by the time the disease becomes evident.

Tick paralysis occurs in the spring and summer months when ticks are most active. It is most often seen in children, primarily in girls, probably because a tick easily can go unnoticed in the long hair of a little girl. The onset of the disease is rapid. Frequently a child will arise in the morning somewhat irritable, anorexic, and complaining of slight pain or paresthesias in the extremities. Limb and gait ataxia are probably the earliest signs of tick paralysis. Within 12 to 36 hours there is a complete, symmetric, flaccid paralysis which has ascended from the lower to the upper extremities and will eventually involve the bulbar musculature unless the tick is removed. Muscle stretch reflexes are absent. Sensory changes may or may not be present but as a general rule they are not very prominent. Blood studies as well as examination of the CSF show no abnormalities.

Mortality from tick paralysis is estimated to be about 12 percent, and thus it behooves physicians to remember this entity in the presence of a child with sudden onset of incoordination, ataxia, or muscle weakness.

Removal of the tick, which is the only treatment of tick paralysis, brings a rapid halt to the process, the paralysis disappearing as a rule in a descending order. Removal is accomplished by (1) application of ether or gasoline to the head of the tick; (2) placing heat from a lighted cigarette or match over the tick; (3) covering the tick with petrolatum; or (4) surgical incision of the skin and subcutaneous tissue if other measures fail to detach the tick.

FAMILIAL PERIODIC PARALYSIS

This is a group of diseases characterized by recurrent, self-limited episodes of flaccid muscle weakness of varying severity and duration. Between episodes of paralysis patients are asymptomatic. The attacks are painless and occur when the patient is at rest. During the post-paralytic period soreness of muscles is a frequent complaint. During an attack muscle stretch reflexes are hypoactive or absent, according to the severity of weakness. Patients suffering from periodic paralysis have a well-developed musculature; a few cases have been reported in which muscle weakness and atrophy occurred after repeated episodes over a period of many years. The electromyogram is normal between attacks; while the patient is paralyzed it may show a markedly decreased number of motor-unit potentials or complete electrical silence, according to the degree of muscle weakness. Nerve-conduction velocity is normal between episodes and may be normal during an attack as long as a contraction can be evoked from stimulated muscles.

All forms of the disease are familial and are genetically dominant. Cold weather increases the frequency of attacks in all forms of periodic paralysis. Classically they have been divided into two main forms according to precipitating factors and the level of serum potassium at the time of the attack (hypokalemic and hyperkalemic). In recent years two other much less common varieties have been recognized, a sodium-responsive paralysis and a periodic paralysis with cardiac arrhythmias. Serum potassium levels are normal in these two forms.

Hypokalemic Periodic Paralysis

Patients with periodic paralysis associated with low serum potassium levels manifest their first symptoms in the first two decades of life. The attacks become less frequent with advancing age. Complete quadriplegia may occur during an episode; respiratory and facial muscles are usually spared. Death may occur from respiratory paralysis or cardiac failure. The attacks are usually precipitated by a meal rich in carbohydrates and tend to manifest themselves after a period of rest or in the early hours of the morning or on awakening. The duration of the attacks is from a few hours to one or two days, and complete recovery takes place within a few hours after the onset of clinical improvement.

The frequency of the attacks varies from one patient to the other; generally they do not occur more often than once a month. Hypokalemic periodic paralysis can be precipitated by the administration of glucose, a combination of glucose and insulin, sodium-retaining hormones, or epinephrine. A diagnosis can be made by the family history, the sudden onset of paralysis of the skeletal muscles with sparing of the bulbar musculature, the absence of sensory findings, clear mentation, and low serum levels of potassium, usually in the range of 1 to 2 mEq./L. Changes in the electrocardiogram parallel the fall in serum potassium. Potassium salts given orally appear to shorten the duration of an attack. A reduced carbohydrate intake, a diet low in sodium, or the daily administration of potassium salts has been suggested as prophylactic measures in this type of periodic paralysis.

Hyperkalemic Periodic Paralysis

Hyperkalemic periodic paralysis has its onset usually in early childhood. The attacks are less severe than in the hypokalemic form and tend to occur during the daytime. Weakness of facial muscles and myotonia are common. The frequency of attacks varies from one a day to one a week and as a rule do not last more than 1 or 2 hours. Precipitating factors are exercise, rest, and the ingestion of potassium-rich foods. Any of the substances (glucose, epinephrine, or calcium gluconate) which promote rapid lowering of serum potassium may terminate an attack. A high-sodium diet, frequent intake of carbohydrates, or the administration of dextroamphetamine and chlorothiazide may be of value in the prophylaxis of this form of periodic paralysis.

A sodium-responsive and a periodic paralysis associated with cardiac arrhythmia have also been reported. They are much less common than other forms. Sodium-responsive periodic paralysis has its onset between 2 and 10 years of age; the attacks are severe, with quadriplegia and involvement of the bulbar musculature, and may last from two to three weeks. The oral or intravenous administration of sodium chloride relieves symptoms in most cases. A few patients with periodic paralysis and cardiac arrhythmia are on record. In this variety the attacks of paralysis begin during the first or second decade, occur in general at monthly intervals, are of moderate severity, and last from one to two days. Cardiac arrhythmias in reported cases have varied from ectopic beats to repeated episodes of complete heart block.

PAROXYSMAL PARALYTIC MYOGLOBINURIA

Paroxysmal paralytic myoglobinuria is characterized by recurrent attacks of muscle cramps, muscle weakness, and excretion of myoglobin in the urine. The first episode usually occurs before age 20 and most patients have fewer than three attacks. More males are affected than females. In some patients the attacks are precipitated by physical exercise. The duration and severity of the muscle weakness is variable. A few patients have died because of renal failure.

ACUTE INTERMITTENT PORPHYRIA

Acute intermittent porphyria (AIP) may cause a rapidly progressing peripheral neuropathy and consequently a flaccid paralysis of acute onset. A typical attack of AIP is characterized by abdominal pain, disturbances of consciousness or mentation, seizures, and signs and symptoms of peripheral neuropathy. The initial episode often occurs in early adolescence but rarely before puberty, although the metabolic defect has been shown to be present since birth. Mental changes are frequently present to the point of psychosis, and generalized convulsions may occur. Oculomotor palsies are uncommon.

The urine shows a burgundy-red or amber color and, if clear, on exposure to light gives a characteristic port-wine color. Examination of the CSF may show a slight increase in protein. The principal metabolic abnormality in acute intermittent porphyria is the excretion of porphyrin precursors (delta-aminolevulinic acid and porphobilinogen) and not the excretion of porphyrins. The latter compounds may form after fresh urine has been exposed to light or to the presence of oxidizing substances. Patients with latent porphyria also demonstrate elevated urinary values of delta-aminolevulinic acid (ALA) and porphobilinogen (PBG). Acute attacks or exacerbations of AIP may be precipitated by a variety of drugs (Sedormid, barbiturates, sulfonamides, estrogens). Death may occur as a result of respiratory paralysis. Mortality rate has been approximately 50 percent in the cases reported. Treatment is entirely symptomatic. Barbiturates should be avoided. Chlorpromazine or morphine can be given to alleviate abdominal or severe pain in the extremities. BAL (dimercaprol) and calcium disodium versenate may be of some value in the treatment of this condition.

EPIDURAL ABSCESS

This is a rare lesion characterized by fever, headache, back pain, weakness in the lower extremities, and finally complete flaccid paraplegia if thrombosis of spinal vessels occurs. The majority of these abscesses result from staphylococci carried by the bloodstream from distant sites of infection. According to some authors an abscess is almost always associated with osteomyelitis of an adjacent vertebra. Symptoms begin days or weeks after the primary infection, which not infrequently may have passed unnoticed. The first symptoms are back pain with local spinal tenderness, followed by stiffness of the neck, malaise, fever, and headache. If the abscess remains untreated at this stage, sudden paralysis may occur in a matter of a few days. There is flaccid paraplegia with complete loss of sensation below the level of the lesion, along with paralysis of the bladder or rectum. Deep and superficial reflexes are absent. Laboratory tests show leukocytosis, and blood cultures are often positive. Lumbar puncture often demonstrates a complete or almost complete subarachnoid block. There may be a slight to moderate pleocytosis, with an increase in the protein levels from 100 to 1500 mg. per 100 ml. The CSF sugar is normal and cultures are sterile. Pus may be aspirated accidentally from the epidural space, and care must be taken not to deposit organisms into the subarachnoid space. The treatment of an epidural abscess is surgical (laminectomy and drainage). The degree of functional recovery will depend on the damage to the cord already present at the time of operation (simple compression or softening of the cord due to thrombosed vessels).

NEUROMYELITIS OPTICA

Acute transverse myelitis is a rare disease which has been described in all age groups including infancy. Neuromyelitis optica (Devic's disease) refers to a demyelinating transverse myelitis preceded, followed, or accompanied by optic neuritis. At the onset there is flaccid paralysis, absence of muscle stretch reflexes, a sensory level, and variable degree of bladder and bowel involvement. Optic or retrobulbar neuritis produces sudden loss of vision with a central scotoma. As in multiple sclerosis, examination of the CSF shows moderate pleocytosis and an elevated protein especially in the gamma globulin fraction. If swelling of the spinal cord is severe, a blockage may be demonstrated by manometry. The initial flaccid paralysis is replaced within days or weeks by a spastic weakness with increased muscle stretch and pathologic reflexes.

DIPHTHERITIC POLYNEURITIS

A rather uncommon form of polyneuritis today is that due to the exotoxin of *Corynebacterium diphtheriae*. The severity of the polyneuritis appears to correlate well with the severity of the infection and the promptness in institution of therapy. The first sign of involvement of the central nervous system following diphtheria is paralysis of accommodation. Diphtheritic polyneuritis characteristically has a latent period of one week to two months following the original infection. This polyneuritis is of the mixed motor-sensory variety, with muscle weakness, decreased or absent muscle stretch reflexes and a stocking-glove sensory loss. An increase in the protein content of the CSF is a common finding. Hence, the clinical findings in this entity are somewhat similar to those of polyradiculoneuropathy. However, palatal and ciliary paralysis are rarely the initial symptoms in the Guillain-Barré syndrome. A history of preceding diphtheritic infection, the type of sensory deficit, and the possible demonstration of myocarditis, a not uncommon complication in diphtheria, are of help in the differential diagnosis.

BOTULISM

The toxin of *Clostridium botulinum* has a paralytic effect on the muscles of the limbs and also in those innervated by the cranial nerves. Botulism is a rapidly evolving afebrile illness, often presenting with abdominal pain following the ingestion of contaminated food products. Signs of involvement of the peripheral nervous system appear within the next 18 to 36 hours and are first manifested by visual disturbances due to loss of accommodation. There is mydriasis, loss of the light reflex, and diplopia; then the child will develop difficulty in swallowing and talking, and generalized weakness. The mental condition of the patient remains intact until the time of death. Examination of the CSF shows no abnormalities. The widespread paralysis seen in botulism is due to failure of transmission at the myoneural junction because of functional block in the terminal nerve fibers, which are incapable of releasing acetylcholine in quantities sufficient to evoke a contraction of muscle fibers. The mechanism by which botulinum toxin interferes with the release of acetylcholine remains unknown.

As soon as the diagnosis of botulism is suspected, polyvalent antitoxin should be administered in a dose of 50,000 units intravenously followed by daily doses of 10,000 to 20,000 units. The antitoxin only neutralizes circulating toxin and has no effect on that which has already temporarily damaged the myoneural junction. Gastric lavage, enema, or catharsis may be of value in removing residual toxin from the gastrointestinal tract. Hypotension and shock are given supportive treatment. Mechanically assisted respiration should be instituted at the first sign of weakness of the respiratory muscles.

TRAUMA

Trauma should be mentioned as an obvious cause of flaccid paralysis. For example, a fracture of the lumbosacral vertebrae can lead to a flaccid paralysis in the lower extremities with atrophy of muscle and loss of reflexes, sensation, and sphincter tone. A similar clinical picture can be seen during the period of "spinal shock" with damage to the spinal cord at higher levels.

MISCELLANEOUS CAUSES OF FLACCID PARALYSIS

1. Postictal hemiparesis (Todd's paralysis).
2. Flaccid paralysis associated with hyperchloremic acidosis and hypokalemia secondary to steatorrhea and loss of potassium by the intestine (gluten enteropathy).
3. Several drugs and vegetal poisons can give rise to a flaccid paralysis. Curare and decamethonium by blocking the action of acetylcholine at the level of the muscle end-plate first produce muscle relaxation and then total neuromuscular block. Coniine (poison-hemlock extract) also paralyzes striated muscle. A number of other substances (lead, arsenic, triorthocresyl phosphate, thallium, and mercury) may also produce a polyneuropathy which usually runs a subacute or chronic course.

COMMENT

The causes of acute flaccid paralysis in children are many. The physician should be aware of the many different diagnostic possibilities and that certain historical and physical findings can be of help in the differential diagnosis. Important clues from the history are (1) recent illnesses, exanthems, and immunization; (2) a history of similar episodes in other members of the family; (3) ingestion of contaminated food products or toxic substances; (4) exposure to ticks; and (5) trauma. Thorough physical examination, including a search for ticks, with special emphasis on the neurologic examination is important (severity, symmetry, and distribution of weakness, presence or absence of sensory changes or a sensory level, incoordination, ataxia, meningeal signs, etc.). Pertinent laboratory tests include roentgenograms of the entire spine and examination of the cerebrospinal fluid and urine, including tests for porphyrin precursors.

REFERENCES

Abbott, K. H. Tick paralysis. *Mayo Clin. Proc.* 18:39, 1943.
Klein, R., et al. Periodic paralysis with cardiac arrhythmia. *J. Pediat.* 62:371, 1963.
Klein, R. Disorders of Potassium and Magnesium Metabolism: Periodic Paralysis. In Gardner, L. I. (Ed.): *Endocrine and Genetic Diseases of Childhood.* Philadelphia: Saunders, 1969.
Lagos, J. C., and Hagood, K. W. Flaccid paralysis of acute onset in children. *Southern Med. J.* 63:451, 1970.

Lagos, J. C., and Thies, R.   Tick paralysis without muscle weakness. *Arch. Neurol.* 21:471, 1969.

Marinacci, A. A.   *Applied Electromyography.* Philadelphia: Lea & Febiger, 1968.

Markland, L. D., and Riley, H. D., Jr.   The Guillain-Barré syndrome in childhood. *Clin. Pediat.* (Phila.) 6:162, 1967.

Markovitz, M.   Acute intermittent porphyria: A report of five cases and review of the literature. *Ann. Intern. Med.* 41:1170, 1954.

Musselman, C. B., et al.   Potassium depletion paralysis associated with gluten-induced enteropathy. *Amer. J. Dis. Child.* 116:414, 1968.

Poskanzer, D. C., and Kerr, D. N. S.   A third type of periodic paralysis with normokalemia and favourable response to sodium chloride. *Amer. J. Med.* 31:328, 1961.

Streeten, D. H. P.   Periodic Paralysis. In Stanbury, J. B., Wyngaarden, J. B., and Fredrickson, D. S. (Eds.):   *The Metabolic Basis of Inherited Disease* (2nd ed.). New York: McGraw-Hill, 1966.

Weiderholt, W. C., et al.   The Landry-Guillain-Barré-Strohl syndrome or polyradiculoneuropathy: Historical review, report on 97 patients, and present concepts. *Mayo Clin. Proc.* 39:427, 1964.

2
Chronic Muscle Weakness

THE NUMBER of known diseases of which flaccid muscle weakness is the only or the most prominent clinical feature has increased considerably in the past few years. Some of these disorders can be diagnosed by simple inspection or by careful physical examination and a few relevant laboratory procedures. Others, however, can only be diagnosed by histologic examination of affected tissue (muscle or nerve).

For the sake of convenience and as an aid in the differential diagnosis of the child with flaccid muscle weakness, it is helpful to divide the nervous system into the classic anatomic subdivisions involved in the control and maintenance of tone and muscle strength. The following is a classification of muscle weakness in infancy and childhood according to the structure of the central or peripheral nervous system primarily involved by the pathologic process.

DISEASES OF THE BRAIN

Trisomy 21

One of the most constant physical findings in trisomy 21 (mongolism) is severe muscle hypotonia. When one of these babies is held in ventral suspension his legs and arms hang limply over the examiner's hand. In the supine position these patients lie in a froglike posture with the arms and legs abducted and externally rotated (Fig. 2-1). The diagnosis of trisomy 21 is in most instances not difficult to make because of the typical facies and the many well-known associated abnormalities of the eyes, skeleton, and heart.

Atonic Diplegia

Congenital atonic diplegia is a nonprogressive disease of central nervous system characterized by generalized muscle weakness (Fig. 2-2). The etiology is unknown. The legs are more involved than the arms.

13

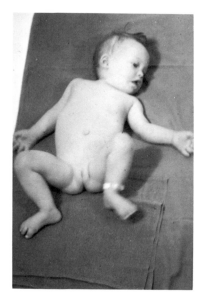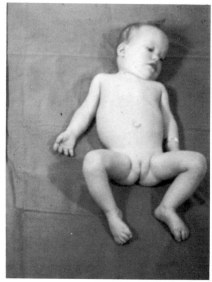

Fig. 2-1. Identical twins, 12 months old, with trisomy 21 (mongolism). Marked hypotonia, froglike posture with arms and legs abducted and externally rotated.

Muscle stretch reflexes are usually hypoactive but may be normal. Associated mental subnormality of a severe degree is almost always present. Laboratory examinations such as serum enzyme levels of glutamic oxalacetic transaminase (SGOT) and creatine phosphokinase (CPK) and the electromyogram are normal.

Congenital Choreoathetosis and Congenital Ataxia

Congenital choreoathetosis and congenital ataxia (secondary to agenesis, hypoplasia, or cerebellar microgyria) are examples of conditions that may produce marked hypotonia and weakness during the first year of life. The true nature of the process is usually not recognized until the infant begins to reach for objects, to sit, to walk, or to perform skilled motor acts during which the characteristic abnormal posturing of the hands and arms and his poor balance on holding up the head, walking, or running become apparent. Speech development is frequently delayed. These infants, especially those with congenital ataxia, are late walkers, have difficulty in learning to chew, and are invariably late in the acquisition of manual and body dexterity. Unless other associated anomalies are present, mental development is not affected and the motor impairment tends to improve with increasing age. Differentiation from other causes of gait ataxia, such as posterior fossa tumors,

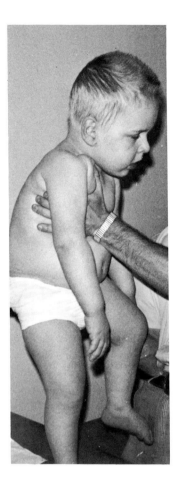

Fig. 2-2. 3-year-old boy with atonic diplegia. Marked generalized hypotonia, normal muscle stretch reflexes, and severe psychomotor retardation.

can be made by the absence of signs and symptoms of increased intracranial pressure, absence of localizing signs such as cranial-nerve palsies in a patient with a condition present for months or years, and by its
tendency to improve as the child gets older.

DISEASES OF THE SPINAL CORD

Infantile Spinal Muscular Atrophy (Werdnig-Hoffmann Disease)

Infantile spinal muscular atrophy, a disease inherited as an autosomal recessive, is probably the most common cause of severe hypotonia

and progressive weakness during the first year of life in an infant who almost always appears unusually bright and alert (Fig. 2-3). In this

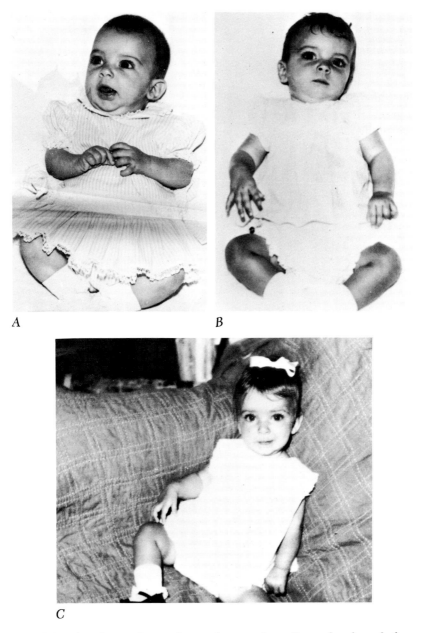

A   B

C

Fig. 2-3.   *A,* infant with spinal muscular atrophy at 3 months of age before onset of symptoms. *B, C,* at 6 and 9 months of age exhibits progressive muscle weakness. Notice position of arms and legs as disease progresses.

condition there is a progressive degeneration of motor cells in the anterior horn of the spinal cord, degenerative changes in surviving neurons,
and diffuse glial proliferation (Fig. 2-4). When the disease begins in
the first few months of life it runs a fairly rapid course with death
taking place in most cases before the second year of life due to respiratory difficulties or lung infections. Nevertheless, there is a great deal of
variation from patient to patient, so that such factors as age and mode
of onset and severity of weakness are of no prognostic significance in
the individual patient. An earlier onset is almost always associated with
a greater degree of physical disability but the rate of progression is often unpredictable. Spinal muscular atrophy starting early in infancy

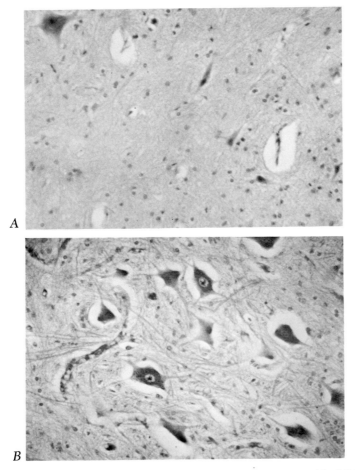

Fig. 2-4. A, transverse section of spinal cord of a 2-year-old child with
spinal muscular atrophy. Motor neurons are few, small, and hyperchro-
matic; normal neuron in left upper corner. B, normal spinal cord in patient
of same age who died from unrelated disease.

may progress rapidly over a 2- to 3-month period and then remain un-changed for several years. Physical examination reveals hypoactive or absent muscle stretch reflexes according to the degree of muscle weak-ness. There is no sensory loss. Fasciculations of the tongue are com-monly present, although they are difficult to demonstrate when the infant is awake or when forceful opening of the mouth is attempted. Fasciculations are best seen at the edge of the tongue and when the infant is asleep. In advanced stages of the disease or when the infant is old enough to cooperate, fasciculations can easily be demonstrated.

During the early stages of infantile muscular atrophy there may seem to be a remarkable discrepancy between the severity of the muscle weakness and the preservation of muscle mass. This phenomenon is more apparent than real, and the bulky extremities consist mostly of fatty tissue. The intercostal muscles are always involved and the dia-phragm is spared, resulting in a typical abdominal or paradoxical (see-saw) type of respiration. Muscle enzyme studies (SGOT and CPK) are normal. The electromyogram shows normal or slightly slow nerve-conduction velocity, decreased number of motor unit potentials as well as the so-called giant motor units. Evidence of denervation (fibrillation potentials) is frequently scant or absent. Muscle biopsy shows evidence of denervation atrophy which is indistinguishable from that seen in dis-eases of peripheral nerves. Muscle biopsy is sometimes misleading and may show myopathic features such as central nuclei, variation in fiber size, and degenerative and regenerative changes. In most cases, how-ever, biopsy changes are typical of neurogenic muscular atrophy (Fig. 2-5). The differential diagnosis of infantile spinal muscular atrophy in-cludes polyneuropathy, congenital myopathies, muscle dystrophies, and juvenile myasthenia gravis. Fasciculations of the tongue, a common

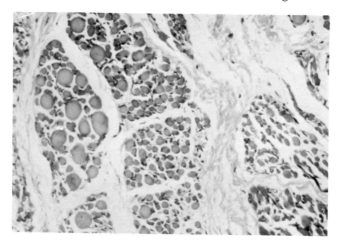

Fig. 2-5. Spinal muscular atrophy. Transverse section of deltoid muscle biopsy showing group atrophy of fibers typical of neurogenic atrophy.

finding in spinal muscular atrophy, is rarely if ever seen in polyneuropathy. Motor-nerve-conduction velocity is always slow in patients with a peripheral neuropathy and significant muscle weakness. In diseases of muscles (myopathies and dystrophies) the electromyogram typically shows an increased number of small polyphasic potentials, and serum enzyme levels (SGOT and CPK) are usually elevated. Myasthenia gravis can be ruled out by a negative response to the Tensilon test and by failure of repeated electrical stimulation of a peripheral nerve to demonstrate a block in neuromuscular transmission.

Juvenile Spinal Muscular Atrophy (Kugelberg-Welander Disease)

In 1956 Kugelberg and Welander described a heredofamilial type of juvenile spinal muscular atrophy. In most reported cases the disease has been inherited as an autosomal recessive character. The age of onset varies from early childhood to adolescence. Because the characteristic proximal muscle weakness and wasting begin first in the legs, this condition is often mistaken for muscular dystrophy. Muscles supplied by the cranial nerves are not involved and no sensory loss is present. Muscle stretch reflexes are hypoactive or absent according to the degree of muscle weakness. Muscle fasciculations are observed at some time in the natural course of the disease in all patients.

A diagnosis of juvenile spinal muscular atrophy can only be suspected on clinical grounds. A definitive diagnosis can be made only by electromyography which shows evidence of widespread denervation with normal motor-nerve-conduction velocity and by muscle biopsy. Juvenile spinal muscular atrophy runs a very slowly progressive course with complete disability taking place anywhere between ten to forty years after onset of symptoms.

Amyotrophic Lateral Sclerosis

Although an extremely rare disease, amyotrophic lateral sclerosis is a well-documented entity in childhood. The clinical picture does not differ from that of adults (Fig. 2-6). Neurologic signs of impairment of the upper and lower motor neurons are present: muscle weakness and wasting, fasciculations, spasticity, hyperactive muscle stretch reflexes, and an extensor plantar response (Babinski sign). On the basis of the clinical course and mode of inheritance two forms can be distinguished —a sporadic variety, which runs a subacute course with death occurring within three years after the onset of symptoms, and a familial form, which runs a more protracted course.

Poliomyelitis

The incidence of poliomyelitis has markedly decreased in the past 15 years. In the great majority of instances poliomyelitis is preceded by

occurs in varying degrees. Examination of cerebrospinal fluid shows the classic albuminocytologic dissociation with normal number of cells and an elevated protein level. Electrodiagnostic studies may show slowing of nerve-conduction velocity and evidence of denervation (fibrillation potentials) 18 to 21 days after the onset of the disease. With the advent of mechanically assisted respiration, prognosis is good in terms of survival. Permanent muscle weakness, however, is not uncommon. Complete functional recovery may take place anywhere from a few months to three years after the onset of the disease.

Polyneuropathy

A number of conditions may produce a polyneuropathy during infancy or childhood. Clinically, signs and symptoms of lower-motor-neuron disease are present (flaccid weakness and absent or decreased muscle stretch reflexes with or without sensory deficit). Electrophysiologic studies show a slow motor-nerve conduction velocity and evidence of denervation (fibrillation potentials). Muscle biopsy reveals a typical pattern of denervation muscle atrophy. There may be elevation of the CSF protein. The onset in most cases of polyneuropathy is usually not as acute as in polyradiculoneuropathy.

Following is a list of some of the most common forms of polyneuropathy in children. Since the causes of polyneuritis in childhood are many, only some of them will be discussed.

PERIPHERAL NEUROPATHIES IN CHILDREN

TOXIC DISORDERS
Infectious: Diphtheria
Heavy metals: Lead, mercury, arsenic, thallium, gold, and zinc.
Nonmetallic compounds: Triorthocresylphosphate, carbon tetrachloride, carbon disulfide, benzene, gasoline, emetine, isoniazid, hydralazine, nitrofurantoin, Dilantin, antimetabolites, antileukemic drugs

INFECTIOUS AND/OR ALLERGIC DISORDERS
Infectious mononucleosis
Polyradiculoneuropathy (Guillain-Barré syndrome)
Herpes zoster
Leprosy

NONINFECTIOUS INFLAMMATORY DISORDERS
Rheumatoid arthritis
Sarcoidosis

ALLERGY
Reactions to insect bites or to injections of vaccines or antitoxins

NUTRITIONAL DEFICIENCY
Vitamin deficiency: Pernicious anemia, thiamine deficiency
Malnutrition: Starvation, malabsorption syndromes

METABOLIC DISEASES
  Diabetes
  Acute intermittent porphyria
  Amyloidosis
  Myxedema

ISCHEMIC VASCULAR DISEASES
  Periarteritis nodosa
  Lupus erythematosus disseminatus

HEREDOFAMILIAL DISEASES
  Peroneal muscular atrophy (Charcot-Marie-Tooth disease)
  Sulfatide lipidosis (metachromatic leukodystrophy)
  Krabbe's leukodystrophy
  Refsum's disease
  Hypertrophic interstitial neuritis

CHRONIC RELAPSING NEUROPATHY

Peroneal Muscular Atrophy (Charcot-Marie-Tooth Disease)

Peroneal muscular atrophy is a familial disease that can be inherited as a dominant or as a recessive trait and is characterized pathologically by degeneration of peripheral nerves and sensory ganglia and clinically by a slowly progressive weakness and atrophy of the evertor and dorsi-flexor muscles (anterior tibial and peroneal) of the feet and toes; foot deformity (high arches, hammer toes); absent or decreased muscle stretch reflexes in the lower extremities and eventual weakness and atrophy of the distal muscles of the arms (Fig. 2-8). Occasionally sensory loss is present, especially for position sense, vibration, and two-point discrimination. Sensory loss is uncommon in children but increases in frequency and becomes more prominent as the patient gets older.

Enlargement and firmness of the peripheral nerves is seen in almost 25 percent of patients. Electrophysiologic studies reveal slow motor conduction velocity of peripheral nerves (ulnar, median, and peroneal).

Serum enzymes and examination of the CSF are normal. Biopsy of a peripheral nerve (sural) shows a large transverse fascicular area with decrease in the number of myelinated nerve fibers. Onion-bulb formations similar to those seen in Dejerine-Sottas disease are not infrequently seen in Charcot-Marie-Tooth disease.

A neuronal type of Charcot-Marie-Tooth disease, in which the primary pathologic process resides in the cells of the anterior horn, has also been described. In this more unusual variety the onset is almost always in middle age or later, the peripheral nerves are not enlarged, and conduction velocity of peripheral nerves is normal or only slightly slow, as often occurs in conditions affecting the anterior horn cells.

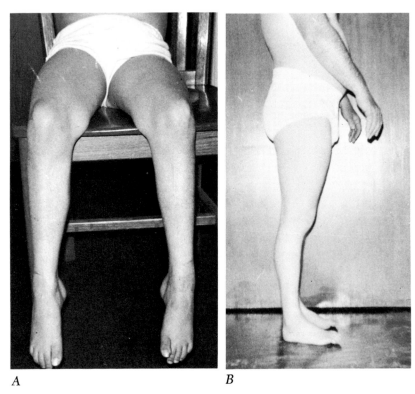

A   B

Fig. 2-8. A, 8-year-old girl with peroneal muscular atrophy (Charcot-Marie-Tooth disease). Onset of symptoms at the age of 4 years with progressive weakness and wasting of muscles below the knee; foot drop due to weakness of dorsiflexor muscles and foot deformity. B, 28-year-old patient with same condition; notice stork-leg appearance due to marked atrophy of muscles below the knee.

Sulfatide Lipidosis (Metachromatic Leukodystrophy)

A peripheral neuropathy may be the initial manifestation of sulfatide lipidosis. There is progressive muscle weakness and hypotonia, sometimes causing a severe degree of genu recurvatum. Sulfatide lipidosis has its onset by the end of the first year of life. Soon, other signs and symptoms of involvement of the central nervous system appear. There is progressive mental deterioration, swallowing difficulties, optic atrophy, third- or sixth-nerve palsy, nystagmus, and ataxia. CSF examination shows an increase in protein levels in the majority of patients. The diagnosis can be made by the demonstration of metachromatic material in biopsy of a peripheral nerve (sural) and/or a decreased or absent arylsulfatase A activity in the urine.

Krabbe's Disease

Krabbe's disease, one of the leukodystrophies of early infancy, may also occasionally present as a peripheral neuropathy.

Refsum's Disease (Heredopathia Atactica Polyneuritiformis)

One of the cardinal signs of Refsum's disease is polyneuritis. Other signs include ataxia, deafness, and retinitis pigmentosa.

Hypertrophic Interstitial Neuritis (Dejerine-Sottas Disease)

Hypertrophic interstitial neuritis is a disease of late childhood and adolescence, but it has been reported as early as one year of age. Characteristically in this condition the peripheral nerves are thickened and easily palpable. Additional clinical features are irregularity of the pupils, a sluggish pupillary reaction to light, nystagmus, scanning speech, intention tremor, and scoliosis.

Chronic Relapsing Neuropathy

Chronic relapsing neuropathy is a disorder of unknown etiology characterized by a slowly progressive distal and symmetrical muscle weakness. Occasionally cranial nerves are affected. There is an elevated CSF protein. The recovery period is prolonged. Recurrences occur within an average time of four years. The administration of steroids appear to suppress the clinical and laboratory manifestations of the disease.

DISEASES OF THE MYONEURAL JUNCTION

Myasthenia Gravis

Myasthenia gravis is a disease characterized by progressive fatigability of striated muscles secondary to a defect in nerve conduction at the myoneural junction. Transient neonatal myasthenia gravis occurs in about 10 percent of babies born of mothers with myasthenia gravis. The disease is self-limited, lasting from one to seven weeks. Good nursing care and specific anticholinesterase treatment (pyridostigmine or neostigmine) should tie over the vast majority of neonates with the transient form of myasthenia gravis. A few deaths, however, have been reported despite appropriate treatment with anticholinesterase drugs. A Tensilon (edrophonium chloride) test should be performed or neostigmine should be administered intramuscularly to any newborn of a mother with known myasthenia gravis and who presents with severe hypotonia, muscle weakness (weak cry, poor sucking), or respiratory difficulties.

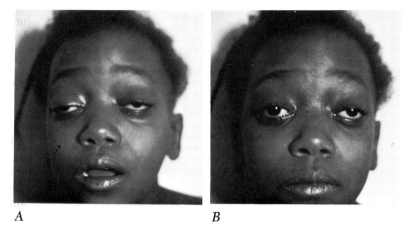

A   B

Fig. 2-9.   7-year-old girl with juvenile myasthenia gravis. Before (A) and after (B) intravenous injection of Tensilon.

Juvenile Myasthenia Gravis

Juvenile myasthenia gravis is uncommon. In one-third of cases symptoms appear at birth or during the newborn period; in the other two-thirds the disease begins in later infancy or childhood. Myasthenia gravis in children in contrast to that in adults is almost always characterized by generalized muscle weakness and partial or complete external ophthalmoplegia. Any child with muscle weakness, ptosis, or external ophthalmoplegia of unknown origin should have a Tensilon test. The injection of 1 mg. to 2 mg. Tensilon intravenously according to age will produce dramatic improvement of signs and symptoms in the great majority of patients with myasthenia gravis within a few seconds to two or three minutes (Fig. 2-9).

Continuous anticholinesterase treatment controls symptoms in most instances. In some patients the disease undergoes spontaneous remission.

DISEASES OF THE MUSCLE

Universal Hypoplasia of Muscles

Universal hypoplasia of muscles is rare. Isolated absence of one or a group of muscles is more common. A diagnosis of congenital muscle hypoplasia can usually be made by inspection alone. Electrophysiologic studies and serum enzymes (SGOT and CPK) are normal.

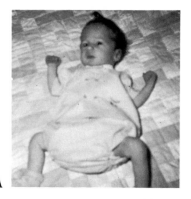
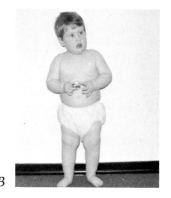

A   B

Fig. 2-10 Benign congenital hypotonia. *A*, infant at 3 months of age had severe generalized hypotonia and muscle weakness; muscle stretch reflexes were normal. *B*, normal psychomotor development at 16 months of age.

Benign Congenital Hypotonia

Benign congenital hypotonia is a poorly defined term used to describe infants with varying degrees of hypotonia which has the tendency to improve with advancing age, carries a good prognosis, and is not associated with intrinsic muscle, nerve, or spinal cord disease. When extensive investigations have been carried out or when patients have been followed for long periods of time, many cases labeled benign congenital hypotonia have been found later to be a muscle disease. The writer has seen only one patient with severe muscle hypotonia and weakness since birth whose condition slowly improved so that by the age of sixteen months motor as well as mental development was normal (Fig. 2-10). Extensive investigation during the third month of life, including serum enzymes, protein-bound iodine, Tensilon test, electromyography, muscle biopsy, and a number of other tests, showed normal results.

Muscular Dystrophy

Muscular dystrophy comprises a group of heredofamilial myopathies characterized by progressive degeneration of somatic muscles. In general, they may be classified as abiotrophies in the sense that for some unknown cause there is a more or less selective degeneration of group of muscles. Muscular dystrophy can be inherited as a dominant, sex-linked, or recessive trait. The age of onset, rate of progression, and degree of disability vary in different types. As a rule, however, these parameters are fairly uniform for each of the several recognized forms.

Pseudohypertrophic Muscular Dystrophy

Pseudohypertrophic muscular dystrophy (PHMD) is a sex-linked (X), recessively inherited, progressive myopathy that occurs only in boys and has its onset between the second and fourth year of life. Loco-motor difficulties are first manifested by weakness of the pelvic girdles (difficulty in rising from a sitting position, climbing stairs, and wad-dling gait). The appearance of a good number of these children is strik-ing. Many of them look like little Herculeses or Japanese wrestlers, their appearance contrasting markedly with their poor motor performance. Children with pseudohypertrophic muscular dystrophy are often late walkers. However, rarely if ever do they not learn to walk. In a young child with progressive weakness, hypotonia, and/or muscle atrophy starting early in life so incapacitating the child that he never was able to walk, the possibility of pseudohypertrophic muscular dystrophy is very remote. Physical examination reveals large calves, thighs, and arms and decreased muscle mass in the shoulder and pelvic girdles and paraspinal muscles (Fig. 2-11), hyporeflexia or areflexia, no sensory loss, and the typical waddling gait as well as the peculiar way of arising from the floor (Gowers' sign). This is not a pathognomonic sign of PHMD since it may be present in any disease associated with weakness of the pelvic girdle and paraspinal muscles. Electromyographic exami-nation shows normal nerve conduction velocity, thus ruling out a pe-ripheral neuropathy, and needle examination reveals the myopathic na-ture of the process (small polyphasic motor unit potentials). Serum enzyme levels (CPK and SGOT) are elevated. Patients with PHMD often have a dull intellect in contrast to those with infantile spinal mus-cular atrophy who are usually of average or above-average intelligence.

Limb-Girdle Muscular Dystrophy

Limb-girdle muscular dystrophy is a myopathy inherited as an auto-somal recessive character. The onset of symptoms is between 4 and 15 years of age (average, 8 years). This is a slowly progressive type of muscular dystrophy. Patients are ambulatory for many years. Age of confinement to a wheelchair varies in different individuals from 12 to 44 years. Muscle weakness is similar in distribution to that of PHMD. Pseudohypertrophy of calf muscles is also a common finding in this type of muscle dystrophy (Fig. 2-12). Levels of SGOT and CPK are usually elevated but to a lesser degree than in PHMD. Carriers do not exhibit clinical muscle weakness in contrast to some carriers of the sex-

---

Fig. 2-11. *A, B,* 9-year-old boy with pseudohypertrophic muscular dys-trophy. Onset of symptoms at age 4 years. He has generalized muscle weak-ness more pronounced in proximal muscles of the extremities, large calves, increased lumbar lordosis due to weak pelvic and paraspinal muscles, and tight heel cords with early foot deformity in the left. Severity of muscle weakness contrasts markedly with his "muscular" appearance. *C,* late stages of the disease in a 17-year-old patient with onset of symptoms at 3 years of age. Severe muscle wasting, kyphoscoliosis, and musculoskeletal contractures.

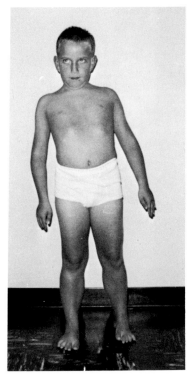

A

B

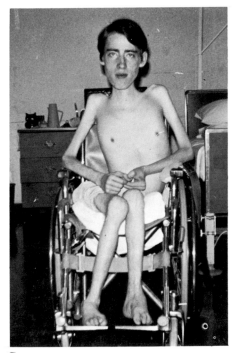

C

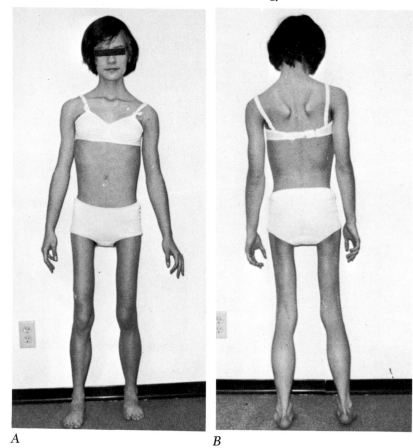

A   *B*

Fig. 2-12. A, 12-year-old girl with limb-girdle muscular dystrophy. The weakness and muscle wasting are more pronounced in proximal than distal muscles. Onset of symptoms at the age of 7 years. B, pseudohypertrophy of calves.

linked recessive type (PHMD). Limb-girdle muscular dystrophy probably does not represent a single disease entity but several different disorders sharing similar clinical features regarding age of onset, distribution of muscle weakness, and course.

Facioscapulohumeral Dystrophy

Facioscapulohumeral (Landouzy-Dejerine) dystrophy (FHD) is inherited as an autosomal dominant. Age of onset of muscle weakness is usually between 12 and 20 years. FHD is a very slowly progressive disease and a normal lifespan can be expected in the great majority of cases. Muscle weakness begins in the orbicularis oris, sternocleidomas-

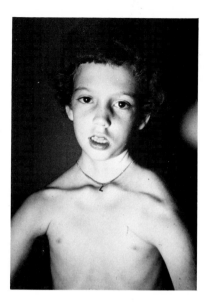

Fig. 2-13. 7-year-old girl with facioscapulohumeral muscular dystrophy. Onset of symptoms at 4 years. Notice expressionless face and atrophy of muscles of the shoulder girdle.

toid, trapezius, and pectoralis muscles (Fig. 2-13). Eventually the shoulders, arms, and pelvic girdle muscles become involved. SGOT and CPK levels are normal or only slightly elevated.

Ocular Myopathy (Progressive Dystrophic Ophthalmoplegia)

Ocular myopathy (progressive dystrophic ophthalmoplegia) should be distinguished, at least on clinical grounds, from nonprogressive congenital external ophthalmoplegia (Fig. 2-14) and the Möbius syndrome of facial diplegia and extraocular muscle palsies. In recent years the first two conditions have been lumped together under the name of progressive ocular myopathy.

Clinical features of ocular myopathy (Fig. 2-15) include (1) onset from infancy to late adulthood, with most cases manifesting the first symptoms during the first two decades; (2) ptosis and progressive symmetrical external ophthalmoplegia with sparing of pupillary reactions to light and accommodation. In about 25 percent of cases there is involvement of facial muscles (especially the orbicularis oculi). Occasionally there is involvement of muscles of the neck and shoulder girdle, trunk, pelvis, or lower extremities. A history of similar disorders in other family members is obtained in about 50 percent of cases.

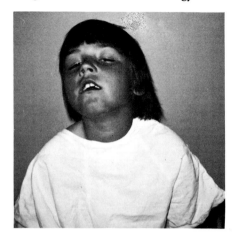

Fig. 2-14. 6-year-old girl with congenital nonprogressive external ophthalmoplegia. There is almost complete ptosis and paresis of extraocular muscles. Normal pupillary reactions to light. No evidence of muscle weakness elsewhere.

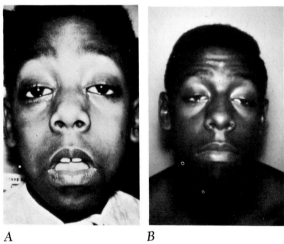

A   B

Fig. 2-15. Ocular myopathy (progressive dystrophy of ocular muscles). Onset of symptoms at age 4 years. *A*, at the age of 6 years patient has partial ptosis and partial paralysis of extraocular muscles. *B*, at the age of 16 years ptosis has increased in severity (note contraction of frontalis muscle to compensate weakness of levator palpebralis), and there is complete paralysis of extraocular muscles.

Congenital Muscular Dystrophy

Benign congenital muscular dystrophy is a nonprogressive or very slowly progressive muscle dystrophy producing very little motor disability. In the few reported cases the diagnosis has been made only after muscle biopsy in patients with slight to moderate hypotonia and muscle weakness of many years' duration. A severe form of congenital muscular dystrophy has also been described. The disease appears to be transmitted as an autosomal recessive trait. In the severe form of congenital muscular dystrophy there is marked physical disability from early life and no pseudohypertrophy is present. A definite diagnosis can be made by electromyography and/or muscle biopsy.

Myotonic Dystrophy

Myotonic dystrophy is a dominantly inherited disease (Fig. 2-16) involving many systems (muscles, inner ear, endocrine glands, eyes, gastrointestinal tract, heart and skin).

The muscle weakness in this type of dystrophy often becomes manifest in early childhood. Myotonic dystrophy is the only muscle dystrophy and one of the few myopathies in which weakness is predominantly distal rather than proximal (neuropathic instead of myopathic distribution). Myotonia can be elicited by percussion with a reflex hammer in the muscles of the thenar eminence, deltoid, or tongue (Fig. 2-17). Electromyographic examination shows normal nerve conduction velocity, myopathic motor unit potentials, and typical myotonic discharges (waxing and waning trains of positive waves). Not infrequently a patient has typical electromyographic findings of myotonic dystrophy and no clinical evidence of myotonia. The reverse is also found—patients with clinical myotonia and a normal electromyogram or an electromyogram which only suggests a diagnosis of a myopathy. Other systems are invariably involved in myotonic dystrophy (cataracts, hypogenitalism, early alopecia, and deafness). The oral adminis-

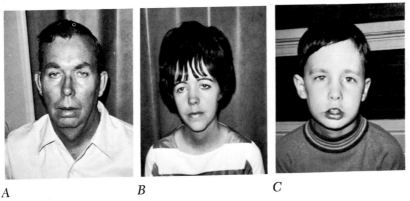

A   B   C

Fig. 2-16. A, B, C, myotonic dystrophy in three generations of one family. Typical myopathic facies: flat, sagging, and expressionless face.

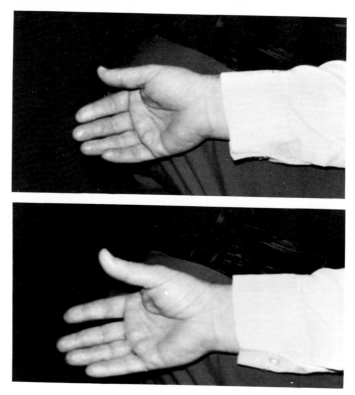

Fig. 2-17. Myotonia following percussion of thenar eminence with reflex hammer in patient shown in Fig. 2-16A.

tration of quinine or procainamide improves myotonia in about 50 percent of patients.

Newly Described Myopathies

In the past few years several new myopathies have been described. They are characterized by muscle hypotonia in early infancy and a slowly progressive muscle weakness. A definite diagnosis can be made only by histologic examination of diseased muscle (central core, megaconial, pleoconial, myotubular, and rod-body myopathy).

Glycogen Storage Disease II

Generalized glycogen storage disease II (Pompe's disease) is a condition characterized by the accumulation of glycogen in many different body tissues (muscle, CNS, heart, etc.) secondary to a deficiency or absence of acid maltase enzyme in lysosomes. The disease produces from early infancy marked hypotonia, muscle weakness, a rubbery consistency of muscles, a large tongue, and cardiomegaly. Because of the large tongue and psychomotor retardation these babies are often confused with infants with cretinism or hypothyroidism. Tests of thyroid function are normal. Chest x-ray shows a large and globular heart. Histologic examination of affected muscle reveals increased glycogen content. A muscle biopsy is indicated in the presence of the above-mentioned signs and symptoms (progressive muscle weakness, large tongue, and cardiomegaly with or without heart failure). Until recently it was believed that Pompe's disease was a rapidly fatal condition and that most patients die before the age of two. Recently several patients with a more chronic course or with symptoms appearing later in life have been reported.

Polymyositis and Dermatomyositis

Polymyositis is an angiitis involving vessels of muscles with secondary inflammation and degenerative changes. Clinically polymyositis is characterized by acute, subacute, or chronic proximal weakness of the pelvic and shoulder girdles. Weakness of the distal muscles of the extremities may also occur. Dysphagia and weakness of the neck muscles are common findings. When associated skin abnormalities are present, the condition is called *dermatomyositis*. In children dermatomyositis is commoner than polymyositis. The age of onset is in the first two decades in about 20 percent of cases. Muscle ache and a low-grade fever are frequent complaints.

Physical examination shows proximal muscle weakness and muscle tenderness, and when the skin is affected, typical lesions may be seen (erythematous rash over the malar bones and the bridge of the nose in a butterfly distribution). A pink or violaceous discoloration of the upper lids is of more diagnostic importance than the paranasal lesions. The skin over the knuckles becomes erythematous and, later on, thickened, atrophic, white, and scaly (Fig. 2-18). Sedimentation rate is usually elevated. Serum enzyme values (SGOT, serum glutamic pyruvic transaminase, aldolase, and CPK) are elevated in more than 50 percent of cases. Serum CPK is elevated in almost all cases of acute or subacute polymyositis.

The electromyogram (EMG) is a highly reliable diagnostic technique in polymyositis. A pathognomonic EMG is observed in a small percentage of cases (small polyphasic motor unit potentials, fibrillation potentials, and pseudomyotonic discharges). In the great majority of cases, however, only two of these diagnostic criteria can be observed (usually evidence of a myopathy and denervation). Muscle biopsy appears to be diagnostically less reliable, showing changes on which to make a definitive diagnosis in only 60 percent of cases. Muscle biopsy may reveal degeneration or regeneration of muscle fibers, relative or absolute in-

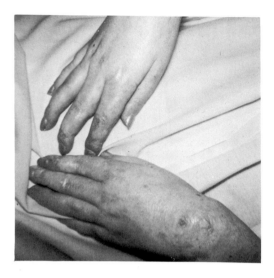

Fig. 2-18. Hands of patient with dermatomyositis showing erythematous and atrophic changes over knuckles.

crease in connective tissue, and infiltration of muscle fibers and bundles with inflammatory cells.

In general the younger the patient at the onset of symptoms of polymyositis or dermatomyositis the more benign its course and the better its prognosis. The clinical course in children is characterized by more frequent remissions than in adults and a better response to steroid therapy. In contrast to adults the incidence of malignancy in children with dermatomyositis is not higher than in the general population. Complications in this condition are relatively uncommon. They include crisis, characterized by fever and severe abdominal pain; multiple perforations of the intestinal tract, including the esophagus, due to occlusion of small blood vessels; acute intestinal obstruction; recurrent obstruction in the pyloric region; and deposition of calcium in the skin and subcutaneous tissues (Fig. 2-19).

Treatment of choice of polymyositis and dermatomyositis is steroids.

COMMENT

The first step in the differential diagnosis of muscle weakness in any age group is essentially the differentiation of involvement of the upper from involvement of the lower motor neurons. Since the terms *hypotonic* and *floppy child* are often used instead of *muscle weakness*, the differential diagnosis is limited to diseases of the motor unit (anterior horn cell, peripheral nerves, myoneural junction, and muscle fibers).

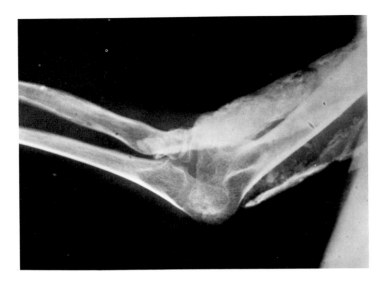

Fig. 2-19.   Deposition of calcium in subcutaneous tissue in 10-year-old girl with dermatomyositis.

Diseases of the brain associated with hypotonia and muscle weakness are few and almost always accompanied by other manifestations of cerebral dysfunction (mental subnormality, chorea, ataxia, and seizures) which greatly facilitate the diagnosis.

Important points in the differential diagnosis of chronic diseases of the motor unit are a history of affected relatives, age of onset, rate of progression, group of muscles involved first, the presence of pseudo-hypertrophy, consistency of muscles, associated anomalies (mental subnormality, cataracts, cardiomegaly, large tongue, nystagmus, deafness, and ataxia), the presence of muscle fasciculations, atrophy of the tongue, and enlarged peripheral nerves. These clinical features are all clues by which a working diagnosis can be made in the great majority of children with severe hypotonia or muscle weakness.

Serum enzyme determinations are particularly helpful in the early diagnosis of PHMD. Often this diagnosis can be made in an infant born of a known carrier by the finding of elevated levels of serum CPK or SGOT months to one or two years before the appearance of clinical weakness.

As previously mentioned, a Tensilon or neostigmine test should be performed on any child with muscle weakness of unknown etiology.

The electromyogram is probably the single most important laboratory test in the differential diagnosis of diseases of the motor unit. This electrodiagnostic procedure consists of two different techniques: (1) the measurement of conduction velocity of peripheral nerves and (2) the

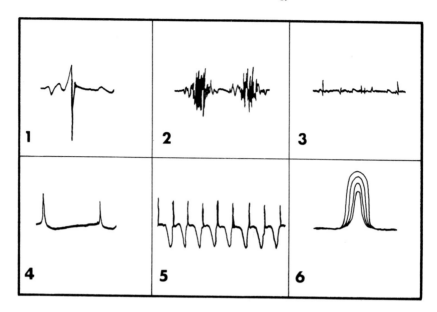

Fig. 2-20. Electromyographic patterns. *1,* normal motor unit; *2,* polyphasic motor unit; *3,* fibrillation potentials; *4,* positive waves; *5,* myotonic discharges: waxing and waning trains of positive waves; *6,* myasthenic response following nerve stimulation at high frequencies showing a decrease in amplitude of evoked muscle potential.

recording, by way of a needle electrode inserted into a muscle, of the electrical potentials and the sound produced by motor units at rest, and during minimal and maximal contraction (Fig. 2-20). Nerve conduction velocity studies permit differentiation between diseases of the muscles and the anterior horn cell from those of the peripheral nerves. The character of the motor unit potentials, on the other hand, is highly reliable in differentiating diseases of the muscles from those of the anterior horn cell. With the exception of myotonic dystrophy and polymyositis the electromyogram does not permit differentiation of diseases of muscles. For this purpose the clinician has to resort to muscle biopsy.

The electromyogram can be an important diagnostic tool in the following clinical situations.

Diseases of the Anterior Horn Cell

In diseases of the anterior horn cell—infantile spinal muscular atrophy (Werdnig-Hoffmann disease), juvenile spinal muscular atrophy, and amyotrophic lateral sclerosis—the electromyogram characteristically shows evidence of denervation (fibrillation potentials, positive waves, and giant motor unit potentials distributed in a widespread manner). Motor conduction velocity is normal or slightly slow.

Peripheral Neuropathies

Slowing of conduction velocity in motor or sensory fibers, according to whether we are dealing with a purely motor, purely sensory, or a mixed type of neuropathy, is the diagnostic hallmark of peripheral neuropathies. Evidence of denervation can be demonstrated in the distribution of one or more nerves according to the type and extent of nerve involvement.

Diseases of the Myoneural Junction

MYASTHENIA GRAVIS.   In myasthenia gravis a defect in neuromuscular transmission can be demonstrated sometimes even when the patient is in clinical remission or when symptoms are under control with anticholinesterase therapy. After a group of muscles is exercised for 1 to 3 minutes or after nerve stimulation at high frequencies there is a decrease in the amplitude of the evoked muscle action potential.

MYASTHENIC SYNDROME (EATON-LAMBERT SYNDROME).   In the myasthenic syndrome, often associated with small-cell carcinoma of the lung, the electromyogram shows the opposite picture of myasthenia gravis. The evoked muscle action potential increases in amplitude following muscle exercise or nerve stimulation at high frequencies. The myasthenic syndrome has not been described in childhood.

Myopathies

In diseases of the muscles, conduction velocity in motor and sensory nerve fibers is normal. Needle electrode examination reveals muscle-action potentials which are polyphasic and small in amplitude and produce a typical cracking sound in the loudspeaker. With the exception of myotonic dystrophy and polymyositis, the electromyogram does not differentiate between different types of myopathies. In myotonic dystrophy in addition to myopathic motor-unit potentials, when the needle electrode is inserted or moved and also during voluntary contraction, pathognomonic waxing and waning trains of positive waves appear on the oscilloscope (Fig. 2-20) and the loudspeaker produces a characteristic sound similar to that of a dive bomber. The triad of polyphasic motor-unit potentials, fibrillation potentials, and pseudomyotonic discharges is pathognomonic of polymyositis. More often than not, however, only myopathic and fibrillation potentials are found. This particular combination is occasionally seen in other myopathies but is a fairly constant finding in active polymyositis and strongly suggests this diagnosis.

REFERENCES

Adams, R. D., et al. *Diseases of Muscle* (2nd ed.). New York: Hoeber, 1962.

Barsy, A. M., and Mouchette, R. On sporadic infantile amyotrophic lateral sclerosis. *Encephale* 56:45, 1967.

Brandt, S. Course and symptoms of progressive infantile spinal muscular atrophy: A follow-up study of 112 cases in Denmark. *Arch. Neurol. Psychiat.* 63:218, 1950.

Brandt, S. *Werdnig-Hoffmann's Infantile Progressive Muscular Atrophy.* Copenhagen: Munksgaard, 1950.

Di Sant'Agnese, P. A., et al. Glycogen storage disease of the heart: I. Report of two cases in siblings with chemical and pathologic studies. *Pediatrics* 6:402, 1950.

Dyck, P. J., and Lambert, E. H. Lower motor and primary sensory neuron diseases with peroneal muscular atrophy: I. Neurologic, genetic, and electrophysiologic findings in hereditary polyneuropathies. II. Neurologic, genetic and electrophysiologic findings in various neuronal degenerations. *Arch. Neurol.* 18:603; 619, 1968.

Gamstorp, I. Progressive spinal muscular atrophy with onset in infancy or early childhood. *Acta Paediat. Scand.* 56:408, 1967.

Gordon, R. G., and Delicatti, J. L. The occurrence of amyotrophic lateral sclerosis in children. *J. Neurol. Psychopath.* 9:30, 1928.

Hernandez, L., and Chavez, M. Amyotrophic lateral sclerosis in a girl seven years old. *Rev. Neuropsychiat.* 7:83, 1954.

Hers, H. G. Recent development in the biochemistry of glycogen storage disease and fructose intolerance. *Chem. Weekbl.* 57:457, 1961.

Huijing, F., et al. Diagnosis of generalized glycogen storage disease (Pompe's disease). *J. Pediat.* 63:984, 1963.

Jackson, C. E., and Strehler, D. A. Limb-girdle muscular dystrophy: Clinical manifestations and detection of pre-clinical disease. *Pediatrics* 41:495, 1968.

Kiloh, L., and Nevin, S. Progressive dystrophy of the external ocular muscles (ocular myopathy). *Brain* 74:115, 1951.

Kugelberg, E., and Welander, L. Heredofamilial juvenile muscular atrophy simulating muscular dystrophy. *Arch. Neurol. Psychiat.* 75:500, 1956.

Marinacci, A. A. *Applied Electromyography.* Philadelphia: Lea & Febiger, 1968.

Markland, L. D., and Riley, H. D., Jr. The Guillain-Barré syndrome in childhood. *Clin. Pediat.* (Phila.) 6:162, 1967.

Millichap, J. G., and Dodge, P. R. Diagnosis and treatment of myasthenia gravis in infancy, childhood and adolescence. *Neurology* 10:1007, 1960.

Muller, S. A., et al. Calcinosis in dermatomyositis; observations on the course of disease in children and adults. *Arch. Derm.* 79:669, 1959.

Munsat, T. L., et al. Neurogenic muscular atrophy of infancy with prolonged survival. *Brain* 92:9, 1969.

Pompe, J. C. Over idiopathische hypertropie van bet hart. *Nederl. T. Geneesk.* 76:304, 1932.

Sections of Neurology, Mayo Clinic and Mayo Foundation. *Clinical Examinations in Neurology* (2nd ed.). Philadelphia: Saunders, 1963, pp. 311–341.

Slatt, B. Myotonia dystrophia: Review of 17 cases. *Canad. Med. Ass. J.* 85:250, 1961.

Teng, P., and Osserman, K. E.   Studies in myasthenia gravis: Neonatal and juvenile types. *J. Mount Sinai Hosp.* N.Y. 23:711, 1956.

Tyler, F. H., and Stephens, F. E.   Studies in disorders of muscle: II. Clinical manifestations and inheritance of facioscapulohumeral dystrophy in large family. *Ann. Intern. Med.* 32:640, 1950.

Watters, G. V., and Williams, T. W.   Early onset myotonic dystrophy. *Arch. Neurol.* 17:137, 1967.

Wiederholt, W. C., et al.   The Landry-Guillain-Barré-Strohl syndrome or polyradiculoneuropathy: Historical review, report on 97 patients, and present concepts. *Mayo Clin. Proc.* 39:427, 1964.

Zellweger, H., et al.   Severe congenital muscular dystrophy. *Amer. J. Dis. Child.* 114:591, 1967.

Zellweger, H., et al.   Benign congenital muscular dystrophy: A special form of congenital hypotonia. *Clin. Pediat.* 6: 655, 1967.

Zundel, W. S., and Tyler, F. H.   Muscular dystrophies. *New Eng. J. Med.* 273:537; 596, 1965.

3
Spastic Weakness

IT HAS BEEN previously mentioned (Chapter 2) that the differential diagnosis in a child who is weak and hypotonic and has decreased or absent muscle stretch reflexes is almost always limited to diseases that involve the motor unit (anterior horn cell, nerves, neuromuscular junction, or muscle). The counterpart of this clinical picture is encountered with greater frequency, that is to say, a child who is weak in one or more extremities but whose physical examination reveals increased muscle tone (spasticity), increased muscle stretch, and pathologic reflexes such as extensor plantar response (Babinski sign). In a child with these findings, all diseases affecting the motor unit can be safely ruled out from the physical examination alone without the need of laboratory tests such as serum enzyme levels, nerve conduction velocity studies, electromyogram, or muscle biopsy. From the standpoint of localization of the pathologic process, a child with spastic weakness may have only a lesion of the spinal cord, the brain stem, or one or both cerebral hemispheres.

Diagnostic problems may, however, arise when one tries to localize the site of the lesion or to determine whether the condition is nonprogressive or progressive. The great majority of children with spastic weakness fall into the general category of motor problems referred to collectively as cerebral palsy. In these patients other signs of cerebral dysfunction are usually present, and the neurologic deficit has the tendency to improve with advancing age. On the other hand, patients with progressive spasticity and weakness often may have had a normal motor development during the first few months or years of life. Patients with progressive spastic weakness may suffer from a disorder affecting the upper motor neuron at its site of origin in the motor cortex or at any level of the corticobulbar or corticospinal tracts. Conditions that may cause progressive spastic weakness include brain and spinal cord tumors, developmental anomalies of the spine, familial disorders affecting the corticospinal tracts, and some progressive degenerative diseases of the central nervous system. Despite the fact that most infants and children with spastic weakness have a nonprogressive motor problem (cerebral palsy), their initial evaluation should always include, as routine

43

procedures, x-rays of the skull and x-rays of the entire spine. If progressive neurologic signs or symptoms are present, additional diagnostic studies are indicated to rule out intracranial or intraspinal pathology.

CEREBRAL PALSY

The term *cerebral palsy* refers to a group of nonprogressive motor disorders due to malfunction of motor centers of the brain characterized by paralysis together with poor coordination, lack of balance, and abnormal posturing of the extremities at rest or motion. Cerebral palsy may be secondary to developmental anomalies of the CNS or may be due to injury to the brain during intrauterine life, the perinatal period, or within the first few months of life. Prenatal etiologies are infections of the fetus by toxoplasmosis, syphilis, rubella, and cytomegalic inclusion disease (CID) and probably by a number of other maternal infections. Perinatal causes include any condition that may decrease the oxygen supply to the fetus (maternal anemia, placenta previa, abruptio placentae, prolapse of the cord), cerebral trauma, anoxia, or intracerebral bleeding during birth secondary to prolonged and complicated labor or delivery and especially difficult breech deliveries. During the first few weeks or months of life important etiologic factors are kernicterus, meningitis, encephalitis, subdural hematoma, and severe head trauma. The chief clinical forms of cerebral palsy are the spastic and the athetoid. The atonic form of cerebral palsy is rare. Spasticity and athetosis may either be found as the sole clinical manifestation or in combination in the same patient.

Spastic weakness is by far the most common clinical manifestation in patients with cerebral palsy. By definition it represents a nonprogressive neurologic deficit which usually becomes manifest or increases in severity when the infant is 6 to 12 months of age and beginning to perform purposeful motor acts such as reaching for objects, crawling, standing up, or walking. Before the age of 6 months these infants are frequently hypotonic. Infants affected with this type of cerebral palsy as a rule have other manifestations of central nervous system involvement such as mental subnormality, ataxia, abnormal movements, or visual difficulties such as esotropia, exotropia, or nystagmus. Physical examination reveals signs of upper motor neuron disease (increased muscle stretch reflexes, spastic weakness, and pathologic reflexes, in one or more extremities). In patients with spastic hemiplegia there is weakness of the arm and leg on the same side, with the leg being involved to a lesser degree than the arm (Fig. 3-1). In double hemiplegia both sides of the body are involved (Fig. 3-2). Infants with spastic diplegia

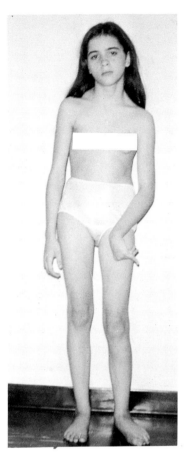

Fig. 3-1.   13-year-old girl with left spastic hemiplegia. Note abnormal posture of hand. Leg is affected to a lesser degree. Normal mental development.

have involvement of all four extremities, but the legs are more affected
than the arms (Fig. 3-3). In spastic paraplegia only the legs are affected
(Fig. 3-4). In infants with monoplegia only one arm or leg is involved
(Figs. 3-5 and 3-6). In these cases the defect is usually not recognized
until the infant is observed to use consistently only one hand when
reaching or playing with objects or appears to favor or to drag one leg
on attempting to crawl or to walk. In retrospect the parents of these
children will almost invariably state that their child moved one arm or
kicked with one leg more vigorously than with the other since very
early infancy. Children are ambidextrous until the age of 12 to 14
months. Any child who is right- or left-handed prior to this age should
be considered to have some sort of motor deficit in one arm until proved
otherwise. In most cases this is due to monoplegia or hemiplegia.

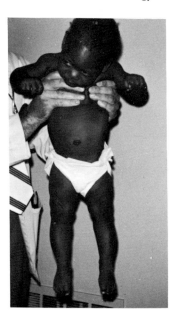

Fig. 3-2.   1½-year-old girl with double hemiplegia. Notice abnormal posture of arms and hands with clenched fingers and hyperextension of the legs. Severe psychomotor retardation.

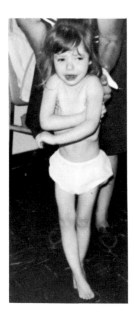

Fig. 3-3.   3-year-old girl with spastic diplegia. Scissoring of legs due to tightness of adductor muscles of the thighs. Arms less affected than the legs.

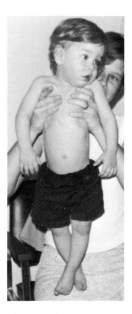

Fig. 3-4. 12-month-old infant with spastic paraplegia. One of identical twins who suffered cerebral anoxia at birth and had seizures during the neonatal period.

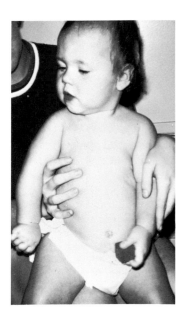

Fig. 3-5. 1½-year-old girl with monoplegia involving the right arm. Notice abnormal positioning of affected arm and hand with flexed fingers. She was noted to be left-handed at 7 months of age.

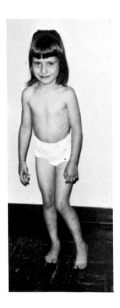

Fig. 3-6. 7-year-old with monoplegia affecting the left leg. Involved extremity is adducted at the thigh and flexed at the knee. Tight heel cord causes her to walk on tiptoe on left foot.

Spastic quadriplegia, a condition in which the four extremities are equally involved, is rarely if ever seen in patients with cerebral palsy. If one sees a child in whom the degree of spasticity and weakness is equal in both upper and lower extremities, the possibility of a lesion of the upper cervical spine should be considered. The evaluation of children with this form of spastic weakness should also include roentgenographic examination of the entire spine to rule out correctable conditions such as congenital anomalies of the upper cervical spine or intraspinal tumors.

BIRTH INJURY

Injury to the upper thoracic or lower cervical cord can occur in difficult breech deliveries as a consequence of hypertension of the neck at the time of the delivery of the head or as the result of traction along the longitudinal axis. Vertebral fractures or subluxations rarely occur. Lesions of the cervical cord may also occur with cephalic deliveries, the mechanism apparently being the application of force in a perpendicular direction of the longitudinal axis. The clinical picture in these infants includes diaphragmatic breathing, respiratory distress, a weak cry, and flaccid extremities. Not infrequently there is also avulsion of roots of the brachial plexus on one or both sides. Examination of these infants a few months after delivery may pose some diagnostic difficulties. Because of the nature and usual location of the lesion the clinical picture is one of flaccid paresis or paralysis of the arms and spastic weakness of the legs, with increased muscle stretch reflexes and an extensor plantar response. A sensory as well as a sweating level can be demonstrated in the great majority of patients. If the lesion involves the upper segments of the cervical cord the clinical picture will be one of spastic quadriplegia with increased tone and increased muscle stretch reflexes in all four extremities. If a clear-cut history of traumatic delivery is not elicited, the possibility of an expanding lesion of the upper cervical cord has to be considered and ruled out by the appropriate diagnostic procedures (x-rays and myelogram).

HYDROCEPHALUS

Patients with hydrocephalus not infrequently exhibit varying degrees of spasticity of the lower extremities. In most instances a diagnosis of hydrocephalus can be made by inspection alone.

BRAIN TUMORS

Tumors of the cerebral hemispheres may produce a slowly progressive unilateral spastic paralysis varying in degree from involvement of one extremity alone, usually the leg, to a complete hemiplegia. On the other hand, brain stem tumors have the tendency to produce a symmetrical spastic paraplegia or quadriplegia and other signs and symptoms of brain stem dysfunction due to involvement of the sixth, seventh, tenth, and twelfth cranial nerves or sensory or spinocerebellar pathways.

SPINAL CORD TUMORS

Tumors of the spinal cord may produce a flaccid weakness at the same level and a spastic weakness below the level of the lesion. In childhood, intraspinal tumors occur one-fifth as frequently as intracranial tumors. Their frequency is greater in the first four years of life because of the many tumors of developmental origin which become manifest during this period. In some large series boys have outnumbered girls by almost two to one.

In children 50 percent of spinal cord tumors are extradural and 50 percent intradural. Two-thirds of intradural tumors are intramedullary and one-third extramedullary. The most common spinal cord tumors in children in order of frequency are (1) tumors of developmental origin (lipomas, dermoid cysts, and teratomas); (2) gliomas (astrocytomas, ependymomas, gangliogliomas); (3) metastatic tumors (neuroblastoma, ependymomas, medulloblastomas); (4) lymphomas and leukemias; (5) sarcomas; (6) neurinomas; and (7) meningiomas.

In general, intramedullary spinal cord tumors produce painless and symmetrical neurologic deficit, while extramedullary tumors usually cause asymmetrical neurologic signs and pain.

The initial complaint in more than 50 percent of children with intraspinal tumors is pain. Any child who complains of persistent localized pain in the back or extremities should be listened to and thoroughly examined. Motor weakness, usually of the spastic variety, is the initial symptom in about 60 percent—muscle spasms in 25 percent, and change in bladder or bowel habits, in a child who is already toilet-trained, in 35 percent of cases. Signs of spinal cord tumors include abnormal muscle stretch reflexes in one or more extremities, musculoskeletal deformities, sensory abnormalities, atrophy of one extremity, tenderness over a localized area of the spine, vasomotor changes in one or more extremities, a visible or palpable paraspinal soft-tissue mass or skin defect overlying the level of the lesion such as nevus flammeus, skin dimples, or a lipoma.

Any child suspected of having a spinal cord lesion should have roentgenographic examination of the entire spine, examination of the CSF, and a myelogram. X-rays of the spine may reveal an increased interpedicular distance with or without erosion of the pedicles. This is one of the cardinal roentgenographic signs of spinal cord tumors. Examination of the CSF shows elevated protein levels in more than 75 percent of cases. Manometry may demonstrate a partial or complete subarachnoid block.

The myelogram in intramedullary tumors may show a complete block or a partial block, in which latter case the swollen cord in the region of the tumor displaces the contrast medium laterally. In extramedullary intradural tumors the myelogram may also demonstrate a complete block, the contrast medium outlining the upper or lower margins of the tumor as a concave filling defect. Extradural tumors show localized unilateral indentations or an asymmetrical tapering of the radiopaque column in cases of partial obstruction. If the block is complete the column has a concave margin (Fig. 3-7).

An increased interpedicular distance with normal-appearing pedicles is not an infrequent finding in patients with nonprogressive neurologic deficit of the lower extremities and/or sphincter disturbances. Examina-

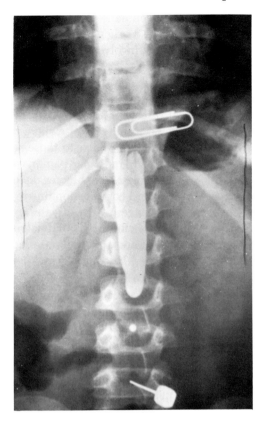

Fig. 3-7. Myelogram in a 5-year-old boy with an extradural sarcoma. There is complete block to the radiopaque column at the level of T_{12}. Onset of symptoms one month prior to admission with pain and stiffness of the back followed by progressive spastic paraparesis and episodes of urinary retention.

tion of the cerebrospinal fluid in these patients is normal, and the myelogram reveals only a wide spinal canal with no evidence of a space-occupying lesion. The neurologic deficit in these patients is almost always due to maldevelopment (myelodysplasia) of the spinal cord.

Spinal cord compression occurs in about 2 percent of patients with lymphomas and leukemias. In patients with lymphomas the level of involvement is usually the dorsal region, followed in order of frequency by the lumbar and the cervical levels. Most patients with lymphomas have radiographic evidence of a lesion at the same level as the spinal cord compression.

Spinal cord disease may occur in lymphomas in one of three ways. Paravertebral involvement may extend along the nerve roots and enter the epidural space through the intervertebral foramina; in this location

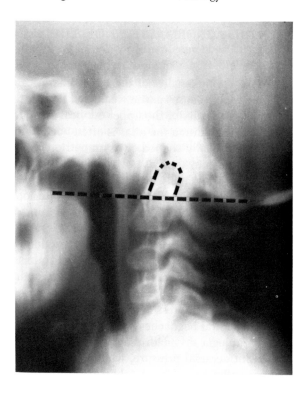

Fig. 3-8.   Basilar impression. Lateral tomogram of the foramen magnum region showing odontoid process of axis about 13 mm. above Chamberlain's line. Also there are hypoplastic vertebral arches and occipitalization of the atlas. Patient is an 8-year-old girl who presented with a 6-month history of nystagmus, occipital pain, and mild locomotor difficulties.

vertebrae. There is also underdevelopment or hypoplasia of cervical vertebrae and occasionally other associated anomalies such as occipitalization of the atlas, thoracic scoliosis, cervical ribs, extraocular palsies, mirror movements of the upper limbs, hydromyelia, or syringomyelia (Fig. 3-10). Patients have a short neck and a low hairline on the back of the neck. Physical examination reveals limitation of head movements due to decrease in the range of motion of the cervical spine. Neurologic symptoms, if present, depend on the associated pathology. These may include spastic paraplegia, sensory deficit, or pyramidal tract signs. The diagnosis can be suspected on clinical grounds (abnormally short neck and low hairline) and confirmed by roentgenographic examination of the cervical spine.

Diastematomyelia

Diastematomyelia is a developmental anomaly of the vertebral column characterized by the presence of a bony or cartilaginous spicule

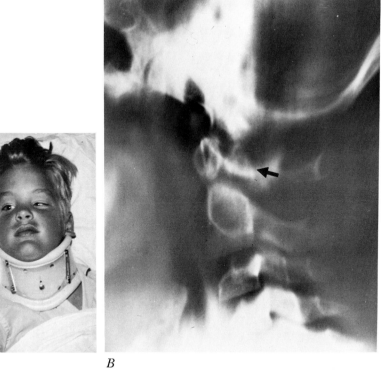

A   B

Fig. 3-9.   A, 10-year-old boy with a history of recurrent episodes of acute flaccid quadriplegia of brief duration following strenuous exercise. On admission to the hospital he had a right peripheral facial paresis, a right abducens paresis, and spastic quadriplegia. B, lateral tomograms of upper cervical spine demonstrated a separated odontoid process of the axis (*arrow*) and marked atlantoaxial dislocation on flexion and extension of the cervical spine.

running dorsoventrally in the spinal canal and dividing the spinal cord in two parts. The bony defect is in the great majority of cases located in the lower thoracic or lumbar spine (Fig. 3-11). The splitting of the spinal cord always extends above and below the bony anomaly over several segments. Associated abnormalities of the spine are invariably present (spina bifida occulta, scoliosis, a wide spinal canal, vertebral fusion, or hemivertebrae). Cutaneous changes overlying the bony defect are common (hair patch, skin dimple, or fat pad).

Diastematomyelia is more common in females than in males. Neurologic symptoms appear before the age of 15. A disturbance of gait is present at one time or another in all patients. Shortening of one leg, muscle atrophy, and bladder dysfunction are frequent signs. Neurologic examination reveals abnormalities in about 80 percent of cases in the form of spastic weakness, decreased or increased muscle stretch reflexes according to the level of the lesion, extensor plantar responses, and sen-

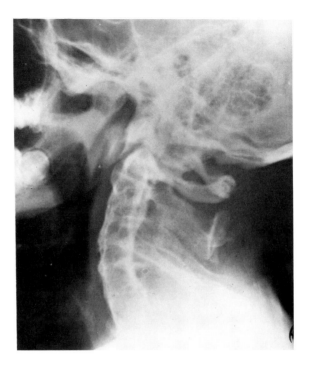

Fig. 3-10. Fusion and underdevelopment of cervical vertebrae (Klippel-Feil anomaly) in an asymptomatic 14-year-old girl.

sory changes. Roentgenographic examination of the entire spine should be done in all patients with the aforementioned signs or symptoms. Since the primary spinal defect cannot always be demonstrated in plain roentgenograms of the spine, the previously mentioned associated anomalies of the vertebral column or the overlying skin assume great diagnostic importance. A myelogram is indicated if any of the previously mentioned spinal abnormalities are present and there are signs of pyramidal tract involvement, such as an extensor plantar response and increased muscle stretch reflexes, or if the neurologic deficit remains otherwise unexplained. Characteristically the myelogram (Fig. 3-12) reveals a double column of contrast medium surrounding the duplicated spinal cord or a large oval filling defect in the midline. The treatment of diastematomyelia is surgical excision of the bony or cartilaginous spur. Surgery prevents further neurologic damage and occasionally relieves symptoms of bladder dysfunction.

FAMILIAL SPASTIC PARAPLEGIA

Familial spastic paraplegia is a condition characterized clinically by progressive spasticity and weakness of the lower extremities without sensory changes and pathologically by selective degeneration of the corticospinal tracts in the spinal cord. The onset is usually in the first or second decade of life and its course is variable. The disease occurs sporadically as well as on a hereditary or familial basis. The diagnosis is made on the basis of progressive spastic weakness of the lower extremities, the absence of sensory changes, and the family history. The differential diagnosis includes multiple sclerosis, other degenerative and familial diseases of the spinal cord, and particularly slowly growing intraspinal tumors which can be ruled out by contrast studies (myelogram).

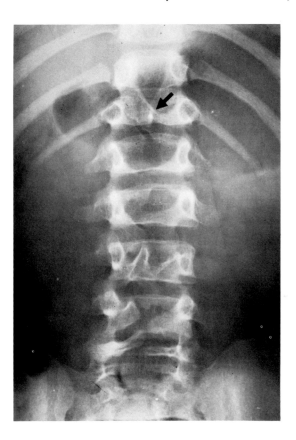

Fig. 3-11. Diastematomyelia. Bony spicule at the level of T_{12} (*arrow*), wide spinal canal at same level, and multiple neural arch defects of lower lumbar vertebrae. (Courtesy of Dr. Sidney Traub)

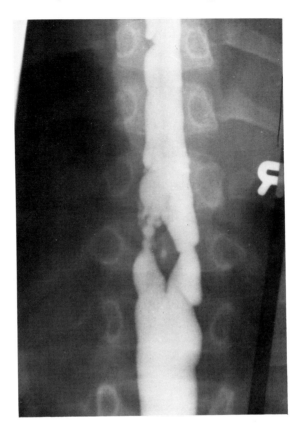

Fig. 3-12. Diastematomyelia. Myelogram showing diamond-shaped defect in radiopaque column. (Courtesy of Dr. Sidney Traub)

NEUROMYELITIS OPTICA

This is a disorder characterized clinically by rapid bilateral loss of vision and an equally rapidly evolving spastic paraplegia and pathologically by plaques of disseminated sclerosis in the optic nerves, brain stem, and spinal cord (Chapter 1).

TRANSVERSE MYELITIS

A transverse myelitis of pyogenic origin (spinal cord abscess) may in rare instances occur during the course of systemic infections such as septicemia, lung abscesses, osteomyelitis, or other infections. The onset of the disease is heralded by back pain and followed by a rapidly evolving flaccid paraplegia, urinary retention, and a sensory level. If the patient survives, the paraplegia become of the spastic variety with increased muscle stretch reflexes and other pyramidal tract signs.

Transverse myelitis is also part of the clinical picture of postinfectious encephalomyelitis, a condition most frequently seen following measles, rubella, and vaccination against smallpox. Infarction of the spinal cord may occur in herpes zoster as the result of thrombosis of a large radicular tributary to the spinal arteries. This complication of herpes zoster is occasionally seen in adults but is extremely rare in children.

A toxic myelitis may occur during aortography when the iodine contrast media is inadvertently injected into the arterial supply of the spinal cord. A similar mechanism of action (retrograde arterial injection) may be responsible for the rare instances in which transverse myelitis has occurred in children following the intragluteal injection of penicillin; in this instance, because of the location of the lesion, a flaccid rather than a spastic paraplegia is more likely to occur. Transverse myelitis may also be a complication of lupus erythematosus disseminatus and periarteritis nodosa.

AMYOTROPHIC LATERAL SCLEROSIS

This is a common disease in adults but is extremely rare in children. When the disease begins in childhood the initial symptoms consist of gait difficulties due to spastic weakness of the lower extremities (see Chapter 2).

TROYER'S SYNDROME

This is a rare disorder inherited as an autosomal recessive and characterized by the onset in early childhood of a slowly progressive spastic paraplegia and distal amyotrophy. Other clinical features are mental retardation, dysarthria, and ataxia. This syndrome has many clinical similarities to amyotrophic lateral sclerosis (Fig. 3-13).

DEGENERATIVE DISEASES OF THE CENTRAL NERVOUS SYSTEM

A common final motor status of a number of degenerative diseases of the central nervous system is spastic weakness (sulfatide lipidosis, Tay-Sachs disease, the leukodystrophies, subacute necrotizing encephalomyelitis). In addition to spasticity, these conditions are characterized

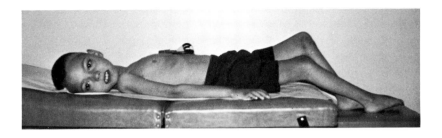

Fig. 3-13.   8-year-old boy with progressive spastic paraplegia, distal wasting in the lower extremities, and flaccid weakness of the upper extremities beginning at the age of 12 months. In addition, he had swallowing difficulties and atrophy and fasciculations of the tongue. Myelogram of entire spine and posterior fossa was normal. The clinical picture in this patient has features common to progressive bulbar palsy, amyotrophic lateral sclerosis, and Troyer's syndrome.

by progressive psychomotor deterioration and a number of other signs indicative of diffuse central nervous system involvement such as ataxia, blindness, deafness, and swallowing difficulties. More than 90 percent of patients with Tay-Sachs disease have a cherry-red spot in the macula; patients with metachromatic leukodystrophy have an increased CSF protein, and often slow nerve conduction velocity can be demonstrated (peripheral neuropathy), even in the presence of spasticity or pyramidal tract signs.

REFERENCES

Aicardi, J., and Lepintre, J.   Spinal epidural abscess in a 1-month-old child. *Amer. J. Dis. Child.* 114:665, 1967.

Caetano De Barros, M., et al.   Basilar impression and Arnold-Chiari malformation: A study of 66 cases. *J. Neurol. Neurosurg. Psychiat.* 31:596, 1968.

Cross, H. E., and McKusick, V. A.   The Troyer syndrome: A recessive form of spastic paraplegia with distal muscle wasting. *Arch. Neurol.* 16:473, 1967.

Dale, A. J.   Diastematomyelia. *Arch. Neurol.* 20:309, 1969.

Grant, F. C.   The diagnosis, treatment and prognosis of tumors affecting the spinal cord in children. *J. Neurosurg.* 13:535, 1956.

Hulme, A., and Dott, N. M.   Spinal epidural abscess. *Brit. Med. J.* 1:64, 1954.

Matson, D. D., and Tachdjian, M. O.   Intraspinal tumors in infants and children. *Postgrad. Med.* 34:279, 1963.

McRae, D. L.   Bony abnormalities in the region of the foramen magnum: Correlation of the anatomic and neurologic findings. *Acta Radiol.* 40:335, 1953.

Morrison, S. G., et al.   Congenital brevicollis (Klippel-Feil syndrome). *Amer. J. Dis. Child.* 115:614, 1968.

Nieri, R. L., et al.   Central-nervous-system complications of leukemia: A review. *Mayo Clin. Proc.* 43:70, 1968.

Perret, G.   Symptoms and diagnosis of diastematomyelia. *Neurology* 10:51, 1960.

Ross, A. T., and Baily, O. T.   Tumors arising within the spinal canal in children. *Neurology* 3:922, 1953.

Schwarz, G. A., and Liu, C. N.   Hereditary (familial) spastic paraplegia. *Arch. Neurol. Psychiat.* 75:144, 1956.

Williams, H. M., Diamond, H. D., Craver, L. F., and Parsons, H.   *Neurological Complications of Lymphomas and Leukemias.* Springfield, Ill.: Thomas, 1959.

Ataxia may be the presenting complaint in a previously healthy child, may follow or complicate various clinical conditions, or may appear at a certain time as part of the natural history of a large number of diseases of the central or peripheral nervous system. Ataxia may be due to impairment in the functioning of many different structures such as peripheral nerves, posterior columns of the spinal cord, posterior columns and spinocerebellar tracts, cerebellum, and cerebellovestibulospinal cord pathways.

From a clinical standpoint ataxia may be classified as acute and chronic. Chronic ataxia can be further subdivided into nonprogressive or progressive.

ACUTE ATAXIA

Intoxications

The most common cause of acute ataxia in all age groups is overdose or intoxication with drugs or toxic compounds. In pediatric practice overdosage of Dilantin, Mysoline, and phenobarbital account in that order of frequency for the great majority of cases of acute ataxia. Overdosage of phenobarbital produces drowsiness and clumsiness rather than a true ataxia. The same is true of overdosage of Mysoline. In rare instances, however, Mysoline may produce a severe truncal and gait ataxia without associated nystagmus. Dilantin intoxication, on the other hand, is a common cause of acute ataxia. It is well known that in young children the therapeutic dosage of Dilantin approaches that at which signs of intoxication appear. Intoxication with Dilantin is manifested by limb and gait ataxia and horizontal and occasionally vertical nystagmus. In rare instances large doses of Dilantin given intravenously for the treatment of status epilepticus may cause permanent damage to the cerebellum and persistent ataxia as the most prominent residual neurologic deficit.

On at least one occasion we have mistaken an acute intoxication with alcoholic beverages in an older child for an acute vascular lesion of the cerebellum.

Bromides are nowadays seldom used in clinical medicine. Formerly they enjoyed popularity as anticonvulsants and sedatives and are still readily available to the general public. Patients receiving bromides manifest drowsiness and marked incoordination when serum levels of bromide are higher than 150–200 mg./100 ml. Diazepam (Valium), a useful drug in the treatment of infantile spasms and myoclonic seizures in older children, commonly produces drowsiness and moderate to severe incoordination at conventional dosage. However, if the dosage of diazepam is slowly increased at weekly intervals most children will eventually be able to tolerate very high dosages without manifesting untoward effects. Other compounds that may produce an acute ataxia are 5-fluorouracil, DDT, and lindane.

Acute Viral Cerebellitis

Viral encephalitis primarily affecting the cerebellum is an uncommon cause of ataxia. Other signs and symptoms of encephalitis such as fever, headache, lethargy, and irritability are usually present. Examination of the cerebrospinal fluid may show a moderate lymphocytic pleocytosis, a normal glucose level, and a mild elevation of the level of protein.

Postinfectious Encephalitis

A postinfectious encephalitis characterized pathologically by perivenous infiltration of cells and demyelination may occur after the common exanthems of childhood, infectious mononucleosis, or an infection with poliomyelitis, Coxsackie, or ECHO viruses. Sometimes the pathologic process may primarily affect the cerebellum. In contrast to the widespread involvement of the CNS seen in cases following measles and rubella, chickenpox tends to produce pathologic changes more marked or limited to the cerebellum. The incidence of postinfectious encephalitis following chickenpox is approximately three per thousand cases. The disease affects children under the age of ten, most patients being under the age of two years. The ataxia has an abrupt onset and usually appears one to three weeks after the original infection, although occasionally it may precede or occur concomitantly with the infection. The child prefers to lie quietly in bed; he may vomit with sudden changes in position; and on attempting to sit up he exhibits marked truncal ataxia. Physical examination reveals incoordination, dysmetria, and intention tremor on finger-to-nose or heel-to-knee tests as well as hypotonia and decreased or pendular muscle stretch reflexes. Nystagmus and slurred speech may or may not be present. Fever, signs of meningeal irritation or increased intracranial pressure are absent. Blood studies and CSF examinations are almost always normal. An occasional patient may show a mild lymphocytic pleocytosis. Postinfectious encephalitis primarily involving the cerebellum is a self-limited disease. The great majority of patients make a complete recovery in 2 to 6 months. In about 25 percent of cases, however, some degree of neurologic deficit in the form of gait disturbances, speech problems, intention tremor, or learning difficulties persists for prolonged periods of time. An acute cerebellar ataxic syndrome in children similar to that produced by postinfectious encephalitis may occur without any signs of preceding infection.

Polyradiculoneuropathy (Guillain-Barré Syndrome)

The first manifestation of polyradiculoneuropathy may be an ataxia totally out of proportion to the muscle weakness exhibited by the patient. This is probably a sensory type of ataxia and is not due to incoordination secondary to muscle weakness. Important diagnostic features of polyradiculoneuropathy are a progressive ascending flaccid paralysis and the classic albuminocytologic dissociation in the cerebrospinal fluid.

Tick Paralysis

The initial clinical manifestation of tick paralysis is commonly a severe ataxia in the absence of any significant muscle weakness. However, since this is a rapidly progressive disease, severe muscle weakness is usually present by the time medical attention is sought.

Prolonged Hyperthermia and Cerebellar Concussion

Prolonged hyperthermia of any cause and cerebellar concussion may in rare instances produce an acute ataxia of variable duration and severity. Following head trauma acute cerebellar ataxia is usually of short duration. Prolonged hyperthermia may cause an acute ataxia of brief duration; in rare instances it may produce a chronic nonprogressive ataxia.

NONPROGRESSIVE CHRONIC ATAXIA

Cerebellar Agenesis

Congenital or developmental ataxia may occur in patients with agenesis or hypoplasia of the cerebellum. Marked incoordination is first noticed at 4 to 5 months of age when the infant begins to reach for objects. These children are usually late walkers, suffer frequent falls, and are overtly clumsy. Speech development is frequently delayed. As the child gets older the cerebellar deficit improves (Fig. 4-1).

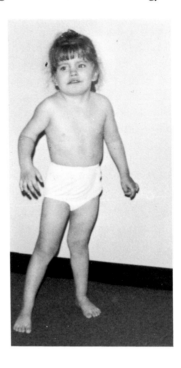

Fig. 4-1. 4-year-old girl with nonprogressive gait and limb ataxia probably due to cerebellar hypoplasia or related developmental abnormality of the cerebellum. Note wide stance and position of trunk and hands. Pneumo-encephalogram done at the age of 2 years showed a large cisterna magna. Her mental development is normal. The ataxia is improving with increasing age.

Dandy-Walker Syndrome

The Dandy-Walker syndrome is a form of obstructive hydrocephalus due to congenital atresia of the foramina of Luschka and Magendie. A frequent pathologic component of this syndrome is congenital hypoplasia or secondary atrophy of the cerebellum due to its compression by a greatly enlarged fourth ventricle. Patients with Dandy-Walker syndrome may have varying degrees of ataxia; however, the clinical picture in most cases is dominated by signs and symptoms of hydrocephalus. Physical examination in these patients reveals a large dolichocephalic skull with an increased ear-to-occiput distance. Roentgenographic examination of the skull demonstrates a large posterior fossa and upward displacement of the lateral sinus. Contrast study (ventriculogram) shows a greatly dilated fourth ventricle and no air in the basal cisterns or subarachnoid space over the convexity of the brain.

Cerebrocerebellar Diplegia

Chronic ataxia may be a prominent clinical feature in patients with cerebrocerebellar diplegia, one of the many forms of cerebral palsy. This is a nonprogressive condition and is in the majority of cases associated with moderate to marked psychomotor retardation as well as with other signs of cerebral palsy.

Hypoglycemia

Frequent and severe episodes of hypoglycemia of any origin during the first years of life may have a devastating effect on the cerebral hemispheres and/or cerebellum and cause permanent nonprogressive ataxia.

Lead Encephalopathy

Mild to moderate ataxia is one of the commonest sequelae in patients surviving from lead encephalopathy.

Marinesco-Sjögren Syndrome

Marinesco-Sjögren syndrome is a rare disorder inherited as an autosomal recessive and characterized by hereditary spinocerebellar ataxia, nystagmus, congenital cataracts, and severe mental retardation.

Maple Syrup Urine Disease (Variant Form)

A variant form of maple syrup disease described by Morris in 1961 is characterized by recurrent episodes of ataxia, lethargy, an odor of maple syrup from the urine, and convulsions instead of the features of the typical form of the disease (severe psychomotor retardation, spasticity, and intractable seizures since early infancy). The episodes appear to be precipitated by infections. During an episode the urine shows increased amounts of the amino acids valine, leucine, and isoleucine. Between episodes levels of urinary amino acids are normal. The child described by Morris was of normal intelligence at 41 months of age.

Hartnup Disease

Hartnup disease is an inborn error of metabolism characterized by impaired intestinal absorption of tryptophan and amino-aciduria. The clinical manifestations of Hartnup disease consist of intermittent episodes of cerebellar ataxia and pellagra-like skin lesions. Plasma tryptophan levels are low. The disease runs a chronic course with remissions and exacerbations. The episodes of ataxia seldom last more than a few weeks. Prolonged administration of nicotinamide appears to be beneficial in preventing attacks.

PROGRESSIVE CHRONIC ATAXIA

Friedreich's Ataxia

Friedreich's ataxia is a heredofamilial disease inherited as a recessive or dominant trait and characterized by the onset of ataxia between 4 and 12 years of age (recessive form) and between 15 and 20 years (dominant form). Friedreich's ataxia is characterized pathologically by degenerative changes in the posterior ganglia and posterior roots of spinal nerves, posterior columns, ventral and dorsal spinocerebellar tracts, and corticospinal tracts. The degenerative changes are more prominent in the dorsal than in the ventral spinocerebellar tracts.

The earliest and most prominent sign is ataxia of gait and ataxia of the lower extremities. Ataxia of the upper extremities is less conspicuous. The ataxia is markedly increased when the eyes are closed. Skeletal abnormalities, such as pes cavus and kyphoscoliosis, occur eventually in almost all patients (Fig. 4-2). Involvement of the cranial nerves occasionally occurs. Nystagmus is present in about 50 percent of patients at some time in the course of the disease. Muscle stretch, abdominal, and cremasteric reflexes are hypoactive or absent. Plantar responses are usually extensor (Babinski sign). Signs of posterior column deficit such as loss of vibration, deep pain, position sense, and two-point discrimination occur in all patients at some stage of the natural course of the disease. The speech frequently deteriorates and becomes explosive and slurred. A typical retinitis pigmentosa and optic atrophy with decreased visual acuity are present in 10 percent of patients with Friedreich's ataxia.

Involvement of the heart is common and may be manifested by sinus tachycardia, arrhythmias, or by a progressive interstitial myocarditis. We have seen one patient with Friedreich's ataxia who had symptoms of angina pectoris for several years and died at the age of 25 of a myocardial infarction. Electrocardiographic abnormalities, present in about 50 percent of patients, consist of T-wave inversion, arrhythmias, and signs of left ventricular hypertrophy (Fig. 4-3).

A diagnosis of Friedreich's ataxia is based on a positive family history, progressive limb and gait ataxia beginning during the first or second decade, signs of posterior column deficit, decreased or absent muscle stretch reflexes, a positive Babinski sign, and progressive skeletal deformities.

Hereditary Ataxia with Muscular Atrophy

Hereditary ataxia with muscular atrophy (Roussy-Lévy syndrome) is a progressive disease with features of both Friedreich's ataxia and Charcot-Marie-Tooth disease (distal muscle atrophy of the legs, ataxia, and variable degree of sensory loss).

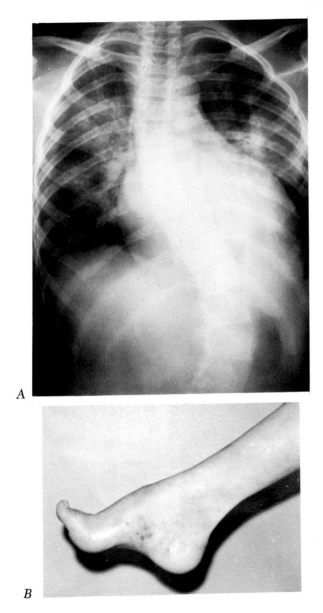

Fig. 4-2. A, chest x-ray showing scoliosis and cardiac enlargement in 10-year-old boy with Friedreich's ataxia. *B,* pes cavus and hammertoe in same patient.

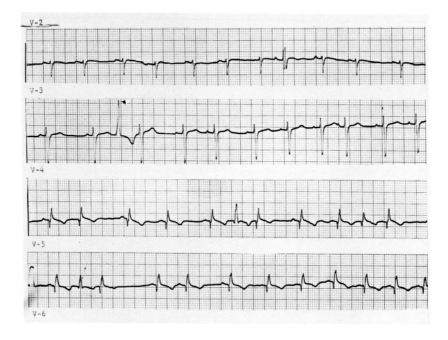

Fig. 4-3. Electrocardiogram in patient with Friedreich's ataxia showing occasional premature ventricular contractions, negative T waves over the left lateral chest leads, and prominent Q waves.

A-beta-lipoproteinemia (Bassen-Kornzweig Syndrome)

A-beta-lipoproteinemia is a rare disease, inherited as an autosomal recessive trait and characterized biochemically by the absence of low-density lipoproteins in plasma. The main clinical manifestations are steatorrhea in early childhood, thornlike erythrocytes (acanthocytosis), a neuromuscular disorder similar to Friedreich's ataxia, atypical retinitis pigmentosa, and abnormal lipid metabolism with absent beta-lipoproteins and decreased serum levels of cholesterol, phospholipids, and triglycerides.

Ataxia-Telangiectasia (Louis-Bar Syndrome)

Ataxia-telangiectasia is an inherited disorder characterized by progressive cerebellar ataxia, oculocutaneous telangiectasia and recurrent sinopulmonary infections. Cerebellar ataxia is the first symptom to appear, usually between the second and fourth year of life. Telangiectasia of the bulbar conjunctiva, eyelids, external ears, neck, elbow folds, and popliteal fossa develops two or three years after the onset of ataxia.

Psychomotor retardation is present in about 50 percent of cases. Patients with ataxia-talangiectasia have low levels of IgA immunoglobulins; their lymphocytes appear to be incompetent and skin homografts exhibit a prolonged survival. In addition, at autopsy structural abnormalities of the thymus gland frequently have been observed. All these findings indicate that patients with this condition have a severe deficiency in immunologic mechanisms. An unusual form of diabetes mellitus has been reported in patients with ataxia-telangiectasia. This is characterized by marked hyperglycemia, absence of glycosuria, and markedly elevated plasma insulin levels after administration of glucose or tolbutamide. Common causes of death in patients with ataxia-telangiectasia have been pneumonia and neoplasias of lymphoid tissue. It is of interest that the patient originally reported by Mme. Louis-Bar developed in early adolescence the first signs and then in early adulthood the full-blown clinical picture of Friedreich's ataxia.

Juvenile Tabes

Juvenile tabes is an extremely rare disease. The first symptoms appear at puberty and consist of decreased visual acuity, urinary incontinence, lightning pains of the extremities, and ataxia. Cranial nerve palsies occur in about 50 percent of cases. In contrast to adults with tabes the Argyll Robertson pupil is not a frequent finding; in children the pupils are more apt to be dilated and fixed. Juvenile tabes runs a slowly chronic course and is a relatively benign condition when compared with the disease in adults. The ataxia of juvenile tabes progresses very slowly over a period of many years.

Posterior Fossa Lesions

A number of space-occupying lesions in the posterior fossa may produce progressive ataxia. Medulloblastomas originate from the posterior vermis of the cerebellum and cause gait and trunk ataxia. Nystagmus in all directions of gaze may be present. Cerebellar astrocytomas, more than 80 percent of which arise from one of the lateral lobes of the cerebellum, produce the so-called lateral cerebellar syndrome, which consists of ipsilateral limb ataxia, ipsilateral hypotonia and decreased muscle stretch reflexes, and nystagmus, with the gross component to the side of the lesion and the fine to the opposite side. Patients with tumors of the cerebellar hemispheres often tilt their head to the side of the lesion.

Ependymomas of the fourth ventricle produce ataxia less frequently than do other posterior fossa tumors. The ataxia with this type of tumor is manifested by gait difficulties only, is of moderate degree, and is almost never the presenting complaint.

Hemangioblastoma of the cerebellum, an uncommon posterior fossa tumor, may be suspected on clinical grounds on the basis of a positive family history (autosomal dominant inheritance), the presence of associated eye disease (glaucoma, retinal detachment), kidney tumors, cutaneous nevi or angiomas, paroxysmal hypertension, and erythrocytemia, which is present in about 20 percent of patients and is due to the production of erythropoietin by the tumor.

Cerebellar hematomas may be caused by trauma of the occiput, may occur in patients with blood dyscrasias such as acute leukemia and thrombocytopenic purpura, or may be secondary to the spontaneous rupture of an angiomatous malformation of the posterior fossa. In cases due to head trauma the clinical course may be acute (hours), subacute (weeks), or chronic (months). In acute cases the onset is apopleptic, with sudden loss of consciousness, cardiorespiratory difficulties, and death. In subacute and chronic cases the clinical manifestations are similar to those produced by tumors of the cerebellar hemispheres (lateral cerebellar syndrome). Cerebellopontine-angle tumors (acoustic neurinomas, cholesteatomas, meningiomas) may cause ataxia by compression of the cerebellum or the brain stem. Long before the appearance of ataxia, however, there is deafness without tinnitus and a peripheral facial paralysis on the same side of the lesion.

Refsum's Disease

Refsum's disease produces a mixed sensory-central type of ataxia. This disease is characterized by a polyneuritis, indistinguishable on clinical or pathologic grounds from that seen in hypertrophic interstitial polyneuritis (Dejerine-Sottas), retinitis pigmentosa, and deafness. In Refsum's disease there is an abnormal accumulation of phytanic acid (3,7,11,15-tetramethyl-hexadecanoic acid) in many body tissues. A definite diagnosis can be made by the demonstration of an elevated serum level of phytanic acid by lipid chromatography.

Multiple Sclerosis

Multiple sclerosis is rare in children. Most cases occur in the third or fourth decade. The disease is characterized pathologically by disseminated plaques of demyelination in the brain and spinal cord and clinically by multiple neurologic signs and symptoms and by remissions and exacerbations. The most common initial complaint in one study of 40 cases of multiple sclerosis with onset prior to age 20 was incoordination, muscle weakness, or both. Additional symptoms during the initial episode included visual disturbances (blurred vision, partial blindness), numbness or tingling of the affected extremities, and transient disturbances of urinary function. Physical findings following the initial episode included muscle weakness affecting more commonly the legs, gait ataxia, extensor plantar response, temporal pallor of optic discs, and sensory deficit. Examination of the cerebrospinal fluid in multiple sclerosis shows a moderate lymphocytic pleocytosis and a normal or slightly elevated protein level with an increase in its gamma globulin fraction. The clinical course of multiple sclerosis in children appears to be similar to that seen in adults. A diagnosis of multiple sclerosis should be entertained when a child presents multiple neurologic deficit indicative of scattered CNS dysfunction.

Pelizaeus-Merzbacher Disease

Pelizaeus-Merzbacher disease, one of the leukodystrophies, is a familial disease inherited as a sex-linked recessive trait with onset in early infancy. The clinical picture consists of nystagmus, tremor of the head, a spastic paralysis, pyramidal tract signs (increased muscle stretch reflexes and Babinski sign), and ataxia. In contrast to other leukodystrophies or degenerative diseases of early infancy, the disease runs a chronic course.

Sulfatide Lipidosis (Metachromatic Leukodystrophy)

Ataxia and nystagmus are prominent signs in patients with sulfatide lipidosis. A normal early psychomotor development is one of the most constant clinical features in patients with this condition. The first symptoms usually appear between 1 and 2 years of age and consist of weakness, hypotonia or spastic paraparesis, ataxia, regression in speech, and swallowing difficulties. Seizures occur in about half and optic atrophy in one-third of patients. Muscle stretch reflexes are hypo- or hyperactive depending on the relative degree of involvement of the central or peripheral nervous system. Patients with sulfatide lipidosis characteristically have elevated levels of CSF protein. A definite diagnosis can be made by the demonstration of metachromatic granules in sural nerve biopsy or by the demonstration of decreased levels or absent arylsulfatase A activity in the urine.

REFERENCES

Baron, D. N., et al.   Hereditary pellagra-like skin rash with temporary cerebellar ataxia, constant renal aminoaciduria, and other bizarre biochemical features. *Lancet* 2:421, 1956.
Bassen, F. A., and Kornzweig, A. L.   Malformation of the erythrocytes in a case of atypical retinitis pigmentosa. *Blood* 5:381, 1950.
Farquhar, J. W., and Ways, P.   Abetalipoproteinemia (Bassen-Kornzweig Disease). In Stanbury, J. B., Wyngaarden, J. B., and Fredrickson, D. S.: *The Metabolic Basis of Inherited Diseases* (2nd ed.). New York: McGraw-Hill, 1966, pp. 509–522.
Gall, J. C., et al.   Multiple sclerosis in children. *Pediatrics* 21:703, 1958.
Hoffmann, W. W.   Cerebellar lesions after parenteral Dilantin administration. *Neurology* 8:210, 1958.

Karpati, G., et al.   Ataxia-telangiectasia: Further observations and report of eight cases. *Amer. J. Dis. Child.* 110:57, 1965.

Morris, M. D., et al.   Clinical and biochemical observations on an apparently non-fatal variant of branched-chain ketoaciduria (maple syrup urine disease). *Pediatrics* 28:918, 1961.

Nevin, N. C., et al.   Refsum's syndrome: Heredopathia atactica polyneuritiformis. *Brain* 90:419, 1967.

Refsum, S. Heredopathia atactica polyneuritiformis. *Acta Psychiat. Scand.* Suppl. 38, 1946.

Rosenthal, I. R., et al. Immunologic incompetence in ataxia-telangiectasia. *Amer. J. Dis. Child.* 110:69, 1965.

Sjögren, T.   Hereditary congenital spinocerebellar ataxia accompanied by congenital cataract and oligophrenia. *Confin. Neurol.* 10:293, 1950.

Thilenius, O. G., and Grossman, B. J.   Friedreich's ataxia with heart disease in children. *Pediatrics* 27:246, 1961.

5

Abnormal Movement
and Posture

ABNORMAL MOVEMENTS or postures are characteristic and constant clinical manifestations of a number of diseases of the central nervous system involving the extrapyramidal system. They may also be the most outstanding sign in several conditions of uncertain etiology which have in common a slow but progressive improvement with advancing age. In other instances abnormal body movements or postures may be temporary, self-limited events as the result of adverse reactions to drug ingestion or in rare occasions be the only apparent manifestation of an underlying emotional disorder.

HABIT SPASMS

Habit spasms are painless stereotyped movements of a group of muscles repeating at variable intervals, and occurring in a background of complete normality. The movements of habit spasms always follow the same pattern with regard to such variables as rhythm, intensity, amplitude, and duration. The repetitive movements of habit spasms may manifest as facial grimaces, winking, shrugging of one or both shoulders or mild extension of the head and retraction of the jaw. As a rule they do not interfere with normal activities.

MUSCLE SPASMS

Muscle spasms or cramps are sudden violent involuntary contractions of a muscle or group of muscles. Muscle spasms are a prominent feature of several clinical entities such as McArdle's disease (myophosphorylase deficiency), neuromyotonia, hypocalcemic tetany (carpopedal spasm), and in the stiff-man syndrome (not reported in children). Ordinary muscle cramps occur frequently in healthy adults and seldom in

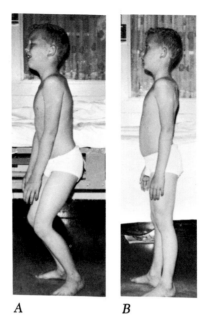

A   B

Fig. 5-1. 8-year-old boy with bilateral painful contraction of hamstring muscles of two days duration. Before (A) and after (B) the administration of Valium (diazepam) intramuscularly.

children. They usually involve the muscles of the limbs, most commonly the legs, and last no more than a few seconds or minutes. Rarely one may see a child with prolonged symmetrical painful spasm of a certain group of muscles lasting for one or more days (Fig. 5-1). The etiology of these prolonged muscle spasms is obscure and all laboratory investigations including serum electrolytes, x-rays of the spine, serum enzyme studies, CSF examination and the electromyogram are normal. It is possible that emotional factors may play a role in such cases. Transient impairment of the inhibitory mechanisms of the anterior horn cells may offer an alternative explanation. A similar etiologic mechanism has been offered to explain muscle spasms in the early stages of poliomyelitis and in strychnine poisoning.

SPASMUS NUTANS

Spasmus nutans is a disorder of movement which occurs during the first 2 years of life and is characterized by involuntary head nodding, tilting of the head, and nystagmus. The onset of spasmus nutans is usually between 4 and 12 months of age. Head nodding may be intermittent or constant and take place in an anteroposterior or lateral direction. The nystagmus is usually horizontal and often more marked in one eye. Spasmus nutans is a self-limited condition; spontaneous improvement occurs by the end of the second year of life.

PAROXYSMAL TORTICOLLIS OF INFANCY

Paroxysmal torticollis of infancy, a newly described condition, is characterized by periodic episodes of torticollis which develop suddenly in an otherwise healthy infant usually between 2 and 8 months of age. The episodes are often associated with irritability, vomiting, pallor, and occasionally an unsteady gait. A single attack may last from a few minutes to 14 days, but the average duration is generally 2 to 3 days. The frequency of the episodes varies in different patients from one every 3 to 6 months to two or three per month. During the attack the child tilts his head to one side and resists attempts to straighten it. There is no loss of awareness, lapse of consciousness, or tonic-clonic movements. Language is not impaired in older children.

Roentgenographic examination of the cervical spine permits ruling out recurrent subluxation as the cause of paroxysmal torticollis. The electroencephalogram shows no abnormalities. CSF examination and a ventriculogram done in one of two patients seen by us were normal. These studies permit ruling out a posterior fossa lesion producing brain stem compression or cerebellar herniation in a patient whose presenting complaints are ataxia and torticollis. One of our patients manifested a moderate to marked ataxia of gait during the attacks, adding support to the suggestion that paroxysmal torticollis of infancy may be an unusual form of labyrinthitis. The attacks cease spontaneously in most patients by 4 to 5 years of age.

FAMILIAL ESSENTIAL TREMOR

Essential hereditary tremor is a familial condition inherited as an autosomal dominant trait and manifested by the onset in childhood or early adulthood of intention tremor of the hand and arms and less frequently of the head. Tremor of the legs is not present. The tremor is slow (4–6 per second) and varies in amplitude and severity from patient to patient and in the same patient under different circumstances. The tremor is not present at rest and is exaggerated by stressful situations. On finger-to-nose test there is usually a terminal tremor which does not have the characteristics of a true ataxia. Many patients with essential tremor have a mild to moderate defect in articulation. Handwriting is invariably affected to varying degrees according to the severity of the tremor. Essential hereditary tremor is a benign condition. A diagnosis can be made on the basis of its character, the absence of other neurologic signs, a positive family history, and its nonprogressive nature.

JUVENILE PARALYSIS AGITANS

Juvenile paralysis agitans is a slowly progressive disease characterized pathologically by degeneration of the large cells of the lenticular nuclei and clinically by a parkinsonian syndrome similar to that of adult patients with Parkinson's disease. Most cases are sporadic, but a few familial cases have been reported. The first symptoms begin usually before the age of 15 years and consist of tremor at rest which decreases by volitional movement. Initially only one extremity may be involved but later on all extremities become affected. As the disease progresses the patient exhibits a masklike facies, rigidity, bradykinesia (abnormal slowness of movements), dysarthria, and gait difficulties. The disease runs a relentlessly progressive course and eventually the patient is bedridden or confined to a wheelchair.

CHOREA

Chorea is the term used to describe a disorder of movement characterized by explosive, involuntary, and purposeless movements. Chorea is a symptom and not a disease.

Congenital Chorea

Congenital chorea or congenital choreoathetosis may be one of the many manifestations of cerebral palsy. The abnormal movements of congenital chorea usually do not become apparent until the infant begins to perform purposeful movements. Marked hypotonia is so commonly associated that during the first few months of life the question of a lower motor neuron disease (floppy infant) is often raised.

Acquired Chorea

Acquired chorea and choreoathetosis may be the end result of a great variety of insults to the brain.

BILIRUBIN ENCEPHALOPATHY.   In the neonatal period (first week of life) chorea is a frequent sequela of bilirubin encephalopathy (kernicterus). Bilirubin encephalopathy is an acute degeneration and pigmentation of nuclei of the brain, brain stem, and cerebellum associated with jaundice in a newborn infant in the first week of life. Most children who survive the acute phase of the disease eventually develop a choreoathetoid movement disorder characterized by involuntary movements of the extremities usually precipitated or aggravated by spontaneous motions or emotions. Additional neurologic sequelae in children surviving bilirubin encephalopathy are paralysis of upward gaze, hearing loss especially for high tones, and mental retardation.

CARBON MONOXIDE INTOXICATION.   Chorea is sometimes seen in patients surviving acute or chronic carbon monoxide intoxication.

DILANTIN INTOXICATION.   Chorea has also been recorded in patients recovering from severe Dilantin intoxication.

Sydenham's Chorea

Sydenham's chorea is one of the many manifestations of rheumatic fever. Since this is a condition in which complete recovery usually occurs there is no clear evidence as to the nature of its pathology. Rheumatic chorea is a disease of early life. More than 75 percent of cases occur between 5 and 15 years. Rheumatic chorea is extremely rare before 3 or after the age of 20 years. Girls are affected twice as frequently as boys.

Sydenham's chorea is characterized clinically by the sudden onset of involuntary, brief, and explosive movements of variable amplitude, involving the extremities, face, and tongue. Physical examination reveals generalized hypotonia and normal, decreased, or increased muscle stretch reflexes. The knee jerk may be pendular. An abnormal posturing of the hands, with the hand flexed at the wrist and the fingers hyperextended (Warner's sign), is seen when the patient stretches out his arms. The inability to maintain a steady muscle contraction or a certain posture can be demonstrated by asking the patient to squeeze the examiner's finger (milkmaid's grip) or to protrude the tongue (darting tongue). Occasionally there is severe weakness of voluntary movements (paralytic chorea) or extreme restlessness, emotional lability, and inappropriate behavior (chorea insaniens). An episode of Sydenham's chorea rarely lasts more than 3 months. Recurrences occur in about 20 percent of cases. With the exception of elevated antistreptococcal antibodies, laboratory studies are normal. Rheumatic heart disease eventually develops in about 25 percent of patients who do not receive prolonged and continuous prophylactic antistreptococcal therapy.

Huntington's Chorea

Huntington's chorea is a familial disease inherited by a single dominant gene. If one generation escapes, the disease does not return in the same family. The average age of onset of Huntington's chorea is 35 years and its duration from 5 to 30 years, with an average of 13 years. Huntington's chorea is characterized by the triad of chorea, which is usually the first symptom, mental deterioration, and psychosis or mental disturbances with suicidal tendencies. Mental changes are manifested by extreme irritability, personality changes, apathy, and a progressive dementia.

The clinical picture of Huntington's chorea in childhood differs in several ways from that seen when the disease begins in adulthood (Fig. 5-2). Convulsive seizures are a common initial manifestation in children. Slowness of movements (bradykinesia), loss of associated movements, and muscular rigidity are much more frequent clinical findings in children than in adults. Other signs such as incoordination, ataxia, and intention tremor due to cerebellar dysfunction are also frequent when the disease begins in early life. The average duration of Huntington's chorea is 8 years in children and 13 years in adults.

Fig. 5-2.   9-year-old girl with Huntington's chorea. Notice abnormal posturing of outstretched arms and hands. Onset of symptoms at the age of 6 years with major motor seizures, progressive mental deterioration and choreiform movements. Father and paternal grandfather also affected.

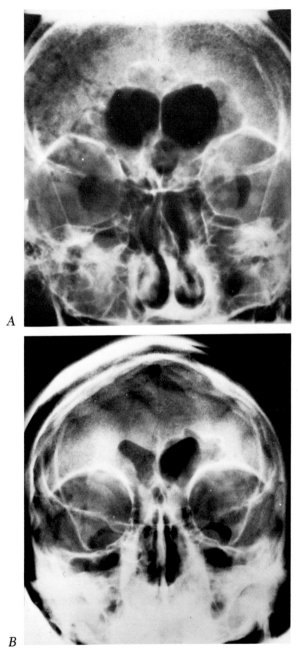

Fig. 5-3. *A*, pneumoencephalogram in 18-year-old patient with Huntington's chorea showing selective enlargement of the anterior horn of the lateral ventricles due to atrophy of the caudate nucleus. *B*, normal pneumoencephalogram in another patient of same age. Note normal-sized temporal horns of lateral ventricles in both cases.

Pathologically there is atrophy of the caudate nucleus and putamen. The globus pallidus and subthalamic nuclei are affected to a lesser degree. In the cerebral cortex there is neuronal degeneration, especially in the frontal lobes. Laboratory studies are normal. The pneumoencephalogram may be of help in the diagnosis by demonstrating selective enlargement of the anterior horn of the lateral ventricles due to atrophy of the caudate nucleus (Fig. 5-3). The diagnosis of Huntington's chorea is made on the basis of the family history, a progressive organic dementia, rigidity, and/or chorea.

HYPERURICEMIA, ATHETOSIS, AND SELF-MUTILATION (LESCH-NYHAN SYNDROME)

Lesch and Nyhan in 1964 described a syndrome occurring only in boys and characterized by mental retardation, bilateral dystonic movements, self-mutilation, and hyperuricemia. Patients with this disorder also exhibit athetoid movements, opisthotonic positioning on stimulation, involuntary bilateral flinging of the arms, and torsion spasms.

HEPATOLENTICULAR DEGENERATION (WILSON'S DISEASE)

Wilson's disease is an inborn error of copper metabolism inherited as an autosomal recessive character. Copper is an essential component of cytochrome oxidase, tyrosinase, and ceruloplasmin. Following absorption in the intestinal tract, copper is first bound to albumin in the liver and then to ceruloplasmin in the plasma. Normal serum values of ceruloplasmin are 23–43 mg./100 ml. The basic pathophysiologic abnormality in Wilson's disease appears to be an increased absorption of copper from the gastrointestinal tract. In Wilson's disease there is a low serum copper content and serum levels of ceruloplasmin of less than 23 mg./100 ml. Urinary excretion of copper, on the other hand, is markedly increased.

Wilson's disease is characterized clinically by cirrhosis of the liver and a variety of neurologic manifestations such as abnormal posturing, muscular hypertonia, tremor, dystonia, chorea, and athetoid movements. The presenting complaint of Wilson's disease is usually tremor in adults and cirrhosis of the liver in children. In the late stages of the disease there is incoordination, ataxia, dysarthria, dysphagia, marked drooling, and retraction of the upper lip (fatuous smile). Wilson's disease is a disease of young people. If, untreated, its course is progressive, with an average duration of 5 to 10 years after onset of the first symptoms.

Pathologically, Wilson's disease is characterized by a postnecrotic cirrhosis of the liver and degenerative changes in the brain, particularly in the basal ganglia, where there are cavitations of the lenticular nuclei, widespread neuronal loss, and marked glial proliferation. In Wilson's disease there is deposition of copper in the brain, kidneys, and iris. A pathognomonic sign of Wilson's disease is the Kayser-Fleischer corneal ring which consists of a greenish-brown discoloration of the periphery of the iris secondary to deposition of copper in Descemet's membrane. Kidney involvement is manifested by amino-aciduria, hyperphosphatemia, glycosuria, and defective acidification with increased potassium excretion and water loss. Hypouricemia is a frequent laboratory finding.

Since Wilson's disease is a treatable disease all siblings of an affected individual should be screened at an early age, probably between 6 and 12 months of age, in an attempt to detect low serum levels of ceruloplasmin. If the ceruloplasmin level is decreased, puncture biopsy of the liver can be performed for definite confirmation of the diagnosis. A hepatic content of copper in excess of 250 μg./gm. dried liver is diagnostic and is usually associated with significant histologic changes. Treatment of Wilson's disease with penicillamine has produced remarkable improvement in many patients.

DYSTONIA MUSCULORUM DEFORMANS

Dystonia musculorum deformans is a clinical entity characterized by spasmodic flexion of the feet, involuntary dystonic movements of the arms, and opisthotonic posturing. Dystonia musculorum deformans occurs most frequently in individuals of Russian Jewish origin. However, cases have been described in other groups. The two sexes are affected with equal frequency. Most cases of dystonia musculorum deformans are sporadic, but families in which several members have been affected are recorded.

The onset of dystonia musculorum deformans is usually between the ages of 5 and 15 years. The great majority of patients exhibit their first symptoms between 5 and 10 years. The dystonic movements, with their writhing and twisting characteristics, produce one of the most bizarre clinical pictures. Owing to the almost unbelievable nature of the movement disorder, some patients with dystonia musculorum deformans are initially diagnosed as psychoneurotic. The dystonic spasms first appear during walking or following spontaneous movement. As the disease progresses they may be initiated by any stimulation or attempts to move an extremity. The feet or an entire extremity may be fixed in a position of flexion; this may eventually lead to permanent deformity.

Marked lumbar lordosis is a constant feature of this disorder. Jaw retraction and torticollis eventually appear in all patients. In the late stages of the disease the thighs become fixed in a position of flexion and abduction and the arms flexed at the wrist, extended at the elbow and abducted and internally rotated at the shoulder. Irregular, slow writhing, purposeless movements may still occur in this background of abnormal posture, leading to grotesque positioning of the entire body. The abnormal movements disappear during sleep, and emotions tend to increase their severity.

Dystonia musculorum deformans is a slowly progressive disease with total incapacity ensuing in the great majority of patients within 5 to 10 years after onset of symptoms. Stereotaxic surgical lesions in the basal ganglia appear to benefit a significant number of patients with this condition. The effect of L-dopa in the treatment of dystonia musculorum deformans is being evaluated at the present time.

SPASMODIC TORTICOLLIS

Spasmodic torticollis is a disorder of posture which rarely begins in childhood. Its onset is usually between the ages of 20 and 60 years with more than half of cases occurring between 30 and 50 years. In this condition the head is drawn into a variety of abnormal positions, most commonly one of lateral flexion with rotation and torsion. Anteroposterior flexion (antecollis) and extension deformity (retrocollis) may also occur. In the more common variety of lateral flexion (torticollis) the involved muscles are the sternocleidomastoid, scalenus, and trapezius. On physical examination these muscles are frequently hypertrophied and tender to palpation. Environmental stimuli tend to precipitate or aggravate muscle contractions. All laboratory studies are normal.

If untreated, the course of spasmodic torticollis is as a general rule progressive. Surgically produced thalamic lesions have relieved symptoms in some patients. Recently encouraging results have been obtained in the treatment of this condition with high dosages of diazepam (Valium). Spasmodic torticollis with onset after birth should not be confused with congenital torticollis secondary to fibrosis and shortening of the sternocleidomastoid muscle.

FAMILIAL PAROXYSMAL CHOREOATHETOSIS

Familial paroxysmal choreoathetosis is a hereditary disorder characterized by the onset during childhood of episodic and short-lasting choreoathetoid movements of the extremities, torsion spasms of the trunk, and facial grimacing. The episodes are usually precipitated by active initiation of movements, especially after a period of immobility. Stressful or startling situations increase the severity of the abnormal movements. The attacks last from a few seconds to a few minutes and are not accompanied by disturbances of consciousness. The general and neurologic examination and laboratory studies are normal. The electroencephalogram may show nonspecific abnormalities. A history of similar episodes or a history of convulsive seizures is often elicited in other family members. Familial paroxysmal choreoathetosis is thought to represent a form of reflex epilepsy. A convulsive etiology is supported by the nature of its clinical features and the excellent response to anticonvulsant therapy. The normal or nonspecific electroencephalographic changes in patients with familial paroxysmal choreoathetosis would indicate that, if this is indeed a form of epilepsy, the seizure discharges must arise from deeply located cerebral structures.

GILLES DE LA TOURETTE'S SYNDROME

Gilles de la Tourette's syndrome (GDTS), one of the most bizarre movement disorders, is characterized by recurrent episodes of rapid tic-like movements involving the face and upper extremities, inarticulate vocalizations such as barking, obscene utterances, and echolalia. GDTS is a rare condition. The movement disorder begins usually between 4 and 16 years of age. Initially, only the muscles of the face are involved, but eventually the arms and legs also become affected. The abnormal movements disappear during sleep, are exaggerated by excitement, and are decreased by concentration and occasionally volition. Prognosis is good in terms of a normal lifespan, and patients are not incapacitated beyond the social limitations imposed by the peculiar tics and obscene utterances. One of the nine patients originally reported by Gilles de la Tourette exhibited her first symptoms at age 7 and died at age 85 still uttering obscenities. Diazepam (Valium) and haloperidol appear to be of some value in the treatment of this condition.

DRUG-INDUCED EXTRAPYRAMIDAL REACTIONS

Temporary and occasionally permanent extrapyramidal dysfunction may occur as a consequence of adverse reactions to the administration of drugs, particularly phenothiazine derivatives. The great majority of cases occur in older patients with psychiatric disturbances treated with phenothiazine derivatives for prolonged periods of time. In children a self-limited movement disorder is not an infrequent complication following the administration of prochlorperazine (Compazine) for the treatment of vomiting. In rare instances intoxication with diphenylhy-

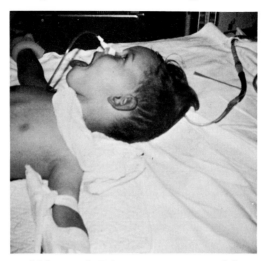

Fig. 5-4.   4-year-old boy with Dilantin intoxication exhibiting agitated behavior, dystonic movements, and intermittent opisthotonos and forceful protrusion of the tongue in various directions.

dantoin (Dilantin) may produce similar clinical manifestations (Fig. 5-
4). The clinical picture consists of one or more of the following: spasms
of the muscles of the neck, extensor rigidity of the muscles of the back,
carpopedal spasms, trismus, and swallowing difficulties. These symptoms gradually subside within a few hours or days after withdrawal of
the drug. The administration of an antihistamine or an antiparkinsonian drug rapidly controls symptoms.

TIPTOE GAIT

Tiptoe gait is an infrequent presenting complaint in early childhood.
Some normal infants walk on the tip of their toes for periods varying
from a few weeks to 3 months after they begin to walk. Rarely an
otherwise normal child will walk and run on the tip of his toes for more
than 3 months (Fig. 5-5). The neurologic examination of these infants
is entirely normal. There is no weakness of the dorsiflexor muscles of
the feet, the Achilles tendon is not tight, and the muscle stretch reflexes
are normal. Sensory examination shows no abnormalities; there are no
sphincter disturbances; and roentgenographic examination of the entire
spine is normal. Nevertheless, several diagnostic possibilities have to be
considered in the differential diagnosis of a child with a persistent unilateral or bilateral tiptoe gait. Following is a list of some conditions
which may cause a child to walk on the tips of his toes from early life or
after a normal gait pattern has developed: spastic diplegia (mild

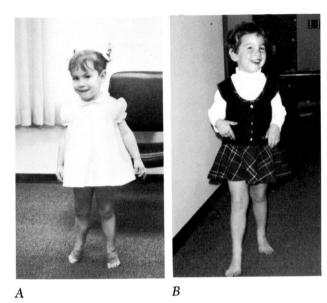

Fig. 5-5.   A, 18-month-old infant who stood and walked on the tips of her toes. *B*, at 3 years of age child is still walking intermittently in the same fashion. Normal neurologic examination and normal x-rays of the spine.

form), spastic paraparesis (mild form), diastematomyelia, myelodysplasia, spinal cord tumors, tight filum terminale, muscular dystrophy, dystonia musculorum deformans, Charcot-Marie-Tooth disease, and juvenile schizophrenia.

REFERENCES

Ayoub, E. M., and Wannamaker, L. W.   Streptococcal antibody titers in Sydenham's chorea. *Pediatrics* 38:946, 1966.

Cooper, I. S.   Dystonia reversal by operation on basal ganglia. *Arch. Neurol.* 7:132, 1962.

Dabbous, I. A., and Bergman, A. B.   Neurologic damage associated with phenothiazine. *Amer. J. Dis. Child.* 111:291, 1966.

Denny-Brown, D.   Hepatolenticular degeneration (Wilson's disease). *New Eng. J. Med.* 270:1149, 1964.

Feild, J. R., et al.   Gilles de la Tourette syndrome. *Neurology* 16:453, 1966.

Healy, C. E.   Gilles de la Tourette's syndrome (maladie des tics): Successful treatment with haloperidol. *Amer. J. Dis. Child.* 120:62, 1970.

Herz, E.   Dystonia: I. Historical review; analysis of dystonic symptoms and physiologic mechanisms involved. *Arch. Neurol. Psychiat.* 51:305, 1944.

Herz, E.   Dystonia: II. Clinical classification. *Arch. Neurol. Psychiat.* 51:319, 1944.

Herz, E., and Glaser, G. H.   Spasmodic torticollis: II. Clinical evaluation. *Arch. Neurol. Psychiat.* 61:217, 1949.

Keats, S.   Dystonia musculorum deformans progressiva: Experience with diazepam. *Dis. Nerv. Syst.* 24:624, 1963.

Lesch, M., and Nyhan, W. L.   A familial disorder of uric acid metabolism and central nervous system function. *Amer. J. Med.* 36:561, 1964.

Lewis-Jonsson, J.   Chorea: Its nomenclature, etiology and epidemiology in a clinical material from Malmohus County, 1910–1944. *Acta Paediat. Scand.* (Suppl.) 76:1, 1949.

Markham, C. H., and Knox, J. W.   Observations on Huntington's chorea in childhood. *J. Pediat.* 67:46, 1965.

Silverberg, M., and Gellis, S. S.   The liver in juvenile Wilson's disease. *Pediatrics* 30:402, 1962.

Snyder, C. H.   Paroxysmal torticollis in infancy: A possible form of laby-rinthitis. *Amer. J. Dis. Child.* 117:458, 1969.

6
Cranial Nerves

OLFACTORY NERVE

CONGENITAL ANOMALIES of the olfactory nerve and related brain structures frequently occur in association with other severe congenital anomalies. In cebocephaly for example there are a rudimentary nose with a single naris, hypotelorism, and holoprosencephaly (incompletely developed forebrain including the olfactory nerves and related rhinencephalic structures). In cyclopia there are a single optic nerve and holoprosencephaly. In trisomy 13–15 there are holoprosencephaly and multiple congenital anomalies. Acquired lesions of the olfactory nerve may not be uncommon in children, but since the sense of smell is difficult to test, especially in young or mentally subnormal children, lesions may often escape detection. Fractures of the cribriform plate and hemorrhage at the base of the frontal lobes secondary to head trauma may cause anosmia by destruction of the olfactory nerves or compression of the olfactory bulbs. Additional causes of anosmia are meningitis at the base of the frontal lobes, lead intoxication, hydrocephalus, brain tumors (especially meningiomas of the sphenoid ridge and olfactory groove), and tumors of the frontal lobes and parasellar region.

OPTIC NERVE

Aplasia or Hypoplasia of the Optic Nerve

Aplasia or hypoplasia of the optic nerve is frequently present in grossly malformed eyes and in association with other severe central nervous system abnormalities such as arhinencephaly, anencephaly, trisomy 13–15, and cyclopia. Congenital hypoplasia or aplasia of the optic nerve in an otherwise normal individual is a rare congenital anomaly. Blindness in the affected eye and a mild degree of internal strabismus are uniformly present. Diagnostic features of congenital hypoplasia of the optic nerve include a nonprogressive amblyopia, an atrophic pale and small disc, a normal retinal vasculature, and a small

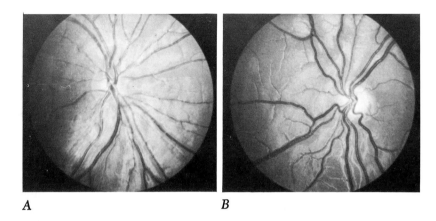

A   B

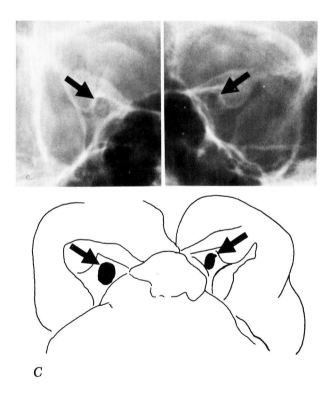

C

Fig. 6-1. Congenital hypoplasia of the optic nerve. Left optic disc (*B*) is pale and smaller than right (*A*). Normal retinal vasculature. *C*, roentgenograms of orbit. The left optic foramen is smaller than the right one. (From Lagos, J. C., *Clin. Pediat.* 9:430, 1970, by permission J. B. Lippincott Company)

optic foramen on the same side of the lesion (Fig. 6-1). In optic atrophy secondary to intrinsic tumors of the optic nerve, optic chiasma, or retroorbital space, there is progressive loss of vision and pallor of the optic disc, which is of normal size when compared with that of the normal eye; in addition, the optic foramen is often enlarged with tumors of the optic nerve such as gliomas or neurofibromas growing within the optic canal.

Optic Atrophy

Optic atrophy may be primary or secondary. Primary optic atrophy may be due to diseases affecting the optic nerve, such as tumors, intoxications, and degenerative diseases of the central nervous system. Funduscopic examination reveals a pale disc with sharply outlined borders and a normal retinal vasculature. The capillaries, however, may be decreased in number. Irrespective of the degree of optic atrophy, the pallor is almost always more pronounced in the temporal side of the optic disc (Fig. 6-2). Secondary optic atrophy is a sequela of prolonged and severe papilledema. In secondary optic atrophy the discs are of a grayish-white color and their borders are blurred. The retinal arteries are thinner than normal, the capillaries decreased in number, and the veins sometimes dilated. A significant degree of primary or secondary optic atrophy is as a rule accompanied by diminution in visual acuity.

Papilledema

Papilledema, or choked disc, is the term used to describe swelling of the optic disc due to increased intracranial pressure (Fig. 6-3). The association between brain tumors and papilledema has been recognized for more than a century (von Graefe, 1866). Since brain tumors in children occur most commonly in the posterior fossa, papilledema is likely to be a fairly early sign due to obstruction of the aqueduct of

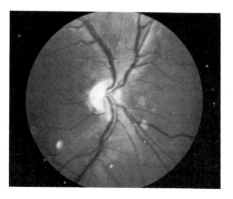

Fig. 6-2. Primary optic atrophy. Pallor of the optic disc more pronounced on the temporal side. Normal retinal vasculature.

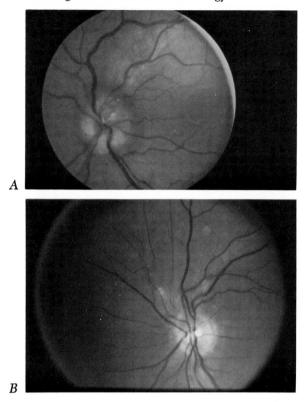

Fig. 6-3. A, papilledema (swelling) of the optic disc and surrounding retina in patient with increased intracranial pressure. Engorged retinal veins. B, compare with normal eyeground. (Courtesy of Dr. James Wise)

Sylvius or the fourth ventricle, with resulting hydrocephalus. Long-standing papilledema may lead to secondary optic atrophy and loss of vision. Peripheral constriction of the visual fields and constriction of the retinal arterioles are early signs of impending optic atrophy; transient attacks of blurred vision are an important symptom. Following is a list of conditions other than intracranial space-occupying lesions which may produce increased pressure and papilledema.

DISEASES OTHER THAN INTRACRANIAL SPACE-OCCUPYING LESIONS WHICH MAY CAUSE INCREASED INTRACRANIAL PRESSURE AND PAPILLEDEMA

DEVELOPMENTAL ANOMALIES
   Craniosynostosis
   Hydrocephalus
   Basilar impression
   Arnold-Chiari malfor-
     mation

METABOLIC CONDITIONS
   Diabetes
   Hypoparathyroidism
   Adrenal insufficiency
   Sudden withdrawal of steroids
     and prolonged steroid therapy

(pseudotumor cerebri)
Puberty (in females, pseudotumor cerebri)
Obesity
Hypervitaminosis A

NEOPLASTIC DISEASES
Meningeal leukemia
Meningeal carcinomatosis
Spinal cord tumors

VIRAL DISEASES
Poliomyelitis
Aseptic meningitis
Encephalitis
Subacute sclerosing panencephalitis

DEGENERATIVE DISEASES
Schilder's disease
Spongy degeneration of the white matter (Canavan's disease)

INFECTIOUS DISEASES
Bacterial and fungal meningitis
Lateral sinus thrombosis (secondary to chronic mastoiditis)
Infectious mononucleosis

HEMATOLOGIC DISORDERS
Polycythemia
Iron-deficiency anemia
Hemophilia

Pernicious anemia
Thrombotic thrombocytopenic purpura

CIRCULATORY CONDITIONS
Congestive heart failure
Dural sinus thrombosis (sagittal sinus secondary to severe dehydration)
Chronic pulmonary hypoventilation
Congenital heart disease

RENAL DISEASE
Chronic renal insufficiency

INTOXICATIONS
Lead and arsenic intoxication
Hypervitaminosis A
Chronic salicylate intoxication

MISCELLANEOUS
Subarachnoid hemorrhage
Prolonged status epilepticus
Opticochiasmatic arachnoiditis
Juvenile Paget's disease
Polyradiculoneuropathy (Guillain-Barré syndrome)
Sarcoidosis
Toxic encephalopathy (acute brain swelling, Reye's syndrome)
Tetracycline therapy

RETINA

Disorders of the retina of importance in pediatric neurology include (1) retinocerebral malformations, (2) retinitis pigmentosa and other pigmentary changes of the retina occurring in association with generalized infections, and (3) the macular and cerebromacular degenerations.

Retinocerebral Malformations

The Wyburn-Mason syndrome is an arteriovenous malformation of the retina and brain stem (Fig. 6-4). Von Hippel-Lindau disease consists of angiomatosis of the retina and cerebellar hemangioma. Malformations of the retinal vessels and glaucoma may occur in encephalotrigeminal angiomatosis (Sturge-Weber syndrome). Astrocytic hamartomas of the retina (phakomas) are a pathognomonic sign of tuberous sclerosis. These glial tumors are usually located at the margin of the optic disc, where they may be confused with drusen (hyaline bodies); less frequently they are found in the periphery of the retina.

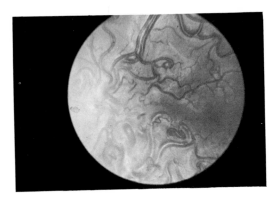

Fig. 6-4. Arteriovenous malformation of the retina in patient with Wyburn-Mason syndrome.

Retinitis Pigmentosa

Retinitis pigmentosa is a degeneration of the neuroepithelium of the retina with onset during the first or second decade of life. In this condition there is accumulation of spicular pigment appearing first in an area of the retina about 15 to 30 degrees from the point of central vision and gradually advancing centrally and peripherally. The retinal vessels undergo progressive narrowing. There is degeneration of the entire retina but primarily of the layer of rods and cones. Constriction of the visual fields and night blindness are present. There is progressive loss of vision leading to total blindness by the fourth or fifth decade. The remainder of the neurologic examination in these patients is normal. Retinitis pigmentosa may be inherited as an autosomal recessive or as an autosomal dominant trait. Sporadic cases also occur.

Retinitis pigmentosa is also an important feature of a wide variety of clinical disorders such as Usher's syndrome (retinitis pigmentosa and deafness); Refsum's disease or heredopathia atactica polyneuriformis (retinitis pigmentosa, polyneuritis, ataxia, increased cerebrospinal fluid protein levels, and an abnormal accumulation of phytanic acid in blood and body tissues); Laurence-Moon-Biedl syndrome (retinitis pigmentosa, mental retardation, obesity, hypogenitalism, and polydactyly); and Bassen-Kornzweig syndrome (retinitis pigmentosa, steatorrhea beginning in early childhood, acanthocytosis (thorny erythrocytes), and ataxia).

Pigmentary changes in the retina may also occur in several congenital infections such as rubella embryopathy, syphilis, toxoplasmosis, and cytomegalic inclusion body disease.

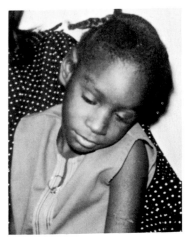

Fig. 6-5. 4-year-old girl with microcephaly, psychomotor retardation, and cataracts due to rubella embryopathy.

RUBELLA EMBRYOPATHY. Pigmentary changes in the retina are present in 20 to 50 percent of children with rubella embryopathy. This is a benign, nonprogressive retinopathy characterized by the abnormal deposition of pigment in the macular and perimacular regions. The changes are limited to the pigment epithelium. Prognosis for vision is excellent. Other diagnostic features of rubella embryopathy are nerve deafness, cataracts, microcephaly, psychomotor retardation, and various forms of congenital heart disease such as patent ductus arteriosus, pulmonary stenosis, and atrial and ventricular septal defects (Fig. 6-5). Early in infancy these infants may have hemolytic anemia, thrombocytopenia, hepatosplenomegaly, and osteolytic lesions in the metaphyses of long bones, especially the femur and tibia.

CONGENITAL SYPHILIS. Syphilitic retinopathy produces pigmentary changes in the retina similar to those of idiopathic retinitis pigmentosa. Syphilitic retinopathy may be unilateral or bilateral. The changes are usually more pronounced in the periphery of the retina. Other neurologic signs of congenital syphilis include nerve deafness and optic atrophy, both of late onset, and varying degrees of psychomotor retardation.

CONGENITAL TOXOPLASMOSIS. Congenital toxoplasmosis causes a chorioretinitis in the form of large white areas surrounded by dark deposits of pigment (Fig. 6-6). The retinal lesions of congenital toxoplasmosis are usually located in the posterior pole of the eye near the macula or the disc. Although acquired toxoplasmosis occasionally may involve the

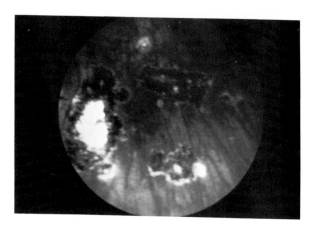

Fig. 6-6. Chorioretinitis in congenital toxoplasmosis. White areas surrounded by dark deposits of pigment. (Courtesy of Dr. James Wise)

central nervous system, it does not produce the retinal lesions seen in the congenital form.

Other clinical features of congenital toxoplasmosis are microcephaly, hydrocephalus, hepatosplenomegaly, psychomotor retardation, neonatal jaundice, and seizures. Intracerebral calcification is present in about 80 percent of cases as multiple punctate deposits scattered in the white matter of the cerebral hemispheres and less frequently in the periventricular region of the occipital, parietal, and temporal regions; curvilinear streaks of calcification may also be seen in the basal ganglia. Laboratory findings include an increased level of IgM in the serum in the newborn period, and an elevated dye-test titer. The complement-fixation test is positive in the mother but may be positive or negative in the infant.

CONGENITAL CYTOMEGALIC INCLUSION BODY DISEASE. Congenital cytomegalic inclusion body disease (CID) may produce a chorioretinitis which is indistinguishable from that seen in congenital toxoplasmosis. Additional clinical features of congenital CID are microcephaly, hepatosplenomegaly, severe psychomotor retardation, spastic diplegia, and intracerebral calcifications which produce a characteristic mold around the ventricular system (Fig. 6-7). Intranuclear and intracytoplasmic inclusion bodies can be demonstrated in affected organs and urine. Serum IgM is increased during the newborn period and complement-fixation antibody titer is positive for cytomegalovirus.

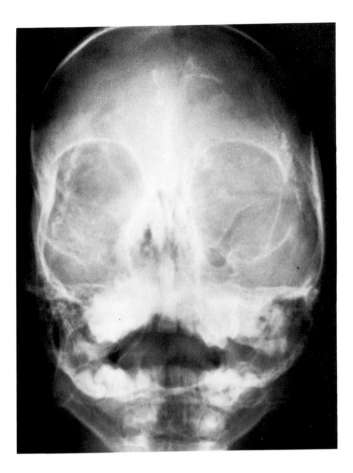

Fig. 6-7. Skull x-ray showing periventricular calcification in infant with congenital cytomegalic inclusion disease and a dilated ventricular system.

CEREBROMACULAR DEGENERATION

Degeneration of the maculae may occur as a familial and isolated clinical manifestation or in association with several progressive degenerative diseases of the central nervous system.

Familial Degeneration of the Maculae

Familial degeneration of the maculae is a disorder inherited as an autosomal recessive trait characterized clinically by loss of central vision beginning during the second decade. Peripheral vision is preserved for many years before the occurrence of complete blindness. In some cases spontaneous arrest may take place. Ophthalmoscopic examination shows progressive degeneration of the maculae. In the initial stages yellowish-gray spots appear in the maculae and later there is deposition of brown pigment in the perimacular regions. In the late stages the maculae become atrophic and exhibit a uniform yellow-gray color.

Amaurotic Family Idiocies

Infantile amaurotic idiocy (Tay-Sachs disease) is a form of ganglioside lipidosis in which there is an abnormal accumulation of a monosialoganglioside in the ganglion cells of the retina. Eventually the ganglion cells are destroyed and the ganglioside lies extracellularly. In the retina, in contrast to the changes seen in the brain, there is no appreciable reactive gliosis. A cherry-red spot in the macula is seen in more than 90 percent of patients with Tay-Sachs disease.

In late infantile amaurotic idiocy (Bielschowsky-Jansky disease), a form of cerebral lipidosis, the maculae become yellowish-gray. In juvenile amaurotic idiocy (Batten's disease), there is a pepper-and-salt deposition of pigment in the retina, optic atrophy, and a grayish-brown discoloration of the maculae.

BLINDNESS OF SUDDEN ONSET

Occasionally the pediatrician is faced with the problem of sudden onset of unilateral or bilateral blindness in a previously healthy child. This is a dramatic occurrence, which in the great majority of cases is, fortunately, a benign and self-limited disturbance.

Head Trauma

Temporary amblyopia (blindness) is occasionally seen in children following trauma of the occiput. In these cases visual loss is sudden and complete. Vision returns to normal in a matter of hours. Electroencephalographic abnormalities localized to the occipital region during the attack suggest that the amblyopia is probably the result of transient cerebral dysfunction of the occipital lobes.

Optic Neuritis

Unilateral or bilateral optic or retrobulbar neuritis is probably the most common cause of sudden loss of vision in children. Optic neuritis invariably occurs without any premonitory symptoms or preceding illness. Physical examination usually reveals total blindness or diminution of vision to light perception or finger counting. Ophthalmologic examination may show a fixed or sluggishly reacting pupil. If the condition is unilateral there is an absent light reflex on the side of the lesion, absent consensual reflex in the normal eye, and a normal consensual reflex in the affected eye. If the loss of vision is not complete a large central scotoma and loss of color vision can be demonstrated. Examination of the eyegrounds reveals a swollen optic disc, no venous pulsations, and engorgement of the retinal veins. This ophthalmoscopic picture is indistinguishable from papilledema due to increased intracranial pressure. Signs and symptoms of increased intracranial pressure, however, are absent.

Initially in the course of optic neuritis there is localized pain in or above the eye and the eyeball is tender to palpation. The remainder of the neurologic and general examination is normal.

Unilateral or bilateral optic neuritis may be a transient and self-limited phenomenon, may be the first manifestation of neuromyelitis optica, or may precede the onset of multiple sclerosis by many years. Vision usually returns to normal following the first attack. Approximately one-third of patients with optic or retrobulbar neuritis make a complete recovery and have no further visual difficulties; one-third develop multiple sclerosis later in life; and in one-third the condition is due to various etiologic factors such as alcohol, diabetes, and syphilis. In recent years optic neuritis has been reported as a complication in children with cystic fibrosis who were on long-term chloramphenicol therapy. The prophylactic use of pyridoxine (vitamin B_6) or cyanocobalamin (vitamin B_{12}) in high dosages may be of value in the prevention of this type of optic neuritis.

The administration of ACTH or steroids for one month appears to shorten the duration of the pathologic process and lead to a more complete recovery of visual acuity. Retroorbital injection of steroids (dexamethasone) has produced in some patients a dramatic improvement in visual acuity within a period of 24 to 48 hours.

The following rule of thumb is helpful in differentiating optic and retrobulbar neuritis from papilledema due to increased intracranial pressure: (1) If the patient's vision is normal and the examination of the eyegrounds shows something that looks like papilledema, it is choked disc (papilledema due to increased intracranial pressure); (2) if the physician is unable to see abnormalities in the eyegrounds and the patient's vision is markedly reduced, it is retrobulbar neuritis; and (3) if the physician sees something that looks like papilledema but the patient cannot see, it is optic neuritis.

Ischemic Optic Neuropathy and Temporal Arteritis

Ischemic optic neuropathy is a disease of late life characterized by painless and sudden onset of blindness, papilledema, and hemorrhages of the optic disc with associated systemic vascular disease and an altitudinal type of field defect with preservation of central vision.

Temporal arteritis, a not uncommon cause of sudden blindness in adult life, has not been reported in young individuals. Prompt recognition and early treatment of this disorder is vital if blindness is to be prevented. The main clinical features of temporal arteritis are headache, tenderness, swelling, and nodularity of one or both temporal arteries and erythema of the overlying skin. By the time the patient seeks medical attention pulsations in the affected temporal arteries are usually absent due to occlusion at one or more points. Low-grade fever, malaise, myalgias, arthralgias, and anorexia are common associated symptoms. Blindness is secondary to occlusion of the central retinal artery. Fifty percent of untreated patients with temporal arteritis become blind in one or both eyes. Steroid therapy started before the onset of visual loss prevents blindness in the great majority of cases. If treatment is initiated once ocular complications have already occurred, little if any improvement in vision can be expected.

Migraine

Sudden, transient loss of vision in one eye may occur during the phase of vasoconstriction which precedes the onset of migraine headaches. During this initial phase there is also vasoconstriction of retinal arterioles. The loss of vision does not last more than 5 to 10 minutes and may or may not be followed by unilateral headache. Prognosis regarding vision is good. In rare instances partial or total visual loss may result from retinal infarction.

Arteriovenous Malformations

Short-lasting episodes of unilateral blindness have been recorded in patients with large ipsilateral arteriovenous malformations. The pathogenesis is probably related to transitory decrease in blood flow in the ophthalmic artery.

Arterial Hypotension

Hypotension of any cause, including episodes of fainting, may produce temporary bilateral loss of vision which may or may not be followed by loss of consciousness. The loss of vision rarely lasts more than a few seconds and is accompanied by a feeling of weakness, lightheadedness, and a clammy and cold skin.

Central Retinal Artery Occlusion

Occlusion of the central retinal artery occurs in adults as a complication of retinal embolism from carotid atheromata. In children it may result from emboli arising in the heart in patients with congenital heart disease. The onset of blindness is abrupt and, unless the obstruction is incomplete, loss of vision is permanent. Examination of the eyegrounds shows a pale disc and narrowed retinal arterioles. A few hemorrhages may be seen around the optic disc.

Miscellaneous

Monocular transient blindness may occur following injections of local anesthetics during dental surgery as well as following intraorbital injections of a local anesthetic. In patients with hysterical blindness the pupillary reactions to light and the ophthalmoscopic examination are normal; visual-field examination with the tangent screen may reveal tunnel vision which does not vary with changes in distance from patient to screen.

OCULOMOTOR PALSIES

Oculomotor or Third Cranial Nerve

Paralysis of the oculomotor nerve produces a dilated and nonreactive pupil, paralysis of accommodation, ptosis, and inability to move the eye upward, downward, and inward. Incomplete paralysis may produce any combination of these signs. Internal ophthalmoplegia refers to paralysis of accommodation and a dilated pupil.

Complete congenital paralysis of the third nerve is extremely rare. Congenital lesions of the oculomotor nerve are usually incomplete, the paralysis involving usually the levator and superior rectus muscles (Fig. 6-8). Acquired lesions of the third nerve may occur within the brain stem or along its course to the eye. Lesions of the third nerve within the brain stem may be associated with other signs of neurologic deficit. If the lesion involves the red nucleus there is a homolateral third-nerve paralysis and contralateral tremor. If the lesion affects the cerebral peduncle there is a homolateral oculomotor paralysis and a contralateral spastic paralysis of the extremities due to simultaneous involvement of the pyramidal tract. When the third nerve is involved within the cavernous sinus by a carotid-cavernous sinus fistula or thrombosis of the cavernous sinus, the other oculomotor nerves (trochlear and abducens) are also usually affected.

Oculomotor paralysis may occur during the course of purulent meningitis and is a common sequela of tuberculous meningitis. Herpes zoster infection may also produce a third-nerve paralysis. Diabetes is a common cause, especially in older people with hemorrhagic retinopathy and other evidence of vascular disease. Other etiologies of oculomotor paralysis are head trauma, polyneuritis of any cause, mumps, aneurysms of the internal carotid artery, subdural hematoma, tumors of the cerebral hemispheres and tumors of the base of the skull, ophthalmo-

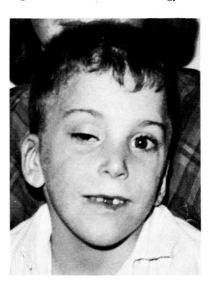

Fig. 6-8.   5-year-old boy with congenital ptosis. No other evidence of third cranial nerve involvement.

plegic migraine, juvenile myasthenia gravis, and intrinsic or metastatic tumors of the orbit.

Trochlear or Fourth Cranial Nerve

Paralysis of the fourth cranial nerve results in weakness of downward gaze and extorsion of the eye. Tilting of the head to the opposite shoulder in order to obtain binocular vision is common in patients with fourth-nerve palsy. Most of the etiologies of oculomotor-nerve paralysis apply also to paralysis of the trochlear nerve.

Abducens or Sixth Cranial Nerve

Paralysis of the sixth cranial nerve results in inability to move the eye outward beyond the midline, with resulting convergent strabismus. If paralysis is complete the patient will experience diplopia. Paralysis of the sixth cranial nerve may be congenital or acquired. Congenital facial diplegia (Möbius syndrome) is often associated with congenital paralysis of one or both abducens nerves; less commonly affected cranial nerves in this condition are the third and twelfth.

Acquired sixth-nerve palsies occur with many of the conditions that cause third- and fourth-nerve paralysis, such as purulent meningitis, diabetes (extremely rare in children), herpes zoster, polyneuritis, poliomyelitis, and skull fractures. Abducens paralysis is not an uncommon sequela in patients who recover from tuberculous meningitis. Thrombosis of the cavernous sinus may involve the sixth as well as the third, fourth, and fifth cranial nerves.

Increased intracranial pressure of any cause may produce unilateral or bilateral sixth-nerve palsy. If it develops after the onset of increased pressure it has no localizing value; if it develops before, it is usually indicative of a lesion in the brain stem, most commonly a slowly growing glioma of the pons. Other causes of sixth-nerve palsy are myasthenia gravis, ophthalmoplegic migraine (less common than third-nerve paralysis), multiple sclerosis, Gradenigo syndrome, nasopharyngeal tumors, intrinsic or metastatic tumors of the orbit, and meningeal leukemia.

Duane Syndrome

Duane syndrome is a congenital condition characterized pathologically by fibrosis of one or both lateral rectus muscles. On examination the palpebral fissure on the affected side widens as the eye is turned laterally and narrows as it is turned medially; there is paralysis of lateral gaze and retraction and elevation of the involved eyeball on adduction (Fig. 6-9).

TRIGEMINAL NERVE

Trigeminal Neuralgia

This is a disorder of the sensory division of the trigeminal or fifth cranial nerve (tic douloureux) characterized by recurrent episodes of sharp short-lasting episodes of pain in the distribution of one of the three sensory branches of the nerve. A not uncommon disease in adults, it is extremely rare under the age of 10 years.

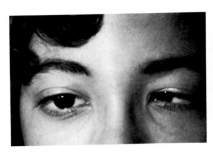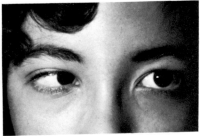

Fig. 6-9.   14-year-old girl with bilateral Duane syndrome. She is unable to abduct either eye beyond the midline. The palpebral fissure narrows and the eyeball retracts as the affected eye is adducted. (Courtesy of Dr. James Wise)

Gradenigo Syndrome

Gradenigo syndrome consists of paralysis of one lateral rectus muscle, pain and swelling of the face in the distribution of the trigeminal nerve, and deafness. Gradenigo syndrome is caused by an inflammatory process of the tip of the petrous pyramid secondary to mastoiditis or middle-ear infection.

FACIAL NERVE

Congenital Facial Paralysis

Congenital facial diplegia (Möbius syndrome) is a paralysis of the facial musculature probably due to agenesis or hypoplasia of the nuclei of the facial nerves. Paralysis of the oculomotor, abducens, and hypoglossal nerves may occur concomitantly. Infants with facial diplegia have an expressionless face, even while crying or laughing; their eyes do not close completely during sleep and constant dribbling of saliva is present. Speech development is delayed and mental retardation is common. Unilateral congenital facial paralysis may occur as a result of maldevelopment of the temporal bone (Fig. 6-10).

Acquired Facial Paralysis

BELL'S PALSY. Peripheral nerve palsy due to damage of the segment of the nerve running within the temporal bone is not an infrequent disturbance in children. Exposure to cold, ischemia secondary to vascular

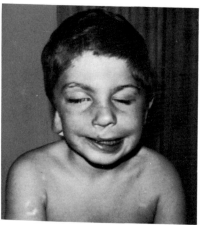

Fig. 6-10. 6-year-old boy with partial congenital right peripheral facial paralysis and hearing loss due to maldevelopment of the temporal bone and external ear.

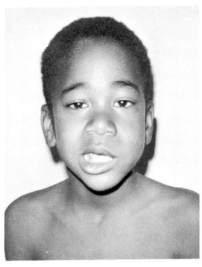
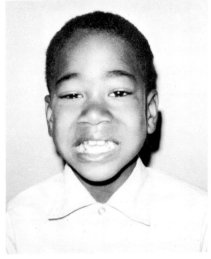

A   B

Fig. 6-11. A, Bell's palsy in a 9-year-old boy. B, one month later there is marked improvement.

spasm, and allergy are among the many etiologic factors incriminated in Bell's palsy. The clinical features, course, and prognosis do not differ from those seen in adults. The paralysis is usually of sudden onset and involves all the muscles of the face supplied by the facial nerve (Fig. 6-11).

OTHER CAUSES OF FACIAL PARALYSIS.   Facial paralysis may occur following *difficult forceps deliveries.* This type of facial paralysis usually resolves spontaneously within a few weeks to two or three months (Fig. 6-12).

A peripheral type of facial paralysis, almost always unilateral, has been described in children in association with *severe hypertension.* The paralysis lasts from a few days to several weeks; some patients may have recurrences corresponding with exacerbations of hypertension. Control of hypertension usually produces a complete recovery. Its pathogenesis is probably related to hemorrhage or edema in the facial canal with subsequent compression of the nerve. Facial paralysis may occur as a complication of intra- and extratemporal bone tumors, infections of the middle ear, parotitis, and trauma to the parotid area or temporal bone. Central nervous system infections such as encephalitis or meningitis may in rare instances be a cause of peripheral facial paralysis.

Facial paralysis is a frequent presenting complaint in patients with *gliomas of the brain stem* (most of them pontine gliomas).

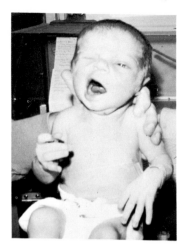

Fig. 6-12. 2-day-old infant with left peripheral facial paralysis secondary to difficult forceps delivery and pressure on the nerve at its exit from temporal bone. Complete recovery in two months.

Polyradiculoneuropathy (Guillain-Barré syndrome) is probably the most common cause of sudden onset of bilateral peripheral facial paralysis in children. Approximately one-third of patients with this disorder develop varying degrees of facial weakness. Ramsay Hunt syndrome (*geniculate herpes neuropathy*) consists of an herpetic eruption in the external ear canal and peripheral facial paralysis. Pathologically there is inflammatory reaction and degeneration of the facial nerve; histologic changes in the geniculate ganglion, however, have not been striking in autopsied cases. *Melkersson's syndrome* is characterized by chronic edema of the face, unilateral or bilateral facial palsy, and in some cases, tongue furrowing (lingua plicata). The facial palsy of Melkersson's syndrome improves spontaneously but has the tendency to recur. *Acoustic neuromas,* a not uncommon cause of facial paralysis in adults, rarely occur in childhood. Their initial clinical manifestation is usually unilateral hearing loss without tinnitus or dizziness. Weeks or months later, a peripheral type of facial palsy develops on the same side of the hearing loss. The initial sign of other cerebellopontine-angle tumors may be facial paralysis or deafness.

ACOUSTIC NERVE

Deafness

The number of known diseases or syndromes of which deafness is the most important feature has increased in the past few years. Deafness may be congenital or acquired. Congenital deafness may be nonhereditary or hereditary. Approximately one-third of all congenital deafness is hereditary and two-thirds acquired. Not all hereditary deafness is congenital.

CONGENITAL NONHEREDITARY DEAFNESS. Congenital nonhereditary deafness may be due to drugs given to the mother during pregnancy, such as quinine and dihydrostreptomycin; to maternal infections during pregnancy, such as rubella, mumps, and syphilis; and to fetal prematurity or basilar skull fracture at birth.

HEREDITARY DEAFNESS. Hereditary deafness is relatively rare. Deafness may be inherited as an autosomal dominant, autosomal recessive, or sex-linked trait. Hereditary deafness may be either conductive or neural. The time of onset varies from birth as in Waardenburg's syndrome to adult life as in otosclerosis. The frequency of the different causes of hereditary deafness varies greatly. The great majority of reported cases are rare entities which have been described only in one or several families. In order of frequency, the most common etiologies encountered in clinical practice are otosclerosis, recessive congenital severe deafness, recessive goiter and deafness, Waardenburg's, Usher's, and Treacher-Collins syndromes, Crouzon's disease, osteogenesis imperfecta, and progressive heart disease and deafness.

Otosclerosis is one of the most important causes of hearing loss. It is inherited as an autosomal dominant trait with a penetrance of about 25 to 40 percent. The onset of hearing loss is generally in the second or third decade. It is estimated that about 4 percent of the general population and 30 percent of individuals with a hearing handicap suffer from otosclerosis.

Recessive congenital severe deafness is said to account for about 25 percent of hearing deficit in children. Pendred's disease is inherited as an autosomal recessive and consists of goiter and deafness. The deafness is congenital, but the goiter usually develops later in life. Hearing deficit is due to a nerve conduction deficit of unknown cause. Most children with Pendred's disease are euthyroid. This condition is said to account for 1 to 10 percent of genetically determined cases of deafness. Waardenburg's syndrome is not an uncommon cause of congenital deafness. The full syndrome consists of lateral displacement of the medial canthi, a broad nasal root, hyperplasia of the medial portion of the eyebrows, heterochromia iridis, and a white forelock. A mild to severe unilateral or bilateral neural hearing loss occurs in 25 percent of patients with this syndrome. Retinitis pigmentosa and deafness (Usher's syndrome) is a recessively inherited disorder characterized by severe neural hearing loss and the gradual development of pigmentary degeneration of the retina with onset in infancy or childhood.

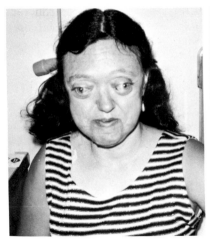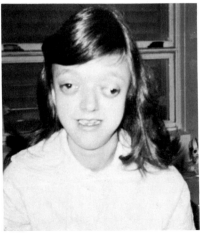

Fig. 6-13. Craniofacial dysostosis (Crouzon's disease) in mother and daughter. Mother is blind as a result of bilateral optic atrophy and daughter has a moderate mixed type of hearing loss.

Craniofacial dysostosis (Crouzon's disease) is a condition inherited as an autosomal dominant and characterized by premature closure of the coronal and other cranial sutures, bilateral proptosis due to shallow orbits, a beaked nose, short upper lip, hypoplastic maxilla, prognathism, and a narrow arched palate (Fig. 6-13). Approximately one-third of patients with this syndrome have a conductive or a mixed hearing loss.

Mandibulofacial dysostosis (Treacher Collins syndrome) is a disorder inherited as a dominant trait characterized by malar and mandibular hypoplasia, colobomas of the outer half of the lower lid, deformities of the earlobes, malformed middle-ear bones, and conductive deafness (Fig. 6-14).

Osteogenesis imperfecta (Fig. 6-15) is a condition inherited as a dominant trait and is characterized by middle-ear deafness, brittle bones subject to frequent fractures, blue sclera, and conductive deafness which usually becomes apparent in the second or third decade. Hearing loss is present in about 20 percent of cases.

Severe bilateral congenital neural hearing loss, a prolonged Q-T interval in the ECG, with Stokes-Adams attacks and sudden death are features of a syndrome described by Jervell and Lange-Nielsen in 1957.

ACQUIRED DEAFNESS. Deafness or hearing deficit acquired after birth may arise from a variety of causes. These include complications following the administration of drugs such as dihydrostreptomycin, kanamycin, and neomycin, all of which may produce permanent deafness, and

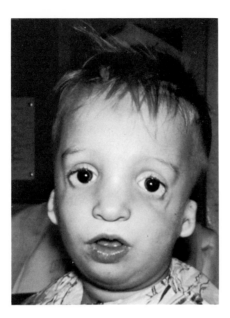

Fig. 6-14. 6-year-old boy with Treacher Collins syndrome and conductive hearing loss. Note typical features: deformed earlobes, colobomas of the outer half of the lower lids, and maxillary and mandibular hypoplasia.

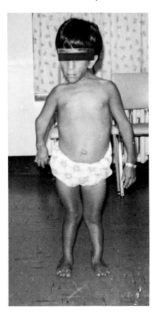

Fig. 6-15. 10-year-old girl with osteogenesis imperfecta. Notice dwarfism and skeletal deformities secondary to multiple fractures.

salicylate intoxication, which may cause a transitory nerve deafness. Other causes of acquired deafness include bilirubin encephalopathy (kernicterus), head trauma with destruction of inner ear by hemorrhage into the temporal bone or severance of the acoustic nerve by a fracture running through the internal ear canal, exposure to sudden loud noise or constant exposure to a noisy environment, bacterial and tuberculous meningitis, encephalitis, mumps (usually unilateral deafness), measles, influenza, serous otitis media, chronic otitis media, and destruction of the acoustic nerve by intrinsic tumors (acoustic neuromas), by tumors arising or extending into the cerebellopontine angle (cholesteatomas, meningiomas, etc.) or by invasion of the inner ear by malignant tumors of the middle ear such as chemodectomas and squamous cell carcinoma.

GLOSSOPHARYNGEAL NERVE

Isolated lesions of the glossopharyngeal nerve are rare and of little clinical significance with the exception of glossopharyngeal neuralgia, which to our knowledge has not been described in children. In nuclear lesions due to conditions such as progressive bulbar palsy, brain stem tumors, syringobulbia, multiple sclerosis, or vascular lesions of the brain stem there is usually associated involvement of the vagus, accessory, or hypoglossal nerves.

VAGUS NERVE

Bilateral vagus paralysis is incompatible with life. Unilateral paralysis is followed by paresis of the soft palate and the muscles of the pharynx on the involved side. There is hoarseness, a nasal speech, and dysphagia. Sensory deficit is localized to the lower pharynx with irritative lesions of the nerve. There may be pain or paresthesias in the pharynx, larynx, or external auditory meatus.

ACCESSORY NERVE

The accessory nerve supplies motor fibers to the sternocleidomastoid and trapezius muscles. A lesion of this nerve is manifested by difficulty in rotating the head toward the opposite side and in shrugging the ipsilateral shoulder.

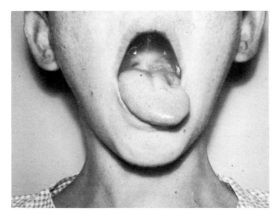

Fig. 6-16.   10-year-old boy with atrophy of the left side of the tongue secondary to damage to the left hypoglossal nerve by purulent meningitis.

HYPOGLOSSAL NERVE

The hypoglossal nerve innervates the muscles of the tongue. In peripheral lesions of the hypoglossal nerve there is ipsilateral paralysis and atrophy of the tongue. On protrusion the tongue deviates to the side of the lesion (Fig. 6-16).

Frequently the last four cranial nerves are simultaneously affected by lesions of the medulla or upper cervical cord as in progressive bulbar palsy, progressive spinal muscular atrophy, amyotrophic lateral sclerosis, syringobulbia, brain stem tumors or hemorrhages, and multiple sclerosis, or by lesions at the base of the skull such as fractures or tumors around the jugular foramen or upper part of the neck.

REFERENCES

Arthur, L. J. H.   Some hereditary syndromes that include deafness. *Develop. Med. Child. Neurol.* 7:395, 1965.

Brody, I. A., and Wilkins, R. H.   Ramsay Hunt syndrome. *Arch. Neurol.* 18:583, 1968.

Cocke, M. J. G., Jr.   Chloramphenicol optic neuritis: Apparent protective effects of very high daily doses of pyridoxine and cyanocobalamin. *Amer. J. Dis. Child.* 114:424, 1967.

Cogan, D. G.   *Neurology of the Ocular Muscles.* Springfield, Ill.: Thomas, 1956.

Henderson, J. L.   The congenital facial diplegia syndrome: Clinical features, pathology and aetiology; a review of sixty-one cases. *Brain* 62:381, 1939.

Jervell, A., and Lange-Nielsen, F.   Congenital deaf-mutism, functional heart disease with prolongation of the Q-T interval and sudden death. *Amer. Heart J.* 54:59, 1957.

Kresky, B., and Nauheim, J. S.   Rubella retinitis. *Amer. J. Dis. Child.* 113:305, 1967.

Lagos, J. C.   Unilateral hypoplasia of the optic nerve. *Clin. Pediat.* (Phila.) 9:430, 1970.

Lathrop, F. D.   Bell's palsy: An otolaryngological problem. Part I. *Trans. Amer. Acad. Ophthal. Otolaryng.* 69:709, 1965.

Lloyd, A. V. C., et al.   Facial paralysis in children with hypertension. *Arch. Dis. Child.* 41:292, 1966.

McLellan, M. S., and Parrino, C. S.   Bell's palsy at 1 month, 4 days of age. *Amer. J. Dis. Child.* 117:727, 1969.

Paine, R. S.   Facial paralysis in children. *Pediatrics* 19:303, 1957.

Saberman, M. N., and Tenta, L. T.   The Melkersson-Rosenthal syndrome. *Arch. Otolaryng.* 84:292, 1966.

Walsh, F. B., and Hoyt, W. F.   *Clinical Neuro-ophthalmology* (3rd ed.). Baltimore: Williams & Wilkins, 1969.

7
Proptosis

PROPTOSIS as an isolated clinical manifestation is not an uncommon presenting complaint in children. Too often a child with proptosis is immediately referred to an ophthalmologist who in turn may refer the child to a neurologist or neurosurgeon. Even though the treatment of the majority of patients with proptosis falls into the domain of the ophthalmologist or neurosurgeon, in most instances a fairly complete diagnostic investigation can be performed in a relatively brief period of time by the pediatrician or the general practitioner. Proptosis can be divided in two main categories: (1) cases due to diseases of the orbit or its contents, and (2) cases secondary to diseases arising from neighboring or more distant structures.

FIBROUS DYSPLASIA OF THE ORBIT

Fibrous dysplasia of the orbit is primarily a disorder of childhood and adolescence. The bony lesions develop during childhood and as a rule grow slowly or not at all after adolescence. The basic defect in fibrous dysplasia is an accumulation of fibrous connective tissue within the bone. Hyperplastic fibrous tissue fills the medullary cavity producing thickening of the affected bone. Patients with orbital or facial involvement tend to have no lesions of the long bones. The characteristic roentgenographic changes of fibrous dysplasia of the orbit are a thickened and trabeculated bone with sclerotic and/or radiolucent areas (Fig. 7-1).

Loss of vision may occur as the result of pressure on the optic nerve. Surgical excision of the lesion is indicated if progressive ocular difficulties develop, such as severe proptosis, loss of vision, paralysis of extraocular muscles, or for cosmetic reasons alone in patients with mild proptosis and who are otherwise asymptomatic.

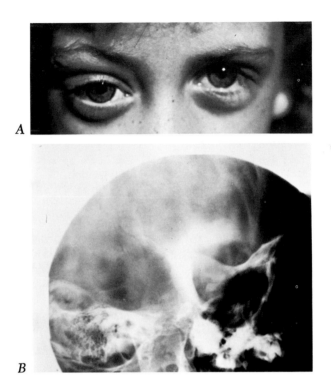

Fig. 7-1. A, 5-year-old girl with proptosis of the right eye due to fibrous dysplasia of the orbit. *B,* sclerosis of the superior and lateral portion of the right orbit.

MUCOCELE

A mucocele is an encapsulated collection of fluid arising from the paranasal sinuses, most commonly the frontal or ethmoidal (Fig. 7-2A). They rarely occur in children. Extension of the lesion into the orbit may result in proptosis. The tumor can often be palpated in the inner angle of the eye and its true nature demonstrated by roentgenographic examination of the orbit (Fig. 7-2B). Mucoceles are one of the most benign and surgically accessible lesions causing proptosis. Excision of the tumor is curative.

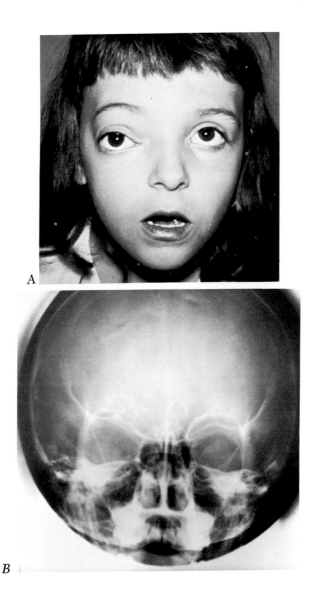

Fig. 7-2. A, 7-year-old girl with proptosis of the right eye of two years' duration due to a mucocele arising from the right frontal sinus. *B*, destruction of the medial portion of the superior right orbit by mucocele of frontal sinus.

MYXOMA

Myxomas arising from the paranasal sinuses are highly malignant and invasive tumors which by direct extension into the orbit may produce proptosis.

TUMORS OF THE ORBIT

The cardinal symptoms of orbital tumors are proptosis, diplopia, loss of vision, and external ophthalmoplegia. Benign tumors, as a general rule, grow slowly, producing a progressive unilateral proptosis over a period of months or years. On the other hand, malignant tumors and inflammatory lesions cause a rapidly increasing proptosis. The ophthalmologic examination of any child with orbital mass may reveal visual disturbances such as loss of vision, extraocular motor paralysis, engorgement of retinal veins, retinal hemorrhages, papilledema, or optic atrophy. Roentgenographic examination of the orbit may show an increased soft-tissue density, erosion of bone, hyperostosis, enlargement of the optic foramen, or abnormalities in the paranasal sinuses.

Congenital Tumors

ENCEPHALOCELE AND TERATOMA.   Congenital tumors, such as teratomas or encephaloceles, are uncommon causes of proptosis. Encephalocele is a developmental anomaly in which a part of the brain with or without a portion of the ventricular system herniates through a bony defect in the orbit, whereas a meningocele contains only the covering membranes of the brain. These abnormalities are evident at birth, are most commonly located in the midline, and present as a soft and pulsatile mass.

HEMANGIOMA.   Hemangioma is the most common tumor of the orbit in children. It usually becomes apparent shortly after birth and may grow rapidly in size during the first few months of life. The eyelid on the involved side may have a purplish discoloration due to the underlying vascular tumor. Because of its usual location in the upper nasal quadrant, outside the muscle cone, hemangioma rarely causes venous engorgement of the retina, papilledema, or a decrease in visual acuity. Occasionally a poorly encapsulated hemangioma may cause pulsations of the eye. This type of tumor is however, in most cases, well encapsulated (fibrohemangioma) and therefore is usually not difficult to remove surgically.

EPIDERMOID AND DERMOID TUMORS. Epidermoids or pearly tumors are cystic structures made up of a capsule of well-differentiated stratified squamous epithelium containing desquamated cells and keratohyalin. Dermoid cysts, in addition, contain sebaceous glands, hairs, and other skin appendanges. Epidermoid and dermoid tumors are relatively common orbital tumors in childhood. Roentgenographic examination of the orbit in a patient with such a tumor may demonstrate bone erosion or intraorbital calcification.

Rhabdomyosarcoma

Rhabdomyosarcoma is a highly malignant tumor which may arise from the muscles of the orbit and also from undifferentiated foci of mesenchymal cells. It may also extend into the orbit from the nasopharynx. It occurs most commonly in children from 5 to 10 years of age. Metastases to the brain and lungs and local recurrences are common even after enucleation of the eye and radiation therapy.

Optic Nerve Glioma

Optic nerve glioma (low-grade astrocytoma) is an occasional cause of proptosis in children. Optic nerve gliomas originate from the intraorbital segment of the optic nerve in one-third and from the intracranial portion of the optic nerve or the optic chiasma in the other two-thirds of cases. Proptosis is almost always preceded by visual loss. Other signs are diplopia, a large pupil on the side of the lesion with an absent or sluggish reaction to direct light and a normal consensual reflex, optic atrophy, and concentric constriction of the visual field. When the tumor involves the portion of the optic nerve within the optic canal roentgenographic examination may show enlargement of the optic foramen (Fig. 7-3). The enlarged foramen characteristically maintains its smooth edges and shows no evidence of erosion or decalcification. A J-shaped sella turcica is a common roentgenographic sign when the glioma involves the intracranial portion of the optic nerve or optic chiasma. However, this roentgenographic abnormality is not a pathognomonic sign of glioma of the optic chiasma, for it is known to be present occasionally in normal individuals and more frequently in patients with conditions such as neurofibromatosis, hypothyroidism, trisomy 21, and skeletal dysplasias. If the tumor involves the optic chiasma, visual loss may be bilateral and various types of visual field defects can be demonstrated. Pneumoencephalogram may show a mass indenting the third ventricle or obstructive hydrocephalus.

Neurofibromatosis

Neurofibromatosis is not a common cause of proptosis. Of all the cranial nerves the optic nerve is the least affected in this condition. In

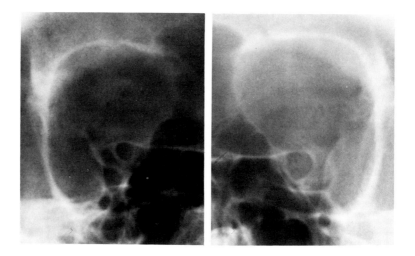

Fig. 7-3. Optic canal views showing enlarged left optic foramen in a 12-year-old girl with a glioma of the left optic nerve growing within the optic canal.

children, however, optic gliomas (astrocytomas and not neurofibromas) are a not-infrequent associated pathologic finding. Neurofibromas of the optic nerve may also produce an enlargement of the optic foramina similar to that seen with optic nerve gliomas.

Meningiomas

Meningiomas which arise from the sphenoidal ridge or within the orbit may cause proptosis. They are exceedingly rare tumors in childhood. In the orbit they may develop from the optic nerve or from heterotopic arachnoidal tissue.

Histiocytosis X

Letterer-Siwe disease, Hand-Schüller-Christian disease, and eosinophilic granuloma of bone are a group of closely related conditions characterized by focal (eosinophilic granuloma) or widespread (Letterer-Siwe and Hand-Schüller-Christian diseases) proliferation of histiocytes throughout the reticuloendothelial system. They are collectively known as histiocytosis X. A diagnosis of histiocytosis X can be made by histologic examination of affected tissue. Any of these three conditions can be a cause of proptosis.

Hand-Schüller-Christian disease has been traditionally associated with the triad of exophthalmos, diabetes insipidus, and membranous bone defects. Although the vast majority of patients with Hand-Schüller-Christian disease do not exhibit this classic triad, proptosis is present in about 10 to 15 percent of cases. Roentgenographic examination reveals an osteolytic lesion of the orbit and sometimes of adjacent bones.

Eosinophilic granuloma, a more benign form of histiocytosis X, is characterized by sharply demarcated areas of bone destruction. Proptosis may occur with eosinophilic granuloma of the orbital bones.

Retinoblastoma

Retinoblastoma is an autosomal dominant, genetically determined tumor arising from the neuroepithelium of the retina. Thirty percent of retinoblastomas are bilateral and 70 percent unilateral. The earliest symptoms of retinoblastomas are loss of vision and/or internal squint due to excessive accommodation. A white pupillary reflex may be the earliest sign of retinoblastoma. Other diagnostic possibilities in a child with a white pupillary reflex are congenital cataract, retrolental fibroplasia, and Coats's disease. Early in its course retinoblastoma appears on funduscopic examination as one or more white elevated masses. Detailed funduscopic examination, with dilated pupils under general anesthesia if necessary, should be performed on any child with an absent red reflex or with an otherwise unexplained squint of sudden onset.

Orbital Pseudotumor

Orbital pseudotumor is a self-limited inflammatory reaction of the soft tissues of the orbit characterized pathologically by edema and pallor of the orbital fat, increased amount of connective tissue, and edema and diffuse infiltration of muscle bundles by chronic inflammatory cells. From a clinical standpoint pseudotumor of the orbit is manifested by proptosis, edema of the lids, chemosis, papilledema, and pain. Orbital pseudotumor may occur at any age but is essentially a disease of middle life. The onset and progression of proptosis are relatively rapid (weeks) when compared to that of orbital neoplasms, in which proptosis develops as a general rule in an insidious and gradual manner (months). The second eye often becomes involved within 4 to 9 months after the first. Biopsy of retroorbital tissue is usually necessary to confirm the diagnosis. Treatment with systemic steroid appears to be beneficial in shortening the duration of orbital pseudotumor. Orbital decompression may be necessary.

Neuroblastoma

Neuroblastoma is a malignant tumor of early childhood which arises from neural crest ectoderm. The most common sites of origin are the adrenal medulla and the sympathetic chain in the chest or abdomen. Neuroblastomas may metastasize to regional lymph nodes, bone marrow, skeleton, and liver. In the head the most common site of metastasis

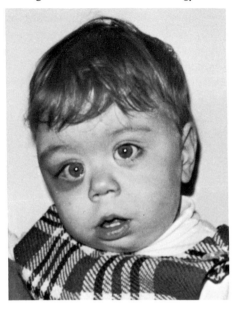

Fig. 7-4. 18-month-old infant with bilateral proptosis more marked on the right side due to metastatic neuroblastoma of the orbits.

is the orbit. Proptosis is not infrequently the presenting sign of metastatic neuroblastoma from a primary site of origin in the abdominal or thoracic cavities (Fig. 7-4). It is then mandatory that a careful examination of the abdomen be performed and that roentgenograms of the chest and abdomen and an intravenous pyelogram be done in any child with proptosis, especially during the first three years of life.

Determination of the urinary output of catecholamine metabolites (VMA test) is a useful screening test for neuroblastoma. The most valuable laboratory test appears to be the determination of the urinary excretion of dopamine and norepinephrine, which is elevated in most patients. In some cases a primary tumor is not found. In such instances bone marrow biopsy may be of help in demonstrating the true nature of the process.

ARTERIOVENOUS FISTULA (CAROTID-CAVERNOUS SINUS)

Carotid-cavernous sinus fistula may be a cause of proptosis. A fistula in this location may be of congenital origin but is more commonly secondary to head trauma. The increase in pressure in the cavernous sinus interferes with the drainage of blood from the eye by way of the superior ophthalmic vein, and a rapidly progressive pulsating proptosis develops. In addition, there is chemosis, engorgement of retinal veins, and papilledema. A bruit can be heard over the involved eye and adjacent skull.

HEMATOMA

Orbital hematomas are usually the result of head trauma, although in rare instances they may develop spontaneously in a patient with a blood dyscrasia.

LEUKEMIA

Orbital involvement in both lymphocytic and myelogenous leukemia may cause unilateral or bilateral proptosis. Occasionally it may be the initial manifestation.

INFLAMMATORY LESIONS

Cavernous Sinus Thrombosis

Proptosis is a cardinal sign of cavernous sinus thrombosis. The venous blood from facial structures has direct access to the cavernous sinus. Thus, the cavernous sinuses are susceptible to bacterial seeding from infectious processes in any of the structures surrounding the eyeglobe. In septic thrombosis of the cavernous sinus, there is high fever, leukocytosis, severe toxicity, and headache. Papilledema is present in about 50 percent of cases. Some degree of proptosis develops in all cases. If the patient has not received antibiotics blood cultures are usually positive. Examination of the cerebrospinal fluid may show changes similar to those seen in aseptic meningitis (lymphocytic pleocytosis, a moderate increase in the level of protein, a normal glucose content, and negative cultures). Cavernous sinus thrombosis of septic origin is almost always secondary to infections of the lower lids and less frequently of the cheeks. A diagnosis of cavernous sinus thrombosis of septic origin is made on the basis of previous infection followed by proptosis, chemosis and edema of the eyelids, partial to complete paralysis of the extraocular muscles resulting from involvement of the third, fourth, and sixth cranial nerves as they pass through the sinus, and progression of signs from one eye to the other made possible by the venous intercommunications between the two cavernous sinuses.

Aseptic thrombosis of the cavernous sinus is usually secondary to trauma or severe dehydration.

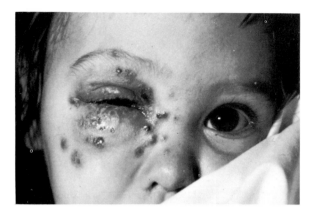

Fig. 7-5. Mild proptosis in a child with orbital cellulitis. (Courtesy of Dr. James Wise)

Orbital Cellulitis

Orbital cellulitis is almost always secondary to inflammation of one of the paranasal sinuses, most commonly the ethmoid. Systemic manifestation of infection such as fever, prostration, and leukocytosis is invariably present. Proptosis is usually minimal (Fig. 7-5). The lids are red and swollen and the conjunctivae red and chemotic. Papilledema and retinal hemorrhages may or may not be present. Blood cultures are frequently positive. Roentgenographic examination of the paranasal sinuses almost invariably shows evidence of an inflammatory process. The treatment of orbital cellulitis includes the administration of antibiotics, frequent applications of warm compresses to the affected eye, and local nasal decongestants.

HYPERTHYROIDISM

Hyperthyroidism is a rare cause of unilateral or bilateral proptosis in the pediatric age group. Thyrotropic exophthalmos results from an increase in volume of orbital tissues, including extraocular muscles. The diagnosis can be suspected on clinical grounds (nervousness, sensitivity to heat, restlessness, overactivity, weight loss in spite of good appetite, tremor, tachycardia at rest in the absence of fever, and palpitations) and confirmed by appropriate laboratory studies (PBI [protein-bound iodine], BEI [butanol-extractable iodine], and ^{131}I uptake).

COMMENT

The evaluation of a child with proptosis includes:

1. Examination of the size and equality of the pupils, pupillary reactions to light and accommodation, and visual acuity.

2. Ophthalmoscopic examination after proper dilatation of the pupils. In many instances this is not necessary since many patients with proptosis have a dilated and fixed pupil.

3. Measurement of the degree of proptosis with the exophthalmodynamometer and, if feasible, visual-field examination by confrontation or with the tangent screen.

4. Auscultation of the eyeball for bruits.

5. Roentgenographic examination of the skull, including basal, orbital, and optic canal views.

6. Skeletal survey, intravenous pyelogram and, in selected cases, especially in children under the age of 3 years, bone marrow examination and determination of the urinary excretion of VMA, dopamine, and norepinephrine.

In many instances a definite diagnosis can be made only by biopsy. Orbital tumors or other lesions causing proptosis can be surgically treated by the ophthalmologic surgeon or by the neurosurgeon. Tumors such as hemangiomas, lipomas, pseudotumor of the orbit, or tumors of the optic nerve which are confined to the orbit can be excised by the Krönlein technique, in which the bone of the orbit is excised temporally for exposure. The same can be accomplished by the neurosurgeon through a small frontal craniotomy and the tumor removed sometimes without opening the dura. If the tumor extends intracranially through the optic canal or superior orbital fissure the anterior middle fossa must be exposed by a frontotemporal craniotomy.

REFERENCES

Chapman, R. B., et al.   Retinoblastoma (Clinical Rounds). *Clin. Pediat.* (Phila.) 5:86, 1966.

Chutorian, A. M., et al.   Optic gliomas in children. *Neurology* 14:83, 1964.

Enriquez, P., et al.   Histiocytosis X: A clinical study. *Mayo Clin. Proc.* 42:88, 1967.

Love, J. G.   Transcranial Removal of Intraorbital Tumors. In Troutman, R. C., Converse, J. M., and Smith, B. (Eds.), *Plastic and Reconstructive Surgery of the Eye and Adnexa.* Washington: Butterworth, 1962.

Masson, J. K., and Soule, E. H.   Embryonal rhabdomyosarcoma of the head and neck: Report on eighty-eight cases. *Amer. J. Surg.* 110:585, 1965.

Matson, D. D.   *Neurosurgery of Infancy and Childhood* (2nd ed.). Springfield, Ill.: Thomas, 1969.

Pugh, D. G.   Fibrous dysplasia of the skull: A probable explanation for leontiasis ossea. *Radiology* 44:548, 1945.

Stern, W. E., et al.   Surgical challenge of carotid-cavernous fistula: Critical role of intracranial circulatory dynamics. *J. Neurosurg.* 27:298, 1967.

8
Meningeal Irritation

SIGNS OF meningeal irritation are with ample reason some of the most feared in the practice of pediatrics. The main cause of meningeal irritation in children is inflammation of the leptomeninges (pia-arachnoid) secondary to their invasion by a variety of microorganisms. Stiffness of the neck has long been recognized as a cardinal manifestation of meningeal irritation. This sign has been variously explained on the basis of increased intracranial pressure, irritation of pain-carrying fibers, or reflex spasms of the paraspinal muscles. Meningeal irritation from any cause also produces several other signs of importance in the diagnosis: the Kernig sign (flexion contraction of the knee) is the inability to extend the leg when the hip is flexed at 90 degrees; the Brudzinski (neck) sign consists of flexion of both legs at the knees and hips when the neck is passively flexed. Passive flexion of the knee and hip joints of one leg produces a simultaneous reflex flexion of the opposite leg. This sign is called the *crossed flexor reflex* of the leg. Lasègue sign consists of pain along the sciatic nerve when the hip is flexed and the leg is hyperextended.

MENINGISM

Signs of meningeal irritation are often present in children at the onset of acute febrile diseases, especially pneumonia. There is fever, severe headache, stiffness of the neck and back, and a positive Kernig and Brudzinski sign. If the diagnosis escapes detection and a spinal tap is performed, the cerebrospinal fluid is usually under mildly to moderately increased pressure, and the cell count and glucose and protein levels are normal. Smears and cultures of the cerebrospinal fluid are negative.

BACTERIAL MENINGITIS

Before the advent of antibiotics bacterial meningitis was, with rare exceptions, a fatal disease. Since then the mortality rate has diminished significantly in all age groups with the exception of the neonatal period. Morbidity, on the other hand, has inevitably risen due to the large number of survivors. This is particularly high in bacterial meningitis among neonates, in whom 50 to 85 percent of survivors are left with severe neurologic sequelae. The most important factor in children relating to the frequency with which pathogenic organisms may produce meningitis is age. In the neonate gram-negative organisms account for more than half of all cases. The most common etiologic agents are *Escherichia coli*, paracolon organisms, proteus, aerobacter, pseudomonas, salmonella, and *Haemophilus influenzae*. Gram-positive organisms in this age group include streptococci, staphylococci, and *Diplococcus pneumoniae*.

The incidence of neonatal meningitis is approximately 1:1000 to 1:2000 full-term births and of 1:250 live premature births. In 75 percent of cases the onset is within the first 10 days of life. Perinatal complications such as premature rupture of the membranes, prolonged and difficult labor, toxemia, third-trimester bleeding, placenta previa, and premature separation of the placenta are more common with infants who have the onset of the disease in the first few days of life. The mortality rate in neonatal meningitis is over 70 percent, and severe neurologic sequelae in survivors are the rule rather than the exception.

There is nothing typical about the clinical picture of meningitis in neonates. Lethargy, respiratory distress, poor sucking and Moro reflexes, hypotonia, jaundice, abdominal distention, vomiting, and diarrhea may be present. The infant is often irritable and anorectic. Fever may be absent, and subnormal temperatures and shock are common. Neurologic signs include a high-pitched cry and slight to moderate fullness of the anterior fontanelle. In the absence of complications such as subdural effusion or cortical thrombophlebitis, focal neurologic signs are lacking. The classical signs of meningeal irritation, almost always present in older children and adults with meningitis, are minimal or absent in neonates and small infants. Blood cultures and examination of the cerebrospinal fluid should be performed in a newborn who is not doing well and in whom there is no obvious cause for his difficulty. Septicemia occurs in more than 90 percent of cases of neonatal meningitis. The leukocyte count is usually elevated above 20,000/cu. ml. Leukocyte counts of less than 5000/cu. ml. are associated with a high mortality rate.

The current treatment of neonatal meningitis includes initially a combination of penicillin or ampicillin and kanamycin and the appropriate antibiotic when the responsible organism and its sensitivity to antibiotics have been determined.

Meningitis under the age of 5 years, neonate excluded, is most commonly due to *H. influenzae*, meningococcus, and pneumococcus. The clinical picture at this age resembles that of adults. Examination of the cerebrospinal fluid is diagnostic, and unless antibiotics have been previously given in insufficient amounts, there is a polymorphonuclear pleocytosis, a low glucose level, and an elevated level of protein. Smear and cultures of the cerebrospinal fluid permit identification of the offending organism.

The incidence of neurologic sequelae following bacterial meningitis in children appears to be higher in those who received inadequate doses of penicillin or a broad-spectrum antibiotic in the early stages of the disease when signs of meningeal irritation may be absent. A diagnosis of infectious disease of unknown etiology is not infrequently made initially and an antibiotic prescribed because of a red throat, a questionable otitis media, or even when no diagnosis at all is entertained in a child with fever. This therapeutic policy serves no useful purpose, delays the diagnosis, and increases the chances of neurologic sequelae. Hydrocephalus, spastic diplegia, hemiplegia, blindness, deafness, seizures, and psychomotor retardation are some of the neurologic sequelae seen in survivors, especially in those in whom a diagnosis is not made in the initial stages of the disease and antibiotics are prescribed in inadequate amounts.

Subdural effusion is a frequent complication of meningitis due to *H. influenzae* but is also seen in meningitis caused by other organisms. The high incidence of subdural effusion in *H. influenzae* meningitis may be more apparent than real and due to the predominance of this type of meningitis in young children. The child who develops a subdural effusion usually becomes febrile after a few days of successful treatment, is irritable, and may have focal or generalized seizures. The anterior fontanelle may be tense or bulging, the head circumference may increase in size and on transillumination of the skull an area of abnormal glowing may be demonstrated in the frontotemporoparietal region. Tapping of the subdural space is diagnostic.

ASEPTIC MENINGITIS SYNDROME

The aseptic meningitis syndrome is caused in the great majority of instances by viruses. The most common etiologic agents are the enteroviruses (poliomyelitis, Coxsackie, and ECHO) and the myxoviruses. Other organisms which may cause this syndrome include rickettsia and leptospira. The clinical picture of aseptic meningitis is similar to that of bacterial meningitis; however, as a general rule the patients appear less acutely ill. The usual signs of meningeal irritation are present. Examination of the cerebrospinal fluid reveals a lymphocytic pleocytosis, a moderate elevation of the protein content, and a normal glucose level.

Smear and culture of the cerebrospinal fluid are negative for bacteria. The disease is usually self-limited and serious neurologic sequelae are rare.

FUNGAL MENINGITIS

Fungal diseases of the brain are always secondary to infection from a focus elsewhere in the body. In most instances the organisms reach the central nervous system by the hematogenous route, usually from a focus in the lungs, the jaw, ganglia, or gastrointestinal tract. Abscess or granulomatous formation of the brain is more common than primary meningitis. The majority of affected individuals suffer from chronic debilitating illnesses, leukemia, or lymphomas or are being treated for various reasons with steroids or antimetabolites. A fungal etiology should be entertained in patients with meningitis or a brain abscess who are suffering from one of the previously mentioned predisposing illnesses. Examination of the cerebrospinal fluid shows a pleocytosis rarely exceeding 1000 cells/cu. ml.; a protein level usually above 100 mg./100 ml., and, with the only exception of mucormycosis, a normal or low glucose level.

The treatment of mycosis of the central nervous system remains unsatisfactory. The intravenous administration of amphotericin B appears to be of value in the treatment of cryptococcosis, blastomycosis, coccidioidomycosis, and mucormycosis. Sulfonamides are effective in the treatment of nocardiosis and amphotericin B or 5-fluorocytosine an experimental drug, in the treatment of candidiasis.

TUBERCULOUS MENINGITIS

Tuberculous meningitis runs a subacute course and is characterized clinically by the gradual onset of listlessness, irritability, malaise, and a low or a moderately high fever. This is followed by the appearance of signs and symptoms of meningeal irritation and increased intracranial pressure (headache, nausea, vomiting, papilledema, convulsions, and coma). The disease occurs most frequently in children under the age of 5 years. Tuberculous meningitis is always secondary to invasion of tubercle bacilli from a distant focus in the lungs, paratracheal nodes, and peribronchial lymph nodes, or as the result of miliary spread.

Examination of the cerebrospinal fluid shows an increased pressure and a pleocytosis of 50 to 500 cells/cu. ml. Early in the course of the disease the cells are chiefly polymorphonuclear; later on lymphocytes predominate. The levels of glucose and chlorides are decreased and the protein content is elevated. The presence of tubercle bacilli can be demonstrated by smear, culture, or guinea pig inoculation. Chest x-ray often reveals a tuberculous focus. The purified protein derivative (PPD) skin test is almost always positive.

The natural course of tuberculous meningitis is death within 6 to 8 weeks after onset. Recovery rate can be expected to be as high as 90 percent if appropriate antibiotic treatment (streptomycin, isoniazid, and para-aminosalicylic acid) is instituted early in the course of the disease. When therapy is initiated in the late stages, recovery rate is less than 25 percent. Neurologic sequelae occur in about one-half of survivors in the form of hemiplegia, epilepsy, deafness, blindness, psychomotor retardation, hydrocephalus, or oculomotor palsies. Visible intracranial calcification eventually develops in about one-third of survivors.

MENINGEAL LEUKEMIA

Leukemic infiltration of the brain substance and meninges has become a common problem in children with leukemia. Invasion of the central nervous system usually occurs when a child with leukemia is in hematologic remission. The main clinical manifestations of meningeal leukemia are progressive headaches, nausea, vomiting, papilledema, meningeal signs, and unilateral or bilateral sixth-nerve palsies (Fig. 8-1.)

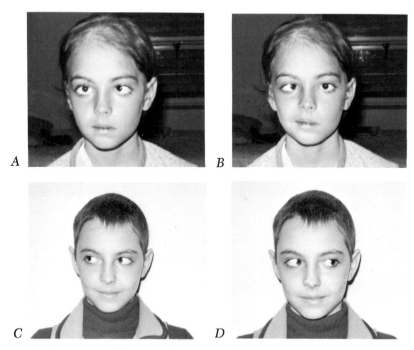

Fig. 8-1. 12-year-old girl with meningeal leukemia. A, B, bilateral sixth-nerve palsy and mild left peripheral facial palsy. C, D, complete recovery 2 months following chemotherapy.

Examination of the cerebrospinal fluid reveals an increased pressure, an elevated protein level, a moderate decrease in glucose level, and a mixed pleocytosis. X-rays of the skull may demonstrate spreading of the sutures in young children. Malignant cells in the cerebrospinal fluid can be demonstrated only in a minority of cases. The treatment of meningeal leukemia consists of external irradiation of the entire neuraxis, intrathecal methotrexate, or intrathecal cytosine arabinoside (Cytosar).

POLIOMYELITIS

Poliomyelitis formerly was the most common viral disease of the central nervous system affecting man. Prominent clinical features initially are fever, headache, muscle ache, stiff neck, and positive Kernig and Brudzinski signs. Examination of the cerebrospinal fluid shows a lymphocytic pleocytosis and increased protein and normal glucose levels. In severe cases these initial manifestations are followed by an asymmetrical flaccid paralysis without sensory loss. The paralysis of poliomyelitis affects most frequently the muscles of the legs followed in order of frequency by those of the arms and the trunk. In approximately 10 to 15 percent of cases of poliomyelitis the muscles supplied by the bulbar nuclei are involved.

BRAIN TUMORS

In rare instances the initial clinical manifestation in a patient with a brain tumor, especially medulloblastomas and ependymomas of the fourth ventricle growing in close proximity to the subarachnoid space, may be similar to that seen in patients with bacterial meningitis (fever, headache, meningeal signs, a predominantly polymorphonuclear pleocytosis, and increased protein levels and a low glucose level in the cerebrospinal fluid). Smears and cultures for bacteria and fungi are negative. Cytologic examination of the cerebrospinal fluid may demonstrate the presence of malignant cells. If an infectious etiology cannot be demonstrated in a child with these symptoms, contrast studies are indicated to rule out an intracranial space-occupying lesion.

SUBARACHNOID HEMORRHAGE

Subarachnoid hemorrhage is an uncommon cause of meningeal irritation in childhood. Spontaneous subarachnoid hemorrhage in this age group is most frequently due to the rupture of a cerebral anteriovenous malformation. Rupture of a berry aneurysm seldom occurs during childhood. Occasionally ependymomas of the lateral ventricles may be the cause of repeated episodes of subarachnoid bleeding before producing signs of cerebral dysfunction or increased intracranial pressure. The onset of symptoms of subarachnoid hemorrhage of any cause is abrupt, with severe headache, seizures, and alteration of consciousness from stupor to deep coma. Signs of meningeal irritation are prominent even in small children. The diagnosis is confirmed by lumbar puncture, which shows a uniformly bloody cerebrospinal fluid with no tendency to clear as the fluid is collected in successive tubes. Cerebral angiography permits demonstration of the source of bleeding in the great majority of patients.

FOLLOWING CONTRAST STUDIES AND LUMBAR PUNCTURE

Headache and backache with or without signs of meningeal irritation are not uncommon complaints or physical findings following contrast studies such as ventriculograms, pneumoencephalograms and myelograms, and after lumbar puncture.

REFERENCES

Dodge, P. R., and Swartz, M. N. Bacterial meningitis; a review of selected aspects: II. Special neurologic problems, postmeningitic complications and clinicopathological correlations. *New Eng. J. Med.* 272:954, 1003, 1965.

Eigler, J. O. C., et al. Bacterial meningitis: I. General review (294 cases). *Proc. Staff Meet. Mayo Clin.* 36:357, 1961.

Lorber, J., and Pickering, D. Incidence and treatment of postmeningitic hydrocephalus in the newborn. *Arch. Dis. Child.* 41:44, 1966.

Mathies, A. W., Jr., and Wehrle, P. F. Management of bacterial meningitis in children. *Pediat. Clin. N. Amer.* 15:185, 1968.

McCracken, G. H., Jr., and Shinefield, H. R. Changes in the pattern of neonatal septicemia and meningitis. *Amer. J. Dis. Child.* 112:33, 1966.

Nieri, R. L., et al. Central-nervous-system complications of leukemia: A review. *Mayo Clin. Proc.* 43:70, 1968.

Swartz, M. N., and Dodge, P. R. Bacterial meningitis; a review of selected aspects: I. General clinical features, special problems and unusual meningeal reactions mimicking bacterial meningitis. *New Eng. J. Med.* 272: 725; 779; 842; 898, 1965.

Todd, M. R., and Neville, J. G. Sequelae of tuberculous meningitis. *Arch. Dis. Child.* 39:213, 1964.

9

Neurologic Deficit of Sudden Onset with Impairment or Loss of Consciousness

THE PICTURE of a healthy child lapsing in a matter of minutes or hours into a deep coma is familiar to all those caring for children. The situation is alarming and has to be dealt with rapidly if a diagnosis and appropriate supportive or specific therapy are to be instituted before the occurrence of irreversible damage to vital cerebral centers.

HEAD TRAUMA

Since in the vast majority of instances external evidence of trauma is apparent, a diagnosis of sudden loss of consciousness secondary to head trauma only rarely presents any difficulties. Occasionally it is difficult to determine whether loss of consciousness is due to head trauma or whether the head trauma is secondary to a fall at the onset of an epileptic attack. Most cases of moderate trauma with or without a skull fracture have no apparent immediate significance. The child is stunned momentarily and within a few minutes may become pale, feel nauseated, and vomit once or several times. He is usually taken to a hospital where the general and neurologic examinations show no abnormalities. Roentgenographic examination of the skull may be either normal or may show a linear skull fracture. This type of fracture is as a rule of no diagnostic or immediate prognostic importance, early or late complications of head trauma being directly related to the severity of cere-

Parts of this chapter are reprinted from J. C. Lagos and R. G. Siekert. Intracranial hemorrhage in infancy and childhood. *Clinical Pediatrics* 8:90, 1969, with permission of J. B. Lippincott Co.

bral or vascular damage produced by the injury (cerebral concussion, cerebral contusion, or associated gross intracranial bleeding).

Cerebral concussion is a clinical term used to describe alteration or loss of consciousness varying from confusion to deep coma according to the degree of functional disruption of brain function. Amnesia for events before and after the accident is common. Coma may last from a few seconds to several days. On awakening the child may be confused and may complain of headache for one or several days. Other symptoms following cerebral concussion are dizziness, vertigo, irritability, inability to concentrate, and changes in personality (posttraumatic syndrome).

The pathophysiology of cerebral concussion appears to be a disturbance in cerebral function related to the displacement of brain structures caused by the sudden movement of the head. Increased intracranial pressure does not seem to play a role. Transient total blindness may occur in children after mild, blunt head trauma.

Cerebral contusion (bruising) may occur on the same side of the brain as the direction of force (coup) or on the opposite side (contrecoup). Often the contrecoup type of injury is more severe. Pathologically in cerebral contusion there is subarachnoid hemorrhage, multiple small hemorrhages in the white matter, lesions of the small perforating arteries, and cerebral edema. Microscopic changes include necrosis of neurons and subsequent scar formation. If lesions are widespread eventually there may be symmetrical dilation of both lateral ventricles.

In patients with cerebral contusion coma may last for several days. Focal neurologic signs when present are related to the area of cerebral damage. On recovering consciousness the patient may be found to have a hemiplegia, hemianopia, aphasia, cranial nerve palsies, or other focal neurologic sequelae according to the site and extent of the cerebral injury. Laboratory findings are normal in head injuries, with the exception of the cerebrospinal fluid, which may be bloody in cases of cerebral contusion, and the electroencephalogram, which may show a flat record immediately after injury and generalized slowing with waves of high amplitude on subsequent days. Vital signs (pulse, respirations, and blood pressure) should be recorded at frequent intervals in any patient with head trauma requiring hospitalization.

Bradycardia, irregular and slow respirations, and a high blood pressure are signs of increased intracranial pressure. A dilated and poorly reacting pupil is usually indicative of a space-occupying lesion on the same side (epidural, subdural, or intracerebral hematoma). Profound coma following head injuries is almost always secondary to brain stem dysfunction due to direct injury to this structure or to its compression by an edematous brain or to the mechanical effects of gross intracranial bleeding.

The immediate treatment of any child with a severe head injury includes (1) the maintenance of an adequate oxygen supply to the brain (tracheal intubation, tracheotomy, aspiration of secretions, and use of oxygen); (2) the maintenance of an adequate cerebral perfusion (vasoconstrictors and administration of blood or plasma); and (3) the reduction of cerebral metabolism and cerebral edema by the use of hypothermia, dehydrating agents such as intravenous urea and mannitol, or parenteral steroids. Neurologic examination and determination of vital signs at frequent intervals should be carried out in all patients in coma due to severe head trauma. This may be the only way to detect at an early stage an expanding mass such as an intracerebral, subdural, or epidural hematoma. These complications of head trauma should be kept in mind at all times and ruled out by appropriate contrast studies.

Head injuries of any severity may or may not produce linear skull fractures. In the absence of impairment of consciousness or neurologic deficit they are as a rule of little immediate diagnostic importance. Depressed skull fractures, on the other hand, should receive immediate surgical treatment. A fracture of the parietal bone crossing the groove of the middle meningeal artery should alert the physician to the possibility of the development of epidural hemorrhage. Complications of skull fractures include (1) cerebrospinal-fluid rhinorrhea with fractures of the cribriform plate; (2) otorrhea with fractures of the temporal bone in the roof of the middle ear; (3) the presence of air in the cranial cavity (pneumocele), usually found in association with fractures of the frontal sinuses; (4) cranial nerve palsies with basilar skull fractures as well as anosmia as a result of fractures of the cribriform plate and injury to the olfactory nerve; and (5) in rare instances a fracture of the base of the skull across the pituitary fossa may damage the pituitary gland, producing transient or permanent diabetes insipidus or pituitary insufficiency. In fractures complicated by cerebrospinal-fluid leak surgical repair is necessary if no spontaneous improvement occurs. Antibiotics should be given to prevent meningitis.

Occasionally following skull factures, especially of the parietal bone, a leptomeningeal cyst develops. This is a cystic mass filled with spinal fluid which accumulates between the arachnoid and the pia mater. At the time of injury there is a tear in the dura mater, with herniation of the arachnoid and subsequent cyst formation. There is progressive enlargement of the fracture line and eventually a gross skull defect results. Roentgenograms of the skull months or years after injury show an irregular bone defect with scalloped margins and some degree of sclerosis of the adjacent bone. Both inner and outer tables are involved, the inner table almost always to a greater extent. The skull defect and the overlying bulging of the scalp may be an accidental finding during a routine physical examination. However, this lesion may produce neurologic deficit in the contralateral side in the form of focal seizures, hemiparesis, increased muscle stretch reflexes, and an extensor plantar response (Babinski sign). The treatment of leptomeningeal cyst is its surgical removal. At surgery the dura mater is absent in the center of the bony defect and markedly thin and adherent to the underlying arachnoid around the margins of the lesion. Because of the possibility of this complication, roentgenographic examination of the skull should be repeated at 3 and 6 months following head injury, particularly if the fracture was diastatic or was located in the posterosuperior portion of the parietal bone where most leptomeningeal cysts seem to develop.

MAJOR MOTOR SEIZURES

Major motor (generalized) seizures are the most common cause of sudden loss of consciousness in all age groups. The attacks seldom last more than 20 minutes and have usually subsided by the time the patient is seen by a physician. In a patient with a known convulsive disorder the sudden loss of consciousness does not usually represent a diagnostic problem. However, when the seizure is the first episode of a chronic convulsive disorder it has to be differentiated from a host of other conditions such as encephalitis, meningitis, toxic encephalopathy, or spontaneous intracranial bleeding, disorders whose first manifestation may be a generalized seizure in addition to other signs or symptoms such as severe headache preceding the attack, progressive deterioration of the level of consciousness, meningeal signs, or signs of focal neurologic deficit.

STATUS EPILEPTICUS

Status epilepticus can be defined as a series of repetitive major motor seizures occurring while the patient is still in the postictal stage of the preceding seizure. Status epilepticus is a medical emergency and a potentially fatal condition requiring prompt and vigorous treatment. It may produce severe focal or diffuse cerebral damage. Experimental status epilepticus has shown serious alternations in the metabolic potential of cortical neurons; despite total muscle relaxation and adequate oxygenation animals suffer irreversible damage ultimately leading to death.

The main cause of status epilepticus in children is sudden withdrawal of anticonvulsants, especially barbiturates, in a patient with a chronic seizure disorder. Patients in status epilepticus have a rise in temperature sometimes as high as 107°F, tachycardia, and progressive deepening coma. If the attack does not cease spontaneously or with anticonvulsant treatment, death ensues.

At present the drug of choice in the treatment of status epilepticus is diazepam (Valium). Diazepam given intravenously or intramuscularly has a potent anticonvulsant activity and causes less respiratory depression than that produced by large doses of barbiturates. The optimal dosage of diazepam in the treatment of status epilepticus has not yet been established. As a general rule, and this also applies to the use of other anticonvulsants in the treatment of status epilepticus, it is desirable to give as much medication as needed to stop seizure activity, taking the necessary precautions to ventilate the patient if severe respiratory depression or respiratory arrest occurs. Diazepam can be given intravenously to infants in a dose of 1 to 2 mg. Older children will usually respond favorably to 2.5 to 10 mg. of diazepam intravenously. In most instances seizure activity terminates rapidly with the initial dose. Diazepam appears to be more effective in patients with prolonged seizure activity associated with idiopathic epilepsy and slowly progressive cerebral disease than in those with prolonged seizure activity complicating acute cerebral disorders such as meningitis, spontaneous subarachnoid hemorrhage, cerebral infarction, or toxic encephalopathy.

If seizure activity is not controlled with diazepam, phenobarbital can be given intravenously in a fairly large initial dose, according to the age of the child, rather than in small repeated doses. Infants and small children tolerate surprisingly high doses of phenobarbital. This tolerance appears to be enhanced by the abnormal cerebral conditions present in status epilepticus. Paraldehyde given intramuscularly or per rectum is also effective in the treatment of status epilepticus (see Appendix 3).

BREATH-HOLDING SPELLS

Sudden loss of consciousness as well as some of the clinical features of major motor seizures occur in so-called breath-holding spells. Breath-holding spells can be defined as stereotyped attacks characterized by transient loss of consciousness and abnormal posturing following an unpleasant stimulus or experience (trauma, spanking, anger). Immediately after a stressful or painful stimulus the child first cries intermittently; a few seconds later his cry becomes sustained and then the child holds his breath at the end of the expiratory phase, becomes cyanotic or pale, loses consciousness, and manifests generalized limpness. If the attack lasts more than a few seconds this is followed by a tonic or opisthotonic phase, which may or may not be accompanied by a few clonic jerks of the limbs. Occasionally there is incontinence of urine or feces. The opisthotonic or tonic phase is followed by another one of limpness. The child usually regains consciousness in a matter of seconds or, less commonly, falls into a deep sleep. Breath-holding spells have their onset usually between 7 and 12 months of age and rarely recur after the age of 4 years. Treatment with anticonvulsants appears to be of little help in the prevention of recurrences. Prognosis in terms of mental development or the subsequent development of convulsive seizures (epilepsy) is excellent. Breath-holding spells can be differentiated from major motor seizures by (1) the constant presence of a precipitating stimulus, (2) the stereotyped nature of the attacks, and (3) by the frequent absence of a postictal state. In addition, opisthotonos is rarely if ever seen in epileptic seizures.

ACUTE INFANTILE HEMIPLEGIA

Acute infantile hemiplegia is not a single disease but a syndrome resulting from a variety of etiologies. Idiopathic acute infantile hemiplegia occurs usually in a child between the ages of 6 months and 2 years and is characterized by the onset of unilateral convulsions, fever, and coma. The disease begins abruptly in an apparently healthy child with focal recurrent seizures on the side which subsequently will become hemiplegic. As a rule the convulsions are severe. In some instances they are initially generalized and later on become lateralized. When the child recovers consciousness, and sometimes while he is still in the postictal state, examination reveals a unilateral flaccid paralysis. In a period of two to three weeks the flaccidity of the involved side is replaced by a slowly increasing spasticity.

Symptomatic hemiplegia in childhood may be secondary to a number of different etiologies. This category can be further subdivided into those cases in which the causal mechanism is known but its origin obscure, such as cerebral thrombosis, and those in which the etiologic mechanism is known, such as cerebral embolism, subdural hematoma, or intracerebral bleeding due to the rupture of an arteriovenous malformation. Thrombosis of the internal carotid or of one of its main branches probably accounts for a large percentage of cases of acute infantile hemiplegia. The rarity with which this diagnosis is made may be in great part due to the infrequency with which angiograms are performed in children with this condition. Subdural hematoma in children is in most instances secondary to head trauma. This is a rare cause of hemiplegia. Patients with chronic subdural hematoma rarely present with hemiparesis. On the other hand, a mild degree of hemiparesis is not uncommonly found in a child with an acute subdural hematoma. Following surgical removal of the hematoma, a persistent hemiparesis is the exception rather than the rule.

Extradural hematoma following head trauma is uncommon in infants and children. The clinical picture is one of progressive deterioration of consciousness from drowsiness to stupor or coma and circulatory and respiratory changes indicative of compression of brain stem centers.

Focal neurologic signs are dilatation of the pupil on the side of the lesion and a hemiparesis on the opposite side. The diagnosis can be confirmed by cerebral angiography. Surgical removal of the hematoma is lifesaving, and neurologic sequelae are rare.

Trauma to the neck in the paratonsillar area may produce thrombosis of the internal carotid artery, with resulting cerebral infarction and hemiplegia. Following fractures of long bones or trauma to subcutaneous tissue, small globules of fat may enter the bloodstream. These emboli may be held up at the capillary level in the central nervous system, producing severe diffuse and focal brain damage. The symptoms of fatty embolism usually begin 2 to 5 days following trauma and consist of headaches, fever, blood-tinged sputum, and progressive deterioration of the level of consciousness from sleepiness to coma and death. Prognosis for life is poor; mortality rate is over 75 percent. Hemiplegia and ocular palsies are some of the neurologic sequelae observed in survivors. A diagnosis can be made on the basis of the history of trauma, the clinical picture, and the demonstration of fat emboli in the retinal vessels and free fat droplets in the urine.

Prolonged status epilepticus may affect one side of the brain more than the other and result in permanent focal damage and hemiplegia.

Gross intracerebral bleeding is not a common complication of head trauma in children, in contrast to adults. This type of bleeding in children is much more likely to occur as a spontaneous event in a child who previously may or may not have had symptoms referable to the central nervous system. Most cases are due to the rupture of an arteriovenous malformation into the subarachnoid space or into the substance of the brain. It may cause a hemiplegia of acute onset. The most common clinical manifestations of arteriovenous malformations before spontaneous rupture are focal or generalized seizures, and neurologic deficit related to local cerebral dysfunction such as aphasia, homonymous hemianopia, or a slowly progressive spastic hemiplegia. Recurrent episodes of migrainoid headaches localized to the side of the lesion occur in 25 percent of patients, and a cranial bruit can be heard in about 40 percent of patients with arteriovenous malformations of the brain.

In many instances of spontaneous intracranial bleeding a definite etiology cannot be demonstrated. It is probable that small arteriovenous malformations or angiomas difficult to demonstrate at surgery or at autopsy are the source of bleeding.

Acute infantile hemiplegia secondary to cerebral thrombosis is a not uncommon occurrence in children under the age of 2 years with cyanotic congenital heart disease (Fig. 9-1). This complication occurs with red blood cell counts above 8 million or an arterial oxygen content below 10 volumes percent. The causal mechanism is probably the increased viscosity of the blood or hypoxia.

Hemiplegia is in general a rare complication of viral encephalitis. It

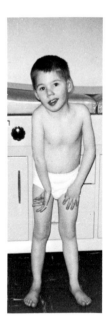

Fig. 9-1. 5-year-old boy with cyanotic congenital heart disease and acute right-sided hemiplegia secondary to cerebral thrombosis at the age of 2 years.

is not uncommonly seen, however, following herpes simplex encephalitis, which may produce extensive destruction in one or both temporal lobes and adjacent areas. Patients who survive herpes simplex encephalitis are usually left with severe neurologic deficit, such as psychomotor retardation, homonymous hemianopia, or hemiplegia (Fig. 9-2).

Bacterial meningitis, especially during early infancy, is not an infrequent cause of unilateral or bilateral hemiplegia of acute onset. Some microorganisms such as *Haemophilus influenzae* and pneumococcus may produce cortical thrombophlebitis and secondary retrograde infarction of cerebral tissue. This complication is manifested by sudden elevation of temperature, seizures, recurrence of meningeal signs, and tension or bulging of the anterior fontanelle. Subdural taps are negative, and examination of the cerebrospinal fluid may show the changes seen during the initial stages of the disease. A more common situation is that in which cortical thrombosis and infarction of brain tissue occur in the absence of clinical or laboratory signs of relapsing meningitis.

Inflammatory diseases of the paranasal sinuses, ear, nose, and throat may produce an inflammatory reaction of the vessels at the base of the skull, with resulting thrombosis and hemiplegia. A noninflammatory cerebral arteritis also leading to hemiplegia may occur in idiopathic

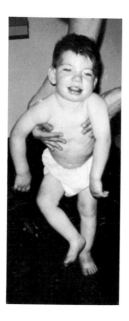

Fig. 9-2.   18-month-old infant who had acute left hemiplegia secondary to herpes simplex encephalitis at the age of 3 months. Moderate psychomotor retardation.

granulomatous arteritis (pulseless disease), a condition characterized by widespread thrombosis of major arterial vessels.

Additional causes of cerebral thrombosis are blood dyscrasias such as sickle-cell disease, thrombotic thrombocytopenic purpura, and collagen diseases like lupus erythematosus disseminatus and periarteritis nodosa.

In idiopathic acute infantile hemiplegia the usual blood, urine, and roentgenographic studies are normal. The electroencephalogram may show evidence of electrical seizure activity or a diffuse slowing on the side opposite the hemiplegia. In symptomatic hemiplegia the electroencephalogram may show similar changes. The echoencephalogram may show displacement of midline structures in herpes simplex encephalitis, in which there may be a severe degree of focal edema and necrosis, and in extradural, subdural, or intracerebral hematoma. The brain scan may demonstrate areas of abnormal uptake of radioactive material in subdural hematomas, arteriovenous malformations, intracerebral hematoma, cerebral infarction, or in areas of localized necrosis as in herpes simplex encephalitis. The arteriogram may reveal occlusion of the internal carotid artery or of one of its main branches or evidence of segmental narrowing of intracranial vessels, especially of the middle cerebral artery.

When all causes of acute infantile hemiplegia are lumped together a mortality rate of about 25 percent is to be expected. Some sort of neurologic deficit is seen in 75 percent of survivors. Irrespective of etiologic mechanisms, months or years following the acute episode the involved cerebral hemisphere may become atrophic. This lack of development produces typical changes in the skull. These consist of thickening of the cranial vault, overdevelopment of the frontal and ethmoidal sinuses, and elevation of the petrous pyramid on the side of the lesion. Motor sequelae of various degrees persist in about 75 percent of patients. Characteristically the arm and hand are more affected than the leg. A significant number of patients are left with permanent severe functional incapacity of the hand. Eventually, however, most children are able to walk without assistance. The hemiplegic limbs develop slowly and in a large number of patients are smaller and shorter than those of the normal side (Fig. 9-3). This difference in size is sometimes difficult to recognize without accurate measurements of the extremities. Careful comparison of the thumbs and great toes often will reveal a difference in size even in cases where there is not an obvious discrepancy in the length and circumference of the extremities.

Sensory loss occurs in more than 50 percent and homonymous hemianopia in 25 percent of cases. Visual-field defects are rarely present in the absence of sensory loss in the hand. Other neurologic sequelae are involuntary movements of a choreoid or choreoathetoid nature. Speech defects may occur, especially in patients with involvement of the domi-

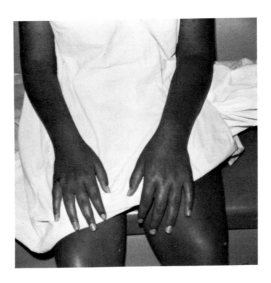

Fig. 9-3.   Right arm smaller than left in 16-year-old girl who had acute infantile hemiplegia at the age of 9 months.

nant hemisphere. Dysphasia is rare under the age of 4 years and is never observed before 2 years unless there is severe associated mental retardation. Generalized or focal seizures develop in 50 percent of cases. Mental or behavioral disturbances are present in about 50 percent of patients.

INTRACRANIAL HEMORRHAGE

As a rule, intracranial bleeding in infants (neonates excluded) and children is secondary to trauma. Some of these children are left with some neurologic deficit, depending upon the site and severity of the bleeding and the promptness of therapy.

The main anatomic locations of intracranial bleeding, in increasing order, are in neonates—intracerebral, intraventricular, subarachnoid, and subdural, and in infants and children—extradural, intracerebral, subarachnoid, and subdural. This is an oversimplified classification, since in many instances there is more than one source of bleeding.

INTRACRANIAL HEMORRHAGE IN NEONATES

Several influences appear etiologically important in the early days of life. These include: (1) circulatory disturbances due to the suction effect secondary to the difference in pressure between the uterine cavity and the atmosphere; (2) moulding of the head, with overlapping or depression of the skull bones accompanied by tears of the falx or tentorium and rupture of the bridging cortical veins, which may result in intracerebral, subarachnoid, or subdural hemorrhage; (3) hypoxia due to maternal complications or difficult delivery; (4) hemorrhagic disease of the newborn due to a diversity of causes which may on rare occasions cause a spontaneous intracerebral or meningeal hemorrhage; (5) infections such as septicemia, particularly in the premature; (6) erythroblastosis fetalis.

Table 9-1 shows the frequency distribution of the different types of intracranial hemorrhage in neonates in Craig's series (1938) of 126 autopsied cases. With the exception of subdural hemorrhage, in which mechanical trauma plays a prominent role, all other types of intracranial hemorrhages are probably due primarily to hypoxia and venous congestion.

Intracerebral Hemorrhage

Intracerebral hemorrhage is the least common of all the intracranial hemorrhages in neonates. They preferentially affect large, full-term in-

Table 9-1.   Sites of Intracranial Hemorrhage in 126 Neonates

	Cases	
Site	No.	%
Intracerebral	6	5
Intraventricular	22	17
Subarachnoid	36	29
Subdural	62	49

This table was based on figures from W. S. Craig (*Arch. Dis. Child* 13:89, 1938) and appeared in an article by J. C. Lagos and R. G. Siekert (*Clin. Pediat.* (Phil.) 8:90, 1969).

fants born after a prolonged labor or a difficult instrument delivery. Multiple petechiae or perivascular hemorrhages are noted at autopsy. According to Craig (1938), these babies do not seem in critical condition at birth but are quiet and inactive. Their color is good but their temperature is difficult to control. Their pulse and respiration rates are slow and their muscle stretch reflexes are decreased. Many have feeding difficulties. This period, which lasts from 6 to 10 days, is followed by a period of agitation and progressive physical weakness. The eyes are constantly open and move restlessly in all directions. Then, the majority of these babies exhibit a typical cerebral cry accompanied by head rolling. In general, this type of intracranial hemorrhage is characterized by an indistinct onset, a fairly prolonged course, and a slow death.

Intraventricular Hemorrhage

Intraventricular bleeding is particularly common in premature infants born by spontaneous delivery. Traditionally it has been accepted that the causative mechanism is generalized venous congestion with damage to the cerebral blood vessels and subsequent rupture of the terminal veins. However, in a series of 30 autopsied premature infants with subependymal hemorrhages, Ross and Dimmette in 1965 found that the terminal veins were responsible for the bleeding in only 2 cases. In the other 28 cases the bleeding originated in the external half of the subependymal matrix, from the transverse caudate veins or their tributaries. Anoxia is the most important factor in this type of hemorrhage, but birth trauma also may play a significant role.

The clinical course of intraventricular hemorrhage in newborn infants may follow one of two patterns. Usually the clinical picture is dominated by signs of asphyxia, and the baby may die shortly after birth or after repeated episodes of cyanosis. Less frequently the clinical course is characterized by a short period of relative well-being (12 to 24 hours) followed by vomiting, jaundice, poor sucking, increasing lethargy, episodes of apnea and progressive respiratory difficulties, and marked hypotonia. Bulging of the fontanelle is commonly seen, and gross twitchings of the face and limbs are present. Death usually occurs after a generalized convulsion.

Intracranial hemorrhages of this type presumably are almost always fatal. In Ross and Dimmette's series the antemortem diagnosis of subependymal hemorrhage with intraventricular rupture was made in only 2 of their 30 cases. These authors suggested that in lethargic premature infants having recurrent episodes of apnea more frequent use of lumbar punctures could make possible the diagnosis of intraventricular hemorrhage; then, treatment of shock and increased intracranial pressure might salvage an occasional premature infant with this type of intracranial bleeding.

Subarachnoid Hemorrhage

Subarachnoid hemorrhage is usually associated with complicated pregnancies with uncomplicated deliveries. The most important etiologic factor is probably anoxia. The clinical picture is characterized by spells of apnea and by a poor color which often improves when the infant cries. Localizing signs are absent. Treatment is entirely supportive. If intracranial pressure is increased, lumbar puncture may be indicated.

It has been postulated that bleeding into the subarachnoid space could be an important etiologic factor in the production of congenital communicating hydrocephalus. This may indeed be true, since approximately 15 percent of newborn infants have some blood in the cerebrospinal fluid (presumably secondary to trauma at birth).

Subdural Hemorrhage

Subdural hemorrhage usually occurs in large babies born of primiparas or elderly multiparas. It is ten times more frequent with breech than with spontaneous deliveries and occurs twice as often in infants of primiparas as in infants of multiparas. Most acute subdural hemorrhages in neonates occur in association with a difficult instrumental delivery.

Subdural hemorrhage in early infancy is characterized by cardiorespiratory symptoms (such as breathing difficulties with periods of dyspnea and cyanosis); a facial expression of anxiety or unusual alertness, with the eyes open and staring; feeding difficulties; irritability; restlessness; increased tension of the anterior fontanelle; and focal seizures, which later may become generalized. Retinal hemorrhages are almost invariably present. Paralysis of the third cranial nerve on the same side as the lesion is common and varies from a dilated or sluggishly reacting pupil to a complete paralysis. Other neurologic findings include unilateral or bilateral flaccidity or spasticity which appears early or late according to the severity and extent of the hemorrhage. Transillumination of the skull to demonstrate abnormal areas of glowing is a simple test and often is a highly successful procedure. Most subdural hemorrhages in neonates are unilateral and supratentorial in location.

If the anterior fontanelle is excessively tense in the presence of one or more of the above signs or symptoms, subdural taps are indicated. Subdural tapping and supportive therapy are generally the only treatments since membranes around the hematoma will not develop with prompt and adequate therapy. Approximately 50 percent of these infants make a good recovery.

Subdural hemorrhage in the neonatal period may be an important etiologic factor in the production of communicating hydrocephalus. It has been suggested that the hydrocephalus which sometimes follows subdural hemorrhage in the newborn or young infant may be due to functional destruction of superficial brain vessels or to alterations of the pacchionian granulations by the vascular lesion or by a process of atrophy following a long period of inactivity.

INTRACRANIAL HEMORRHAGE IN INFANTS AND CHILDREN

Intracerebral Hemorrhage

As in adults, intracerebral hemorrhages in children can be grouped according to whether they are spontaneous or secondary to trauma. Intracerebral hemorrhages of traumatic origin are rare in children. Ingraham and Matson did not find a single case of gross intracerebral bleeding (hematoma) in a series of 1330 cases of head injury requiring hospitalization. In the same group of patients they found 30 cases of extradural and 319 cases of subdural hemorrhage.

On the other hand, spontaneous intracerebral hemorrhage appears a much more common entity. This sort of hemorrhage almost invariably occurs in a child who previously has enjoyed good health. Arteriography or pathologic examination rarely gives any clue as to the possible underlying etiologic factors. Margolis and co-workers in 1951 and in 1961 described 6 cases of spontaneous intracerebral hemorrhage, 4 of which were in children. In all cases they were able to demonstrate small vascular malformations. From these and other reports it seems that cerebral angioma represents the most important, if not the sole, etiologic factor in the production of spontaneous intracerebral hemorrhages in children.

Spontaneous subcortical hemorrhage is a variety of intracerebral hemorrhage which seems to occur predominantly in adolescents or in young adults. The immediate and the long-term prognoses (in terms of further bleeding or of neurologic deficit) in spontaneous subcortical hemorrhage are in general excellent. Its occurrence at an early age suggests some kind of vascular anomaly as the most probable etiologic factor.

Intracerebral hemorrhage is said to be a frequent complication of thrombosis or thrombophlebitis of the dural sinuses. Other conditions which may produce bleeding into the substance of the brain are various blood dyscrasias such as leukemias, sickle-cell anemia, idiopathic thrombocytopenic purpura, thrombotic thrombocytopenic purpura, and hemophilia. Bleeding into a neoplastic tumor with or without vascular components or into a nonneoplastic growth (tuberous sclerosis) may in rare cases give rise to intracerebral bleeding in an infant or child. Intracerebral hemorrhage secondary to arterial hypertension also occurs in children with renal disease or coarctation of the aorta.

Subarachnoid Hemorrhage

Subarachnoid hemorrhage is a type of intracranial bleeding which is rare in infants or children. It was once thought that this lesion was usually secondary to infection, rheumatic fever, or blood dyscrasias, but rupture of an intracranial aneurysm or arteriovenous malformation may occur at practically any age in childhood, including the neonatal period.

In children, as in adults, the majority of proved ruptured aneurysms have arisen from the branches of the anterior part of the circle of Willis. Superficially located arteriovenous malformations constitute probably the most important etiologic factor in the production of subarachnoid hemorrhages in children. We have seen several patients who had repeated episodes of subarachnoid hemorrhage as the first manifestation of brain tumor, particularly ependymoma, before the true nature of the process was recognized (see Chapter 8).

Extradural Hemorrhage

Extradural hemorrhage is relatively uncommon. The frequency varies in different reports from 1:305 to 30:1330 cases of head injury requiring hospitalization.

Ingraham and associates in 1949 in an analysis of 20 cases stated that the clinical picture in children differs in several aspects from that in adults. Of their 20 patients, only 3 had initial loss of consciousness followed by the classic lucid interval. They pointed out that in children the amount of blood collected in the extradural space may be more than sufficient to produce shock and for this reason anemia or shock

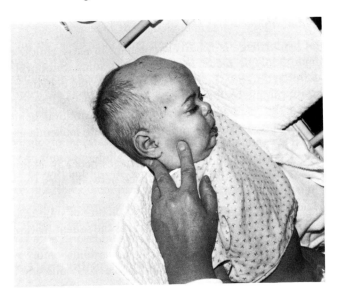

Fig. 9-4. 7-month-old infant with idiopathic thrombocytopenic purpura and subarachnoid and subdural hemorrhage. Note marked bulging of the anterior fontanelle.

that caused by chronic subdural hematoma. Subhyaloid or preretinal hemorrhages are common in acute and subacute cases, but papilledema is rare during infancy even in the presence of very high intracranial pressure.

It is well accepted that the source of bleeding in subdural hemorrhage is the rupture of bridging veins, with slowly increasing size of the hematoma. A semipermeable membrane begins to form around the hematoma in a relatively short time (18–20 days), and the osmotic activity of the collected blood increases with hemolysis. The albumin in the subdural space is derived mainly from the plasma proteins; a minimal part is derived from the breakdown of the erythrocytes of the hematoma. Abnormal capillaries are also present in the membranes of the subdural hematoma (especially parietal), with secondary effusion of fluid into the cavity.

Some authors believe that, because of the rapid growth of the infant's brain and the compression of the subarachnoid space by the inelastic abnormal membrane, the latter eventually interferes with the normal development of cortical function, with a normal and adequate blood supply, and with the normal reabsorption of cerebrospinal fluid. Hence, the membrane must be removed or at least widely excised. However, long-term results in children who had had subdural hemorrhages have shown that a large number of children with retained membranes are

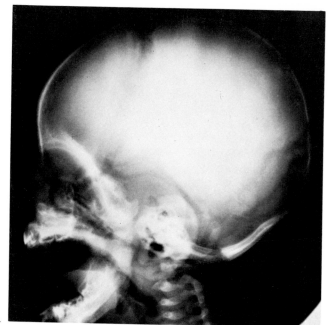

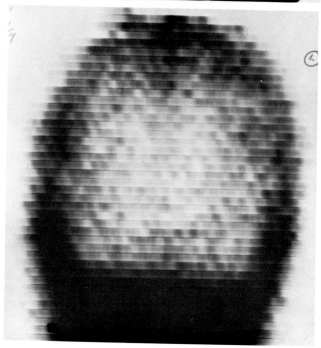

Fig. 9-5. *A,* skull x-ray showing spreading of cranial sutures in 3-month-old infant with chronic bilateral subdural hematoma. *B,* brain scan in same patient shows increased uptake of radioisotope over the convexity of the brain bilaterally.

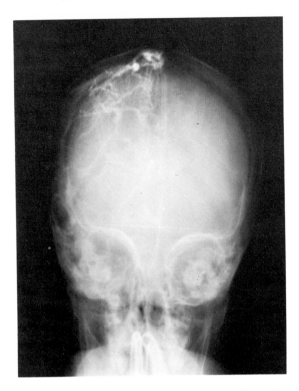

Fig. 9-6. Right carotid angiogram in 14-month-old infant showing separation of arteries from inner table of skull by subdural hematoma. A similar type of picture was observed on the left side by Lagos and Siekert in 1969.

neither subject to reaccumulation of fluid nor mentally retarded or neurologically handicapped.

The ultimate prognosis in cases of chronic subdural hematoma seems to depend not so much on the presence of retained membranes as on the underlying cortical damage at the time of surgical treatment. The condition of the brain at the time of the operation seems to be the determining factor so far as the long-term prognosis is concerned. In most cases, removal of the membrane is probably not indicated. Several subdural taps will dry out the subdural space in the great majority of cases. If this does not occur trephination and evacuation of the hematoma are indicated.

VIRAL INFECTIONS OF THE CENTRAL NERVOUS SYSTEM

The viral agents causing central nervous system disease in man are in general opportunistic and invade it only when a propitious parasite-host relationship exists. Certain viruses, such as the agent responsible for rabies, have a special affinity for invading and destroying central nervous system structures. Viruses can invade the central nervous system via peripheral nerves (rabies and possibly polioviruses). The neural route, once believed to be the most important if not exclusive route for virus infection, is probably of secondary importance in man. It is uncertain whether viruses can invade the central nervous system via the olfactory nerve. This mode of spread has been suggested to explain the predilection of herpes simplex virus for the temporal lobes. Finally, viruses could reach the central nervous system by the hematogenous route by one of several mechanisms: through invasion of the choroid plexus, by proliferation of the virus in the endothelium of cerebral capillaries, or by passive passage across the blood-brain barrier. The hematogenous route is probably the most important in human disease. Central nervous system infections of viral etiology can be divided into four major clinicopathological categories: (1) encephalitis, (2) aseptic meningitis, (3) encephalomyelitis, and (4) paralytic syndrome (poliomyelitis in its broader sense).

Encephalitis

The most important agents causing encephalitis are the arthropodborne viruses, herpes simplex, lymphocytic choriomeningitis, mumps, Coxsackie B, and ECHO viruses. Poliomyelitis viruses, in rare instances, may produce an encephalitic picture without paralysis.

Viral encephalitis is characterized clinically by fever, headache, nausea and vomiting, convulsions, and disturbances of consciousness ranging from somnolence and lethargy to profound coma. It is not uncommon to see a child with viral encephalitis presenting with sudden loss of awareness or delirium and a clinical picture simulating an acute psychotic reaction. A mild respiratory infection may or may not precede the onset of symptoms. Headache is a prominent complaint in patients with a clear sensorium. Cerebrospinal fluid examination shows a moderate lymphocytic pleocytosis, a normal glucose level, and a mild elevation of protein. Approximately 50 percent of survivors show significant disability. Histologically there is meningeal infiltration with mononuclear cells and perivascular lymphocytic infiltration and collection of glial or histiocytic cells in the substance of the brain. Varying degrees of neuronal damage may occur, especially in the areas where cellular infiltration is greater.

In general, the agents responsible for most types of encephalitis produce diffuse damage to the brain manifested clinically by nonlocalizing signs and symptoms. A common exception to this rule is infection with herpes simplex virus, which preferentially affects one or both temporal lobes, causing focal areas of necrosis and severe brain edema. Herpes simplex encephalitis can occur at all ages but is essentially a disease of adolescents or young adults. An upper respiratory infection precedes the onset of the disease by hours or days in about one-third of cases. Cutaneous herpetic lesions are seen in less than 10 percent of patients.

The onset of neurologic symptoms is abrupt. In addition to the usual signs and symptoms of encephalitis (fever, headaches, lethargy, confusion, and coma) there may be focal signs or symptoms suggestive of involvement of the temporal lobe or adjacent areas, such as motor or mixed aphasia, adversive eye or head movement, focal seizures, abnormal motor or psychic behavior suggestive of temporal lobe seizures, olfactory and auditory hallucinations, hemiparesis, or a homonymous visual-field defect. Papilledema is present in about 15 percent of cases. There may be a moderate elevation of the white blood count. Cerebrospinal fluid examination shows a normal pressure in about two-thirds of cases, a lymphocytic pleocytosis, a normal glucose level, and an elevated protein. The electroencephalogram may show generalized nonspecific abnormalities or focal slowing in one or both temporal regions. Because of the focal signs and symptoms a diagnosis of a space-taking lesion is frequently suspected on clinical grounds and often confirmed by arteriography, which may show displacement of midline structures to the side opposite the lesion.

At surgery the true nature of the process is recognized. On gross inspection there is softening of one or both temporal lobes and related rhinencephalic structures. Microscopically there is extensive necrosis of affected areas. Mortality in herpes simplex encephalitis is about 70 percent. Neurologic sequelae are present in almost all survivors. These include psychomotor retardation, personality changes, focal motor deficit, incoordination, and seizures. The differential diagnosis in herpes simplex encephalitis includes other forms of encephalitis, as well as space-occupying lesions such as brain abscesses, brain tumors, or subdural hematoma. Treatment is entirely supportive (antipyretics, anticonvulsants, urea or mannitol infusions and steroids to treat cerebral edema, or surgical decompression). Some recent reports indicate that antiviral agents (idoxuridine) may be effective therapy in this form of encephalitis.

Aseptic Meningitis

This is rarely associated with impairment or loss of consciousness. Aseptic meningitis is an acute febrile illness characterized by headache, stiff neck, and a positive Kernig or Brudzinski sign. This is as a rule a benign self-limited disease and neurologic sequelae are the exception. Aseptic meningitis is most commonly caused by enteroviruses and agents of the myxovirus group. Less common etiologic agents are those of the arthropod-borne group, lymphocytic choriomeningitis, and herpes simplex. Examination of the cerebrospinal fluid shows abnormalities in the great majority of cases. There is a pleocytosis ranging from 10 to 2000/cu. ml., a normal glucose, and a moderate elevation of the protein of 50 to 100 mg./100 ml. The virus can be isolated from the throat, feces, or cerebrospinal fluid. A definite etiologic diagnosis, however, can be established in only half the cases.

Encephalomyelitis

Encephalomyelitis may be the result of direct invasion of the central nervous system by viruses like herpes simplex; Eastern, Western, and Venezuelan equine viruses; and many others. Encephalomyelitis may also follow a number of common infectious diseases of childhood or vaccination (smallpox, rabies, pertussis), or be the manifestation of an acute widespread demyelinating process of unknown etiology which is probably etiologically related to multiple sclerosis.

In children encephalomyelitis occurs most frequently as a complication following acute infections like measles, rubella, chickenpox, infectious mononucleosis, and after vaccination against smallpox. This type of postinfectious encephalomyelitis resembles pathologically experimentally produced encephalomyelitis. The underlying pathology is similar irrespective of the preceding illness and consists chiefly of widespread foci of perivascular demyelination with phagocytosis of the broken-down lipoid products by the microglia. Onset of symptoms is usually during convalescence from a childhood exanthem or one to two weeks following vaccination.

As a rule symptoms begin abruptly with fever, headache, blurred vision, convulsions, and progressive deterioration of consciousness, often leading to coma. Involvement of brain stem structures is manifested by cranial nerve palsies, pupillary changes, and episodes of decorticate or decerebrate rigidity. Involvement of the spinal cord is evident by paralysis or weakness of the extremities, muscle stretch reflex and sensory changes, and sphincter disturbances. An extensor plantar response is common. Examination of the cerebrospinal fluid may show an increase in pressure, elevation of the protein levels, and a lymphocytic pleocytosis. Skull x-rays are normal and the electroencephalogram shows diffuse and occasionally focal nonspecific changes. The illness may be of mild or moderate severity or lead to death in a few days. According to the part of the central nervous system most severely affected the patient may present primarily encephalitic, cerebellar, brain stem, or spinal cord symptoms or any combination of them in cases where widespread involvement occurs. The severity of symptoms is usually greater following measles and after smallpox vaccination. Duration of the disease is brief, lasting in the average case from one to two weeks.

The incidence of encephalomyelitis has been estimated at 1:1000 following measles, 1:6000 after rubella, and 1:700,000 cases following vaccination. Mortality rate in encephalomyelitis following measles is 15 percent, and about 20 to 30 percent of survivors are left with some kind of neurologic sequelae such as mental impairment, hemiplegia, spastic paraplegia, deafness, or seizures. Mortality rate in the postvaccinal form is about 40 percent, deaths almost always occurring with primary vaccination and as a rule in children one year of age or older. There is no specific treatment. A diagnosis of encephalomyelitis can be suspected on the basis of a previous illness or vaccination and the presence of signs and symptoms referable to the cerebrum, brain stem, and spinal cord. The clinical picture of other forms of encephalomyelitis do not differ essentially from that described above.

In acute disseminated encephalomyelitis the pathologic changes are similar to those seen in multiple sclerosis and consist of patchy demyelination and a cellular reaction similar to that seen in the postinfectious form; however, the lesions are not perivascular in location. The pathologic lesions in those cases secondary to actual viral invasion of the central nervous system are similar to those seen in other forms of encephalitis and consist chiefly of perivascular cellular infiltration, with little if any evidence of demyelination.

Poliomyelitis

Severe impairment or loss of consciousness is not a clinical feature of poliomyelitis (see Chapter 1).

TOXIC ENCEPHALOPATHY (ACUTE BRAIN
SWELLING, REYE'S SYNDROME)

Toxic encephalopathy is the name given to an acute organic brain syndrome characterized by the sudden onset of seizures, fever, delirium and alteration of consciousness progressing in a matter of hours to 1 or 2 days from lethargy to profound coma. Death in 24 to 72 hours after the onset of coma is a frequent occurrence. Toxic encephalopathy is characterized pathologically by diffuse brain swelling in the absence of any signs of inflammation, bleeding, or demyelination. In 1963, Reye and co-workers described patients with a syndrome which included the aforementioned signs and symptoms who at autopsy had fatty infiltration of the liver and kidneys. At the present time this syndrome is the prototype of toxic encephalopathy or acute brain swelling. In Reye's original report, the disease was usually preceded by an upper respiratory infection and followed after 1 to 3 days by abrupt clinical deterioration, with severe vomiting, delirium, seizures, coma, and death in 17 of 21 patients. It soon became apparent that this syndrome was not as new as many authors had believed, and a search of the literature disclosed reports of similar cases as early as 1929. Since 1963, a large number of additional cases have been reported, some of them representing retrospective reports of patients who had exhibited before death a clinical picture compatible with this syndrome and whose organs showed the typical histologic changes.

Children with Reye's syndrome are usually stuporous or comatose on admission. In a large number of cases a mild upper respiratory infection or chickenpox precedes the onset of symptoms. Fever and repeated episodes of vomiting are common. Major generalized convulsions occur in a large percentage of patients and may either be the initial clinical manifestation or follow deterioration of the level of consciousness. Physical examination reveals increased muscle tone in some patients and flaccidity in others. Muscle stretch reflexes may be decreased or increased. An extensor plantar response (Babinski sign) is a common sign. Focal or lateralizing neurologic signs are conspicuously absent. Papilledema is not seen early but eventually develops in all patients. Blood sugar levels are low in 75 percent of cases. Cerebrospinal fluid examination reveals no abnormalities except for a low glucose content in patients with low levels of blood glucose. Respiratory arrest often precedes cerebral death and many of these patients are maintained with the aid of mechanical devices (such as a heart-lung preparation) before circulatory collapse ensues. In spite of the markedly swollen and edematous brain, which is the pathologic hallmark of this syndrome, cerebrospinal fluid pressure may be normal during the first or second day after the onset of coma, and papilledema may not develop in some patients until shortly before death.

In many instances, cerebral death occurs within hours or one to two days following the onset of coma. Mechanically assisted respiration for more than 24 hours is probably a contributing factor of cerebral edema. Liver involvement is manifested clinically by moderate hepatomegaly and by a moderate or marked elevation of serum SGOT. Blood urea nitrogen levels are usually moderately elevated in the range of 40–50 mg./100 ml. Respiratory difficulties (hyperpnea and irregular respiration) usually precede the onset of respiratory arrest. The presence of fixed and dilated pupils is ominous, and very few patients with this sign recover.

Cultures of the cerebrospinal fluid for bacteria, viruses, and fungi as well as laboratory investigations for exogenous toxic substances have so far yielded negative results. The electroencephalogram shows diffuse abnormalities in the form of generalized slowing. An isoelectric tracing is invariably present following respiratory arrest. Attempts to correct hypoglycemia and to decrease cerebral edema by the intravenous administration of urea, mannitol, or parenteral steroids appear to be of little benefit once the patient is already in profound coma.

At autopsy the brain is grossly edematous, with flattening of the cerebral convolutions. Microscopic examination reveals swollen neurons and fat-filled endothelial cells in the cerebral capillaries. The liver is slightly to moderately enlarged, firm, and yellow, and its lobules are filled with fat in a diffuse and uniform distribution. Similar histologic changes are seen in the kidneys in the proximal convoluted tubules and proximal loop of Henle.

The etiology of this syndrome is obscure. A toxic or viral etiology and an immune reaction to a preceding viral infection have been suggested as possible etiologic mechanisms. However, up to now, no toxins, viruses, or viral particles have been isolated from affected organs. The pathologic changes in the liver are different from those seen in acute yellow atrophy or fulminating hepatitis. Despite the massive fatty infiltration of the liver, present evidence indicates that liver failure is probably not a likely cause of death in these patients or that it is responsible for the cerebral changes. With the exception of hepatomegaly, low blood glucose levels, and high serum levels of SGOT, toxic encephalopathy or acute brain swelling without fatty infiltration of the viscera is indistinguishable on clinical grounds from the syndrome described by Reye.

ACUTELY DECOMPENSATED HYDROCEPHALUS

Acutely decompensated hydrocephalus produces a rapid rise in intracranial pressure with nausea, vomiting, lethargy, headache, and ataxia (frontal lobe type). This may occur in a patient with a partially compensated or arrested hydrocephalus. More often than not, however, it happens as a complication in patients who have undergone a shunting procedure. The shunt may stop functioning for a variety of reasons, such as obstruction of its distal end by a thrombus, obstruction of the vena cava in patients with a ventriculo-auricular shunt when the distal end of the catheter has been pulled away from the right auricle, or by obstruction of the proximal end by debris. If the valve of the shunt depresses without difficulty but does not refill in one or two seconds the proximal end of the shunt is nonfunctioning. If the valve feels hard to digital pressure and resists compression the distal end of the shunt is obstructed. In practically all instances, if a shunt ceases to function, a revision is necessary.

METABOLIC DISTURBANCES

Water Intoxication

Water intoxication occurs most frequently in clinical practice during the first 48 hours in the postoperative period when it is a common practice to administer solely 5% glucose in water. Other contributing factors are increased secretion of antidiuretic hormone and the administration of anesthetics and analgesics (Demerol and morphine), which promote retention of water and a decrease in urinary volume. The administration of intravenous fluids under these circumstances bypasses the thirst mechanism and the patient is no longer able to control his fluid intake. Water intoxication is also seen following the administration of salt-free water by subcutaneous clysis and of tap water enemas in the control of hyperpyrexia. Water intoxication is accompanied by a rise in intracranial pressure which may reach levels of 400 mm. H_2O or higher. The clinical manifestations of water intoxication include headache, nausea, vomiting, confusion, irritability, delirium, convulsions, and coma. Muscle stretch reflexes may be decreased or increased and an extensor plantar response may or may not be present. Laboratory findings include low serum sodium and chloride, decreased serum osmolarity, and nonspecific electroencephalographic changes (intermittent generalized slow-wave activity). Lumbar puncture reveals a cerebrospinal fluid under increased pressure usually between 200 and 400 mm. H_2O.

It seems likely that the neurologic symptoms produced by water intoxication are due to a fall in serum osmolarity rather than to the associated hyponatremia and hypochloremia. This is supported by the fact that the administration of mannitol causes a rapid improvement of symptoms while lowering the serum sodium and chlorides still further. Treatment consists of correction of the water and electrolyte abnormalities.

Hypernatremia

Hypernatremia exists when the serum level of sodium is above 150 mEq./L. The clinical features of hypernatremia are in many ways similar to those of water intoxication. Central nervous system manifestations consist of disturbances of the level of consciousness varying from lethargy to coma. Muscle tone and muscle stretch reflexes are increased. Seizures are seen in about half of the cases. Twitching of the facial muscles, rigidity, and opisthotonos are common signs. The child with hypertonic dehydration, in contrast to the child with hypotonic dehydration, presents few of the clinical signs traditionally associated with dehydration, such as decreased skin turgor, sunken eyeballs, lethargy, or circulatory collapse. Sudden shrinkage of the brain may cause subarachnoid or subdural bleeding due to tearing of bridging veins.

Pathologic findings in hypernatremia include gross and microscopic hemorrhages in the cerebral hemispheres, cerebellum, and brain stem. Venous congestion is prominent. Many of the neurologic findings seen in hypernatremia are probably explained by neuronal dysfunction due to the electrolyte imbalance rather than to the gross morphologic changes which take place in the brain. The diagnosis can be established by the demonstration of a sodium level above 150 mEq./L. The hematocrit is usually elevated and the serum calcium is low in about two-thirds of the cases. Treatment consists of correction of the electrolyte abnormality.

Diabetic Coma

This complication may be the initial manifestation of diabetes in children or young adults. Symptoms include nausea, vomiting, dehydration, tachypnea, circulatory collapse, and deterioration of the level of consciousness leading to coma and, if untreated, to death. Diagnosis is confirmed by the finding of severe glycosuria, the presence of ketone bodies and diacetic acid in the urine, a high blood glucose level, and acetone in the serum or plasma.

Hypoglycemic reactions in diabetics may also give rise to neurologic symptoms. These are usually due to overdosage with insulin or omission of meals. The onset of symptoms is sudden, consisting of sweating, a feeling of hunger, weakness, blurred vision, pallor, shallow respiration, extensor plantar response, psychotic behavior, stupor, and convulsions. Laboratory tests show absent urinary glucose, acetone, and diacetic acid, and a blood glucose level of 60 mg. or less per 100 ml.

Hypoglycemia

Hypoglycemia in nondiabetics may be due to hyperinsulinism secondary to islet-cell tumors or hyperplasia of the pancreas, glycogen depletion secondary to hepatic insufficiency of any cause, adrenal cortical insufficiency (Addison's disease), hypopituitarism, and hypothyroidism. It is also seen in association with extrapancreatic tumors of mesodermal origin usually located in the thoracic or retroperitoneal area. Spontaneous symptomatic hypoglycemia of infancy is an entity of obscure origin. Other causes of hypoglycemia during infancy and childhood include leucine-sensitive hypoglycemia, some of the glycogen storage diseases, hereditary fructose intolerance, and ketotic hypoglycemia. Once a diagnosis of hypoglycemia is made the appropriate laboratory tests should be done to rule out the many diagnostic possibilities previously mentioned.

Hypocalcemia

Hypocalcemia may cause focal or generalized major motor seizures during the newborn period. Formerly it was seen with greater frequency during the first year of life in infants with rickets. In older children it is a rare cause of seizures. Carpopedal spasm and laryngospasm are the usual manifestations in this age group; these attacks are not accompanied by loss of consciousness. Hypocalcemia in childhood is most commonly seen in the late stages of chronic renal disease, hypoparathyroidism, and persistent fatty diarrhea with loss of calcium by the intestine. A diagnosis can be suspected on clinical grounds and confirmed in the laboratory by low blood levels of calcium. Normal values are from 8.9–10.1 mg./100 ml. Treatment of the acute episode consists in the administration of calcium gluconate, 5–10 cc. of a 10% solution intravenously. Prevention of attacks can be accomplished by treatment of the underlying disorder.

SYNCOPE

Syncope or fainting is the temporary loss of consciousness due to cerebral hypoxia, which may occur as a result of extreme fatigue, prolonged standing in a hot environment, getting up after prolonged bed rest or with sudden changes to the erect position, severe pain, anemia, and not infrequently the sight of blood or other psychologic or emotional stress. Before losing consciousness the patient feels weak and lightheaded and breaks out in a cold sweat. Within seconds there is blurring of vision or total blindness followed by loss of consciousness, which as a rule does not last more than one minute. Physical findings during the attack are pallor, a clammy skin, and a slow pulse and low blood pressure. If the episode lasts longer than a few minutes clonic convulsive movements or loss of bladder or bowel control may occur. Syncope can be differentiated from epileptic seizures by the constant presence of premonitory symptoms. Ordinary fainting spells rarely, if ever, occur suddenly. Syncope occurs with greater frequency in adults than in children.

STOKES-ADAMS SYNDROME

Sudden onset of dizziness or temporary loss of consciousness sometimes associated with major motor seizures may occur as the result of complete atrioventricular block. The symptoms are due to a decreased cardiac output with resulting impairment of cerebral circulation. In children complete heart block is usually of congenital origin due to a defect in the main stem of the bundle of His; it seldom causes symptoms. Nevertheless, an occasional child has been reported with repeated episodes of sudden loss of consciousness and generalized tonic-clonic seizures due to intermittent attacks of complete heart block of unknown etiology.

Intermittent or permanent atrioventricular block can be treated medically with sympathomimetic drugs (epinephrine, isoproterenol) or surgically by the implantation of a cardiac pacemaker.

HEATSTROKE

Heatstroke is a serious disorder which can be seen in association with surgical procedures, febrile illnesses, congenital absence of sweat glands, during treatment with anticholinergic drugs, and following physical exertion or prolonged exposure under high environmental temperatures. Symptoms of heatstroke include headache, anorexia, ataxia, mental confusion, somnolence, delirium, stupor, and coma. Body temperature as a rule exceeds 106°F but may vary from 99° to 111°F. The skin is hot and dry. Convulsions occur in 60 percent of patients. Physical examination may reveal an extensor plantar response in comatose patients, stiffness of the neck, decorticate posturing or flaccid muscles with decreased muscle stretch reflexes. Examination of the cerebrospinal fluid and the electroencephalogram are normal. In addition to the neurologic symptoms, rarely absent in patients with heatstroke, there may be cardiovascular complications such as hypotension, cardiac and renal failure, shock, hepatic damage, and hematologic abnormalities (leukocytosis and thrombocytopenia). Widespread hemorrhages may occur. These have been attributed to capillary fragility, thrombocytopenia, and low prothrombin levels secondary to hepatic damage.

A diagnosis of heatstroke should be suspected when a patient exposed to high environmental temperature or under the circumstances previously mentioned has fever without other apparent cause. Treatment consists of therapy of complications and reduction of body temperature by immersion in or sponging with cold water. Sedatives are contraindicated except to control seizures. Mortality rate is as high as 20 percent.

INTOXICATIONS

Barbiturates

Barbiturate intoxication, a leading cause of accidental or suicidal ingestion of hypnotic drugs in adults, is uncommon in children. Symptoms of barbiturate intoxication are largely related to the nervous and cardiovascular systems. Barbiturates depress activity of nerves and skeletal, smooth, and cardiac muscle. In children a period of hyperactivity and excitement may precede the central nervous system manifestations of barbiturate intoxication. When barbiturates are used in therapeutic dosages their action on structures other than the central nervous system are negligible. However, their depressant action on the cardiovascular and respiratory systems constitute a major problem in intoxicated patients.

Moderate intoxication is characterized by drowsiness and motor incoordination. In severe intoxication the patient is usually comatose. Muscle stretch reflexes are decreased or absent. Initially the pupils may be myotic and react normally to light. As coma deepens the pupils become fixed and dilated. Respirations may be slow or rapid, shallow or of Cheyne-Stokes type. There is a fall in blood pressure, probably due to depression of medullary vasomotor centers and to the peripheral action of the drug on the sympathetic ganglia and myocardium. This results in vascular collapse, a weak and rapid pulse, and a cold and sweaty skin. Vesicular and bullous skin lesions have been observed in 50 percent of patients dying from barbiturate intoxication. Respiratory complications, especially pneumonia, are a frequent cause of death. Renal failure and hyperthermia resistant to antipyretic therapy may develop. The electroencephalogram may show a predominance of fast rhythms in mild cases and severe suppression of electrical activity in severe ones.

The treatment of barbiturate intoxication includes: (1) gastric lavage, which is indicated within two hours following ingestion of the drugs; (2) maintenance of a patent airway with a pharyngeal or endotracheal tube; (3) administration of oxygen by a nasal catheter or through the end of the tracheal tube; (4) assisted respiration if ventilation is inadequate; (5) administration of blood transfusions or vasopressor drugs if circulatory collapse supervenes; (6) hemodialysis if renal failure occurs; (7) water diuresis and alkalinization of the urine to promote increased excretion of barbiturates; (8) prophylactic antibiotics to prevent respiratory infections. Peritoneal or hemodialysis is the most effective way to promote elimination of barbiturates and is recommended in patients with progressive central nervous system depression, respiratory failure, and/or cardiovascular collapse.

Diphenylhydantoin

Mild to moderate intoxication with diphenylhydantoin (Dilantin) occurs frequently in infants and small children treated with this drug for seizure disorders. It is well known that the therapeutic dosage of diphenylhydantoin in young children approaches that at which signs and symptoms of intoxication appear. Serious intoxications are infrequent when compared with the large number of patients who develop mild or moderate toxic reactions. In contrast to the slow onset of anticonvulsant activity, symptoms of overdosage with diphenylhydantoin appear usually within hours after ingestion of the drug. Mild to moderate intoxication is characterized by drowsiness, nystagmus, and ataxia.

In severe cases drowsiness progresses rapidly to a profound coma. The risk of intoxication appears to increase when the liquid form of the drug is used. Diphenylhydantoin intoxication may, in rare instances, produce permanent damage to the cerebellum.

The treatment of mild to moderate diphenylhydantoin intoxication includes reduction of the dosage or its withdrawal and replacement by another anticonvulsant. Signs and symptoms of intoxication usually disappear within 24 to 78 hours. Peritoneal dialysis which promotes rapid elimination of the drug is recommended in patients who have ingested large amounts of the drug and who are in profound coma.

Phenothiazines

The phenothiazine drugs are some of the most widely used in the practice of medicine. They are used primarily as antiemetics and in the treatment of psychiatric disorders.

Phenothiazine derivatives may produce extrapyramidal manifestations by two different mechanisms, (1) a hypersensitivity reaction and (2) a dose-related reaction. Sudden onset of extrapyramidal reactions is seen frequently following the administration of prochlorperazine (Compazine). These side effects may manifest as a parkinsonian-like syndrome with bradykinesia, tremor, rigidity, trismus, and shuffling gait, or as dystonias and dyskinesias (torticollis, retrocollis, oculogyric crises, facial grimacing, and generalized dystonic postures). Phenothiazine-induced extrapyramidal reactions are rapidly reversed by the administration of an antiparkinsonian or an antihistaminic drug. Intoxication with phenothiazine derivatives rarely causes serious alteration of the level of consciousness. Syncopal attacks may occasionally occur from postural hypotension even at therapeutic dosages of phenothiazine.

Salicylate Intoxication

Salicylates (aspirin) are the most widely used of all medications. Aspirin is responsible for over 20 percent of all poisonings reported in the United States. Intoxication occurs most frequently among young children as a result of accidental ingestion or therapeutic excess. Salicylates exert a direct stimulating effect on the respiratory center in the brain stem. Initial symptoms are related to this action and consist of an increase in the rate and depth of respiration. This leads to loss of carbon dioxide and respiratory alkalosis, followed by a metabolic acidosis. Other metabolic changes include hypoglycemia or hyperglycemia, glycosuria and accumulation of ketone bodies, and lactic and pyruvic acids in the blood. In young children ketosis develops so rapidly that the alkalotic phase is rarely seen.

Signs of central nervous system dysfunction usually appear with salicylate levels in the blood higher than 25 to 35 mg./100 ml. Central nervous system manifestations are hyperventilation, vomiting, tinnitus, mental confusion, and disorientation. As intoxication becomes more severe there are restlessness, hallucinations, convulsions, depression of all cerebral functions, coma, respiratory failure, and death. Prognosis is directly related to blood levels. In infants and young children a level of 35 mg./100 ml. is usually associated with toxic symptoms; levels above 45 mg./100 ml. may cause severe and often fatal intoxication.

Treatment of salicylate intoxication includes the promotion of drug elimination by the kidneys (administration of glucose and sodium bicarbonate intravenously) and the correction of water, acid-base, and electrolyte imbalance. In severe cases large amounts of the drug can be eliminated by exchange transfusion, peritoneal dialysis, or hemodialysis.

Amphetamine Poisoning

In recent years amphetamine derivatives such as Benzedrine, Desoxyn, and Dexamyl, a combination of dextroamphetamine and amobarbital, have accounted for an increasing number of cases of poisoning, especially among adolescents. All amphetamine preparations exert their toxic effects by stimulation of the central nervous system and by a sympathomimetic action. Mild intoxication is manifested by restlessness, insomnia, tremor, sweating, and flushing. Moderately intoxicated patients exhibit, in addition, confusion, hyperactivity, tachycardia, tachypnea, and hypertension. In severe intoxication there is delirium, marked hypertension, hyperpyrexia, convulsions, and coma, followed by circulatory collapse and death.

Patients with mild intoxication need no treatment other than protection against injury and rest in a quiet environment. In the absence of serious symptoms, gastric lavage or induction of emesis to remove the drug from the stomach is beneficial. Remarkable decrease in excitement and other behavioral disturbances can be obtained with chlorpromazine (Thorazine) in a dose of 1 mg./kg. body weight intramuscularly. This dose can be repeated after 30 minutes if necessary. Peritoneal dialysis or hemodialysis should be performed in severely ill patients who do not respond to the above-mentioned measures.

Lead Poisoning

Lead poisoning continues to be a serious problem in large urban communities. Ingestion of lead-containing plaster and flakes of old paint and inhalation of fumes produced by the combustion of battery casings are the most common causes of lead poisoning. Lead intoxication occurs most frequently in children between the ages of 1 and 6 years who have an abnormal craving for nonnutritious substances such as dirt and plaster and in those in the lower socioeconomic classes who live in old, badly maintained houses. The highest incidence is in children between 1 and 3 years, with most deaths occurring in 2-year-olds. Lead poisoning accounts for about 5 percent of accidental poisoning in some large urban communities and for about 80 percent of the total deaths due to accidental poisoning.

The clinical picture of lead intoxication in children differs from that seen in adults. Lead intoxication in adults causes unilateral or bilateral wrist drop due to paralysis of one or both radial nerves. A peripheral neuropathy in children is extremely rare and when it occurs involves the peroneal nerves, causing unilateral or bilateral foot drop. In the early stages of intoxication symptoms are vague and nonspecific— anorexia, lethargy, pallor, abdominal pain, vomiting, constipation, irritability, and motor difficulties, especially ataxia. An acute or subacute encephalopathy is the usual clinical manifestation of severe lead poisoning in children. Characteristically, this is heralded by drowsiness, lethargy, and repeated focal or generalized major motor seizures. There may be clumsiness, severe ataxia, and repeated falling. This is followed by progressive deterioration of the level of consciousness, leading to coma. Signs and symptoms of increased intracranial pressure are prominent, and focal or lateralizing neurologic signs minimal or absent. A history of pica can be elicited in the great majority of cases.

Laboratory findings include a microcytic hypochromic anemia and basophilic stippling of erythrocytes, which is found in 60 percent of cases. Punctate basophilic stippling is a normal finding in a number not exceeding 800 stippled cells per million erythrocytes. Red cell basophilic stippling greater than 1000 per million is abnormal. Urinalysis shows proteinuria, excretion of reducing substances, elevated coproporphyrin, and increased amounts of delta-aminolevulinic acid. The latter appear to correlate better with high blood levels of lead than does the excretion of coproporphyrins in the urine. Lead lines are seen in adults with chronic lead intoxication but rarely in children. They are most frequently encountered in the lingual gum opposite the lower bicuspids and molars. X-rays of the abdomen may show radiopaque flecks of lead in the intestine or lines of increased density at the ends of long bones. Areas of increased density are occasionally seen in the angle of the scapula. Confirmation of the diagnosis requires the demonstration of increased amounts of lead in blood or urine. Blood levels of more than 80 μg./100 ml. of serum indicate intoxication; values between 60 and 80 μg. are highly suspicious. Normal values for lead in the urine are less than 40 μg. per liter. Recently the determination of lead concentration in hair has been found to be a reliable screening device. Hair concentrates more lead per unit of weight than any other body tissue. The lead content of hair in lead intoxication is two to five times higher than bone and thus can provide readily available material for determination of elevated tissue levels. Treatment should be initiated in any child with blood levels above 60 μg./100 ml. and clinical symptoms suggestive of lead poisoning and in any child with abnormally high blood levels, even if he is symptom-free.

Organic lead intoxication (gasoline sniffing or exposure to gasoline fumes) may also produce an encephalopathy. There is irritability, insomnia, emotional instability, hallucinations, low blood pressure, marked tremor and, finally, coma and death. In contrast to inorganic lead poisoning there is no anemia or red cell basophilic stippling, and coproporphyrins are not excreted in abnormal amounts in the urine.

The treatment of lead encephalopathy is essentially that of acute brain edema and convulsions and the removal of lead from the blood as well as that stored in other body tissues, especially bones.

Cerebral edema can be treated by the intravenous administration of urea or mannitol or parenteral steroids (see Appendix 3). Hypothermia of about 90° to 92°F may be helpful. Excessive cooling, however, may precipitate circulatory collapse. As the last resort, and if these measures fail to relieve increased intracranial pressure, a subtemporal decompression may be performed. Seizures due to lead intoxication are particularly resistant to barbiturates and Dilantin. Furthermore, phenobarbital may produce respiratory arrest. Morphine is contraindicated. Paraldehyde 0.3–0.6 cc./kg. body weight (up to 10 cc.) can be given by rectum in equal amounts of olive oil or chloral hydrate 50 mg./kg. body weight by mouth in a dose not exceeding 1 gm. per day. If these measures fail to control seizures an inhalation anesthetic may be used.

The removal of lead from the brain as well as other body tissues can be accomplished by the simultaneous administration of calcium disodium versenate and BAL (dimercaprol). A combination of these two chelating agents appears to be more effective in removing lead from the body and brain cells than either agent alone. With this treatment, supplemented by means of controlling cerebral edema, the mortality from lead poisoning has been markedly reduced. However, approximately 40 percent of survivors are left with some kind of neurologic sequela, such as seizures, mental retardation, motor difficulties, or optic atrophy.

Thallium

Thallium is used as a rodenticide, pesticide, and formerly was used in depilatory creams. The lethal dose is approximately 1 gm. of absorbed thallium. Thallium poisoning causes a peripheral neuropathy giving rise to paresthesias or pain in the extremities, muscle weakness, ptosis, dysarthria, and ataxia. Other symptoms include nausea, abdominal pain, hematemesis, and bloody diarrhea. In severe cases progression of symptoms is manifested by lethargy, generalized tremors, convulsions, respiratory failure, and death. Alopecia in the presence of signs and symptoms of a peripheral neuropathy is characteristic of thallium poisoning. The demonstration of thallium in the urine confirms the diagnosis. The administration of a combination of cystine, methionine, potassium chloride, and a multivitamin preparation may be helpful in the treatment of thallium poisoning. BAL and thiosulfate, drugs formerly used, have not proved of great value in the treatment of thallium intoxication.

Arsenic Poisoning

Arsenic is a constituent of many insecticides, weed killers, and rodenticides. It was formerly used in dyes and paints and at one time enjoyed popularity in the treatment of syphilis and a number of other diseases. In acute intoxication, the clinical picture is dominated by gastrointestinal symptoms. Following ingestion symptoms appear within a few minutes to one hour. There is a metallic taste, burning pain in the esophagus and epigastrium, projectile vomiting, and profuse diarrhea with rice-water stools and bloody discharges. Other symptoms are vertigo, headache, muscular cramps, a rapid and weak pulse, cyanosis, dyspnea, stupor, convulsions, circulatory collapse, and coma. Treatment consists of gastric lavage, supportive measures, and administration of BAL (dimercaprol) intramuscularly in a dose of 2.5 mg./kg. every 6 hours for 2 days, every 8 hours for 1 day, and every 12 hours for a total period of 10 days.

Chronic poisoning is manifested by malaise, progressive fatigue, nausea and vomiting, diarrhea, and prominent skin changes in the form of increased pigmentation, hyperkeratosis of palms and soles, and whitish transverse lines in the nails (Mee's lines). Leukopenia, with neutropenia and a relative eosinophilia, and thrombocytopenia are common blood changes. A peripheral mixed sensory-motor type of peripheral neuropathy develops in patients with chronic arsenic poisoning. This may also occur in patients who recover from acute intoxication. A diagnosis can be made by the determination of levels of arsenic in the urine (normal, less than 100 μg./L.) and its content in hair and nails.

Acute Iron Poisoning

Accidental overdosage of iron preparations account for about 2000 cases of poisoning yearly in the United States. Mortality rate in severe cases has been estimated to be about 45 percent. As little as 1 gm. of ferrous sulfate may cause severe intoxication. In general the amount ingested in reported cases has been greater than 3 gm. of ferrous sulfate or ferrous gluconate. Symptoms of acute iron poisoning are vomiting and diarrhea, both of which may or may not be bloody, restlessness, irritability, drowsiness, lethargy, pallor, cyanosis, disorientation, convulsions, shock, and coma. Shock and coma are usually seen in patients with serum iron levels higher than 500 μg./100 ml. The intravenous administration of deferoxamine is specific treatment for acute iron poisoning. Deferoxamine combines with iron to form ferrioxamine, a substance readily soluble in water and easily eliminated by the kidneys. Additional therapeutic measures include induction of emesis, gastric lavage, the maintenance of a clear airway, and treatment of shock.

Ethyl Alcohol (Ethanol)

Intoxication with ethanol may be the result of accidental ingestion of alcoholic beverages, tinctures, perfumes, colognes, mouthwashes, or alcohol-vehicle medications to which a young child may have access. Ethanol produces initially a period of excitement, incoordination, ataxia, followed by central nervous system depression, stupor, delirium, a weak rapid pulse, subnormal temperature, dyspnea, and cyanosis. In severely intoxicated patients death results from respiratory failure. Severe hypoglycemia may occur. A diagnosis of ethanol poisoning may be suspected by the odor of alcohol on the breath and the associated hypoglycemia. Treatment is entirely supportive. Stimulants such as caffeine and sodium benzoate or ephedrine subcutaneously may be used. Hypoglycemia can be corrected by the intravenous administration of 50% glucose.

Methanol

Methyl alcohol (wood alcohol) is present in paints, paint removers, varnishes, and canned fuels. Symptoms of intoxication appear between 8 and 24 hours following ingestion and include vomiting, violent gastric and abdominal pain, headache, disturbed vision progressing to blindness, pain in the eyes, dilated pupils, delirium, cyanosis, dyspnea, weak and irregular pulse, and hypotension. In severe cases the patient is in profound coma. Death may occur from respiratory or circulatory failure. Metabolic acidosis is a prominent feature of methanol intoxication and is due to the formation of formaldehyde and formic acid, both oxidative metabolic products of methanol. A transitory or permanent toxic amblyopia is a characteristic finding and is due to reversible changes or degeneration of the ganglion cells in the retina and optic nerve fibers. Treatment consists of supportive care, the administration of sodium bicarbonate to combat acidosis, and ethanol orally or intravenously, which by a competitive action prevents or delays the oxidation of methanol. In severe cases peritoneal dialysis or hemodialysis are indicated.

Isopropyl Alcohol (Rubbing Alcohol)

Symptoms, signs and treatment of intoxication with isopropyl alcohol are similar to those of intoxication with ethanol.

Carbon Monoxide Poisoning

Carbon monoxide poisoning results from inhalation of this gas formed by the incomplete combustion in stoves, furnaces, and automobile fumes. Mild intoxication (concentration of 0.05%) causes severe headache, vertigo, weakness, drowsiness, and sometimes vomiting. Severe intoxication (concentration of 0.2% or higher) produces muscle twitchings, elevated blood pressure, mydriasis, stertorous and rapid respiration, stupor, convulsions, and muscular rigidity. The lips are blue, pale, or pink and the skin is dusky with bluish-red patches. Death usually follows respiratory arrest. The toxic effects of carbon monoxide are due to its great affinity for hemoglobin, with resulting formation of carboxyhemoglobin which interferes with the exchange of gases between blood and body tissues. Most patients who recover from carbon monoxide poisoning are left with no neurologic sequelae. A few patients develop a parkinsonian syndrome, aphasia, or a choreiform movement disorder. Focal neurologic deficit is rare.

In fatal cases the viscera, blood, skeletal muscles, and other organs have a pink-red color due to the presence of carboxyhemoglobin. The brain is markedly congested, with numerous petechial or gross hemorrhages in the white matter, corpus callosum, and basal ganglia.

Treatment includes immediate removal from toxic environment, artificial respiration, and the administration of 100% oxygen.

Mushroom Poisoning

Mushroom poisoning is not common in the United States. The situation is different in other countries, e.g., Germany, where approximately 200 people per year die from mushroom poisoning. Of approximately 3000 types of mushrooms, 70 to 80 are known to be toxic to man. Most deaths occur following ingestion of *Amanita phalloides* or its close relatives, *A. verna* and *A. virosa*. Symptoms of poisoning with these three amanitas begin about 10 hours after ingestion with severe abdominal pain, watery diarrhea, vomiting and severe dehydration. These manifestations are followed by a latent period of relative well-being after which gastrointestinal, hepatic, renal, and neurologic signs and symptoms appear. Central nervous system involvement is manifested by somnolence, confusion, convulsions, increased intracranial pressure, and finally coma. The natural course of the disease is 6 to 8 days in adults and 3 to 4 days in children. Mortality rate is between 50 to 90 percent.

Symptoms of intoxication with amanita muscaria consist of violent gastrointestinal cramps, vomiting, nausea, and watery stools, beginning shortly after ingestion. This is followed by increased salivation, sweating, myosis, dyspnea, and a weak and slow pulse. Some patients exhibit confusion, vertigo, hallucinations, psychic manifestations, convulsions and coma.

No effective antidote is available for intoxication with mushrooms. Therapeutic measures include supportive care, gastric lavage to remove undigested mushrooms, and atropine to counteract the muscarinic effects in intoxication with A. *muscaria*.

Organic Phosphates

These compounds are present in insecticides and include chiefly parathion, malathion, chlorthion, and diazinon, of which the first is particularly dangerous. Poisoning can occur by ingestion, inhalation, or absorption through unbroken skin. Organic phosphates exert their toxic effects by a muscarinic, nicotinic, and anticholinesterase action. Symptoms are headaches, dizziness, pinpoint pupils, muscle weakness, fasciculations, diarrhea, sweating, and salivation. In severe poisoning there is pulmonary edema, convulsions, coma, and death. A diagnosis can be suspected on the basis of the clinical picture and a history of ingestion or exposure to insecticides containing organic phosphate and confirmed in the laboratory by the determination of cholinesterase activity in red cells or plasma. Treatment consists of the administration of atropine to counteract muscarinic effects and cholinesterase reactivators such as PAM (pyridine-2-aldoxime methiodide).

Kerosene

Poisoning with kerosene or other petroleum distillates is not uncommon. Intoxication with these products causes central nervous system depression which develops soon after ingestion and a chemical pneumonitis which becomes manifest within a few hours to one or two days later. If death occurs, it is usually due to pulmonary insufficiency rather than central nervous system depression. Treatment includes the administration of antibiotics to prevent bacterial pneumonitis and steroids which may have a favorable effect on the chemical pneumonitis.

See textbooks of toxicology in regard to other less common causes of poisoning in children.

REFERENCES

Bax, M., and Mitchell, R. (Eds.). *Acute Hemiplegia in Childhood.* London: Spastics Society, Heinemann, 1962.

Buck, R. V. Mushroom toxins: A brief review of the literature. *New Eng. J. Med.* 265:686, 1961.

Cann, H. M., and Verhulat, H. L. Mushroom poisoning. *Amer. J. Dis. Child.* 101:128, 1961.

Carter, S., and Gold, A. P. Acute infantile hemiplegia. *Pediat. Clin. N. Amer.* 14:851, 1967.

Christensen, E., and Husby, J.   Chronic subdural hematoma in infancy. *Acta Neurol. Scand.* 39:323, 1963.

Coffin, R., et al.   Treatment of lead encephalopathy in children. *J. Pediat.* 69:198, 1966.

Cornblath, M., and Schwartz, R.   *Disorders of Carbohydrate Metabolism in Infancy.* Philadelphia: Saunders, 1966.

Craig, W. S.   Intracranial haemorrhage in the newborn: A study of diagnosis and differential diagnosis based upon pathological and clinical findings in 126 cases. *Arch. Dis. Child.* 13:89, 1938.

Crawford, J. D., and Dodge, P. R.   Complications of fluid therapy in neurologic disease; water intoxication and hypertonic dehydration. *Pediat. Clin. N. Amer.* 11:1029, 1964.

Ellis, F. H., et al.   Treatment of Stokes-Adams disease. *Mayo Clin. Proc.* 39:945, 1964.

Espelin, D. E., and Done, A. K.   Amphetamine poisoning. Effectiveness of chlorpromazine. *New Eng. J. Med.* 278:1361, 1968.

Ford, F. M.   *Diseases of the Nervous System in Infancy, Childhood and Adolescence* (5th ed.). Springfield, Ill.: Thomas, 1966.

Glick, T. H., et al.   Acute encephalopathy and hepatic dysfunction associated with chickenpox in siblings. *Amer. J. Dis. Child.* 119:68, 1970.

Gottschalk, P. G., and Thomas, J. E.   Heat stroke. *Mayo Clin. Proc.* 41:470, 1966.

Greengard, J.   Lead poisoning in childhood: Signs, symptoms, current therapy, clinical expressions. *Clin. Pediat.* (Phila.) 5:269, 1966.

Heyman, A., et al.   Peripheral neuropathy caused by arsenical intoxication: Study of 41 cases with observations on effects of BAL (2,3 dimercaptopropanol). *New Eng. J. Med.* 254:401, 1956.

Hjern, B., and Nylander, I.   Acute head injuries in children: Traumatology, therapy and prognosis. *Acta Paediat. Scand.* Suppl. 152, 1964.

Ingraham, F. D., et al.   Extradural hematoma in infancy and childhood. *J.A.M.A.* 140:1010, 1949.

Ingraham, F. D., and Matson, D.   *Neurosurgery of Infancy and Childhood.* Springfield, Ill.: Thomas, 1954.

Ingraham, F. D., and Matson, D. D.   Subdural hematoma in infancy. *Advances Pediat.* 4:231, 1949.

Jacobs, J., et al.   Acute iron intoxication. *New Eng. J. Med.* 273:1124, 1965.

Johnson, R. T., and Mims, C. A.   Pathogenesis of viral infections of the nervous system. *New Eng. J. Med.* 278:23, 84, 1968.

Kirtley, W. R.   Clinical aspects of diabetic coma. *J. Indiana Med. Ass.* 48:1408, 1955.

Lagos, J. C., and Riley, H. D., Jr.   Clinical and electroencephalographic study of irreversible coma secondary to encephalopathy. Read at the 24th Annual Meeting of the American Electroencephalographic Society, Sept. 17–19, 1970, Washington, D.C.

Lagos, J. C., and Siekert, R. G.   Intracranial hemorrhage in infancy and childhood. *Clin. Pediat.* (Phila.) 8:90, 1969.

Laxdal, O. E., et al.   Reye's syndrome: Encephalopathy in children associated with fatty changes in the viscera. *Amer. J. Dis. Child.* 117:717, 1969.

Lombroso, C. T.   Treatment of status epilepticus with diazepam. *Neurology* 16:629, 1966.

Margolis, G., et al.   Further experiences with small vascular malformations as a cause of massive intracerebral bleeding. *J. Neuropath. Exp. Neurol.* 20:161, 1961.

Margolis, G., et al.   The role of small angiomatous malformations in the production of intracerebral hematomas. *J. Neurosurg.* 8:564, 1951.

Meyer, H. M., Jr., et al.   Central nervous system syndromes of viral etiology: Study of 713 cases. *Amer. J. Med.* 29:334, 1960.

Miller, H. G., et al.   Parainfectious encephalomyelitis and related syndromes: A critical review of the neurological complications of certain specific fevers. *Quart. J. Med.* 25:427, 1956.

Nolan, D. C., et al.   Herpesvirus hominis encephalitis in Michigan: Report of thirteen cases, including six treated with idoxuridine. *New Eng. J. Med.* 282:10, 1970.

Perlstein, M. A., and Attala, R.   Neurologic sequelae of plumbism in children. *Clin. Pediat.* (Phila.) 5:292, 1966.

Prensky, A. L., et al.   Intravenous diazepam in the treatment of prolonged seizure activity. *New Eng. J. Med.* 276:779, 1967.

Reye, R. D., et al.   Encephalopathy and fatty degeneration of viscera: A disease entity in childhood. *Lancet* 2:749, 1963.

Ross, J. J., and Dimmette, R. M.   Subependymal cerebral hemorrhage in infancy. *Amer. J. Dis. Child.* 110:531, 1965.

Schwartz, P.   *Birth Injuries of the Newborn, Morphology, Pathogenesis, Clinical Pathology and Prevention.* New York: Hafner, 1961, pp. 14–20.

Shulman, K., and Ransohoff, J.   Subdural hematoma in children, the fate of children with retained membranes. *J. Neurosurg.* 18:175, 1961.

Tenckhoff, H., et al.   Acute diphenylhydantoin intoxication. *Amer. J. Dis. Child.* 116:422, 1968.

Wenzl, J. E., et al.   Methanol poisoning in an infant: Successful treatment with peritoneal dialysis. *Amer. J. Dis. Child.* 116:445, 1968.

Wenzl, J. E., and Rubio, T.   Encephalitis due to herpesvirus hominis in an infant: Treatment with idoxuridine. *Southern Med. J.* 63:457, 1970.

Westlin, W. E.   Deferoxamine in the treatment of acute iron poisoning: Clinical experiences with 172 children. *Clin. Pediat.* (Phila.) 5:531, 1966.

10

Increased Intracranial Pressure

INCREASED INTRACRANIAL PRESSURE in children is in most instances secondary to space-occupying lesions (brain tumor, brain abscess, chronic subdural hematoma) or hydrocephalus. The signs and symptoms of increased intracranial pressure in infancy differ from those seen in later childhood because of the capacity of the infant's skull to increase in size by spreading of its sutures in response to a chronic increase in intracranial pressure. In infants signs of increased intracranial pressure are enlargement of the head, separation of the cranial sutures, and an increase in size and tension of the anterior fontanelle. Papilledema rarely if ever occurs during infancy as long as spreading of the sutures is possible. In older children, as in adults, headache, nausea, and vomiting are the common symptoms of increased intracranial pressure. Funduscopic examination may show papilledema, and visual-field examination with the tangent screen may demonstrate an enlarged blind spot. Unilateral or bilateral sixth-nerve paralysis may also occur; when it develops after the onset of symptoms of increased intracranial pressure it is a sign of no localizing value. Between 1 and 5 years of age skull x-rays in children with chronic increased intracranial pressure may show spreading of the sutures without significant enlargement of the head, in addition to demineralization of the sella turcica, and erosion of the posterior clinoid processes.

BRAIN TUMORS

Approximately two-thirds of brain tumors in children are infratentorial and one-third supratentorial in location. This is the opposite frequency of location of brain tumors in adults. Pituitary adenomas, meningiomas, and neuromas, common intracranial tumors in adulthood, are extremely rare in childhood.

Since the great majority of brain tumors in children are cerebellar in origin, the most common sign is limb or gait ataxia. Vomiting and head-ache are the most common symptoms and eventually occur in almost all patients when the cerebrospinal fluid pathways become obstructed as a result of compression of the aqueduct or the fourth ventricle by a poste-rior fossa tumor, or compression of the foramen of Monro or the third ventricle by supratentorial tumors. Vomiting occurs in about 85 percent of children with brain tumors and is usually associated with nausea and sometimes with abdominal pain. In the early stages it tends to occur early after arising and later on at any time during the day. The projec-tile type of vomiting traditionally linked with cerebral neoplasms is the exception rather than the rule. In patients with midline neoplasms of the posterior fossa vomiting may occur in the absence of increased intracranial pressure as a result of direct irritation of medullary centers. Because of the previously mentioned capacity of the skull of the infant and young child to spread its sutures and thereby reduce increased intracranial pressure vomiting may be intermittent or recurrent.

Headache is present in about 75 percent of children with intracranial neoplasms. The two most frequent locations of headache are the frontal and the occipital regions. The pain is probably the result of irritation of the meningeal branch of the ophthalmic division of the trigeminal nerve and pressure on pain-sensitive structures in the posterior fossa, or herniation of the cerebellar tonsils and the medulla through the fora-men magnum. Headache may occur early in the morning after awaking or at any time during the day. The headache, like vomiting, may be intermittent or recurrent and may or may not be precipitated by factors which increase intracranial pressure such as coughing or sneezing.

Increased intracranial pressure of any cause may produce convergent strabismus, which is the result of direct pressure on one or both abdu-cens nerves. Papilledema occurs at some stage in the course of the dis-ease in the great majority of children with brain tumors. Loss of vision due to optic atrophy secondary to longstanding papilledema seldom occurs.

General signs of increased intracranial pressure are a slow pulse, a high blood pressure, and slow and irregular respirations. These changes are present in the late stages in all patients with brain tumors; in the early stages they may be a manifestation of tumors located in the brain stem or hypothalamus.

Convulsions are not a common symptom in children with brain tu-mors. This is readily explained by the fact that the majority of brain tumors in this age group are infratentorial in location. Focal or jackso-nian seizures, on the other hand, are not uncommon in patients with tumors of the cerebral hemispheres. So-called cerebellar fits are seen in patients with tumors of the cerebellum and are the result of acute and intermittent compression of brain stem structures or sudden and tem-porary increase in intracranial pressure. During these attacks the child's extremities suddenly become extended, the head is retracted and the entire body assumes a position of opisthotonos. During the attack the child is unconscious or becomes agitated and exhibits irregular respirations, a high blood pressure, a slow pulse, and fixed and dilated pupils.

Examination of the cerebrospinal fluid in patients with a brain tumor may reveal an increase in pressure and an elevation of the level of protein in the range of 100–500 mg./100 ml. Occasionally, particularly in patients with ependymomas and medulloblastomas, the cerebrospinal-fluid glucose level may be low and a moderate mixed pleocytosis (polymorphonuclear and lymphocytes) may be present. These findings may be misleading and may suggest a diagnosis of subacute meningitis (cryptococcus, coccidioidal, or tuberculous). In these cases cytologic examination of the cerebrospinal fluid may reveal the presence of malignant cells.

The most common brain tumors in children in order of decreasing frequency are: cerebellar astrocytomas, medulloblastomas, ependymomas, craniopharyngiomas, pontine gliomas, gliomas of the optic chiasma, and tumors of the cerebral hemispheres, pineal gland, and hypothalamus.

INFRATENTORIAL TUMORS

Cerebellar Astrocytomas

Cerebellar astrocytomas are the most common brain tumors in childhood. They usually originate in one cerebellar hemisphere. Pathologically, they may be either solid structures or consist of a cyst with a mural nodule representing the tumor. Clinical manifestations are ataxia, incoordination, and hypotonia of the ipsilateral extremities, decreased or pendular muscle stretch reflexes on the affected side, and nystagmus, which is slow and coarse on the side of the lesion and fine and rapid on the opposite side (lateral or hemispheric cerebellar syndrome). Cerebellar astrocytomas occur as frequently in boys as in girls. Patients with this tumor often tilt their head to the side of the lesion (Fig. 10-1A) with the chin pointing to the opposite side; on walking they may show a tendency to deviate toward the side of the involved cerebellar hemisphere.

X-rays of the skull may show spreading of the cranial sutures due to chronic increased intracranial pressure secondary to obstructive hydrocephalus. The electroencephalogram may show diffuse and bilateral nonspecific abnormalities. Brain scanning is rarely helpful in localizing tumors in this location. Air-contrast studies may reveal evidence of hydrocephalus and/or displacement of the aqueduct or fourth ventricle away from the side of the lesion (Fig. 10-1B).

Cystic astrocytomas of the cerebellum can be surgically removed in

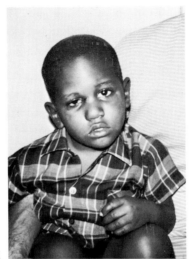

A

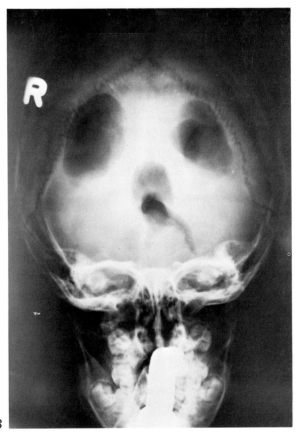

B

toto and a complete cure accomplished. In this respect they are probably the only truly benign intracranial tumors in childhood. Solid astrocytomas can rarely be removed completely. Partial excision followed by
radiation therapy may produce long remissions.

Medulloblastomas

Medulloblastomas are highly malignant, undifferentiated tumors arising from the posterior vermis of the cerebellum. Medulloblastomas are
more common in boys than girls and have a peak incidence at between
5 and 8 years of age. Vomiting is the most common initial symptom,
followed in order of frequency by vomiting and headache, and gait
ataxia. When vomiting alone is the initial manifestation it is usually due
to direct pressure on medullary centers rather than to increased intracranial pressure. Physical examination of patients with medulloblastomas reveals truncal and gait ataxia. No ataxia or incoordination of the
extremities can be demonstrated if the patient is tested in the supine
position. Muscle stretch reflexes are decreased or are pendular in character and as a rule there is generalized hypotonia (midline cerebellar
syndrome). When nystagmus is present it is rapid, fine, and symmetrical. Contrast studies show changes similar to those seen in patients with
cerebellar astrocytomas.

Medulloblastomas cannot be removed completely and exhibit a
strong tendency to seed along the neuraxis. Partial removal followed by
irradiation with or without shunting procedure permits decompression
of the aqueduct and fourth ventricle, sometimes with remarkable although temporary improvement of symptoms. The average survival of
patients with this type of tumor is approximately one to two years.

Ependymomas

Ependymomas may occur at any age from early infancy to adulthood. They occur most frequently in the fourth and less commonly in
the lateral ventricles. In the fourth ventricle they arise from its floor in
the region of the anterior medullary velum. Vomiting is the most common initial symptom. This is at first an isolated finding and many
months may lapse before other signs such as papilledema or ataxia appear. Nystagmus is a constant clinical feature in tumors arising in the
cavity of the fourth ventricle including ependymomas. Partial removal
of the tumor followed by radiation therapy may produce long remis-

Fig. 10-1. A, 3-year-old boy with a cerebellar astrocytoma of the right
hemisphere. Notice tilting of the head toward the side of the lesion. B,
ventriculogram in same patient showing hydrocephalus and displacement of
the fourth ventricle toward the left by a mass in the right side of the posterior fossa.

sions. Seeding along the neuraxis is also common with this type of tumor.

Brain Stem Gliomas

Brain stem gliomas usually originate in the pons but have the tendency to invade neighboring structures, especially the medulla. The most common initial clinical manifestation of brain stem gliomas is abducens paralysis, either alone or accompanied by headache or ataxia. Less frequent presenting signs are facial, abducens and facial, or glossopharyngeal and vagus palsies. Hemiparesis is the initial complaint in about 10 percent of cases. Cerebellar signs like ataxia and nystagmus develop sooner or later in the great majority of patients. Pyramidal signs, in the form of spastic weakness and an extensor plantar response (Babinski sign) occur also in the majority of patients. Sensory deficit is an uncommon finding. Because gliomas of the brain stem grow slowly, signs and symptoms of increased intracranial pressure such as headache, vomiting, and papilledema develop late but may occur relatively early in the course of the disease in about 20 percent of cases. A diagnosis of brain stem glioma should be considered in any child who develops progressive multiple paralysis of cranial nerves with or without pyramidal tract signs. A similar clinical picture can be produced by progressive bulbar palsy, a condition akin to spinal muscular atrophy and characterized by progressive degeneration of cranial nerves nuclei. Other signs of brain stem and cerebellar dysfunction or signs of increased intracranial pressure, however, do not develop in the latter disorder.

Skull x-rays, the electroencephalogram, and examination of the cerebrospinal fluid usually show no abnormalities until late in the course of brain stem gliomas. Air ventriculography is the diagnostic procedure of choice if the clinician suspects a tumor of the brain stem. The ventriculogram shows upward and backward displacement of the aqueduct or fourth ventricle or failure to fill these structures (Fig. 10-2). If the diagnosis can be substantiated on the basis of the clinical and radiologic findings, the only available form of therapy is radiation. This frequently produces a remarkable, although temporary, improvement, especially of cranial nerve palsies.

Cerebellopontine Angle Tumors

Cerebellopontine angle tumors are unilateral in the great majority of cases and are most commonly found in early adulthood and middle life. The most common tumor in this region is the acoustic neuroma. Bilateral acoustic neuromas may occur in association with neurofibromatosis. The initial complaint in patients with acoustic neuroma is in most instances hearing loss followed weeks or months later by an ipsilateral peripheral facial paralysis. Pain in the distribution of the trigeminal

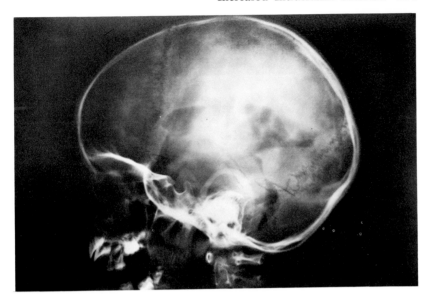

Fig. 10-2. Pneumoencephalogram in 4-year-old child with a brain stem glioma showing posterior displacement of the fourth ventricle.

nerve is uncommon. However, a decreased corneal reflex on the same side of the lesion is found in a small number of cases. Enlargement and/or erosion of the internal auditory meatus is a characteristic roentgenographic sign. Less common cerebellopontine angle tumors are cholesteatomas, meningiomas, tumors arising from adjacent structures (flocculus, lateral recess, choroid plexus) or the petrous bone, and tumors of the glomus jugulare. Special views of the skull (Stenver, etc.) to demonstrate the size and configuration of the internal auditory meatus are indicated in any patient with an acquired and unexplained sensory hearing loss.

SUPRATENTORIAL TUMORS

Craniopharyngioma

Craniopharyngiomas, also known as suprasellar cysts or hypophyseal duct tumors, are the most common supratentorial tumors in childhood. They arise from embryonic remnants of Rathke's pouch (an outpocketing of the stomodeum) above the sella turcica and seldom in it or near the tuber cinereum. Because of their location craniopharyngiomas may compress or invade suprasellar or intrasellar structures such as the optic chiasma, the hypothalamus, or the pituitary gland. Occasionally the tumor grows into the retrosellar space and may produce symptoms due

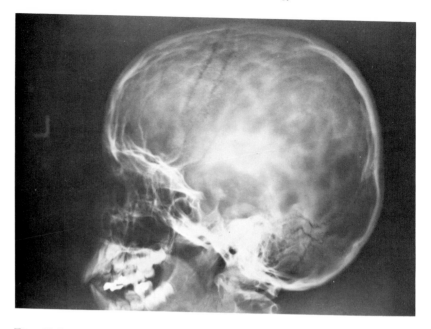

Fig. 10-3. Lateral view of the skull in patient with craniopharyngioma showing suprasellar calcification and spreading of the sutures due to hydrocephalus and increased intracranial pressure.

to compression of the brain stem. Approximately 50 percent of craniopharyngiomas become clinically manifest during the first two decades of life. The most common signs and symptoms are diabetes insipidus, bitemporal hemianopia due to pressure on the optic fibers coming from the nasal retinae which decussate in the midline of the chiasma, growth retardation, and hydrocephalus due to obstruction of the cerebrospinal fluid pathways by pressure and distortion of the third ventricle, with signs and symptoms of increased intracranial pressure. Primary optic atrophy may occur due to pressure on the optic chiasma or optic nerves. Symptoms referable to hypothalamic or pituitary involvement include sleepiness, obesity, small stature, and genital infantilism. Craniopharyngiomas are as a rule cystic tumors. X-rays of the skull show areas of spotty calcification above the sella turcica in 85 percent of cases; from a roentgenographic standpoint they are rarely simulated by any other disorder. Enlargement of the sella turcica may also occur (Fig. 10-3). A diagnosis of craniopharyngioma is generally easy to make from the typical localizing clinical signs and the characteristic roentgenographic changes. Total surgical removal is rarely possible. Cyst evacuation or partial removal of the tumor followed by radiation therapy is the treatment of choice.

Pituitary tumors like eosinophilic adenoma (gigantism), basophilic adenoma (Cushing's syndrome), and chromophobe adenoma are rare tumors in childhood. The first two produce hyperfunction of the pituitary (growth hormone in eosinophilic adenoma, and adrenocorticotropic hormone in basophilic adenoma). Chromophobe adenoma is a nonfunctioning tumor and gives rise to clinical manifestations by destruction of the pituitary gland, causing signs of hypopituitarism, and by compression of the optic chiasma, producing bitemporal hemianopia. Enlargement and ballooning of the sella turcica are common roentgenographic signs of chromophobe and eosinophilic adenomas but are rarely seen in basophilic adenoma. Pituitary tumors almost always remain confined to the pituitary fossa and rarely if ever cause increased intracranial pressure.

Gliomas of the Optic Chiasma

In advanced stages and when there is compression of the third ventricle, a large glioma of the optic chiasma may produce hydrocephalus and increased intracranial pressure (see Chapter 7).

Hypothalamic Tumors

The most common tumors in this location are low-grade astrocytomas, oligodendrogliomas and teratomas. They may cause the diencephalic syndrome of infancy described by Russell in 1951, which consists of severe loss of weight, normal linear growth, euphoria, and locomotor overactivity (Fig. 10-4A). Profound emaciation, especially in an active and often overaffectionate child with normal or increased appetite, has rarely been described in any other condition. Pallor without anemia, sweating, tachycardia, and hypotension are less common clinical features. Focal neurologic signs are usually absent. The roentgenographic appearance of the soft tissues of these patients is characteristic. In most patients there is complete absence of the subcutaneous fat lines of the extremities. This phenomenon is said not to occur in any other situation with the exception of imprisonment in concentration camps. Patients with cachexia due to other pathologic conditions, such as marasmus, celiac disease, or malignancies, always show persistence of a thin line of subcutaneous fat. About 80 percent of cases of diencephalic syndrome are due to slow-growing astrocytomas of the hypothalamus. Examination of the CSF may show an elevated level of protein from the early stages. A diagnosis can be suspected on the basis of the clinical picture and confirmed by ventriculography or pneumoencephalography, which shows a mass in the hypothalamic area indenting the third ventricle with or without hydrocephalus (Fig. 10-4B). Occasionally contrast studies fail to reveal the tumor.

Because of the location and the nature of these tumors, treatment is

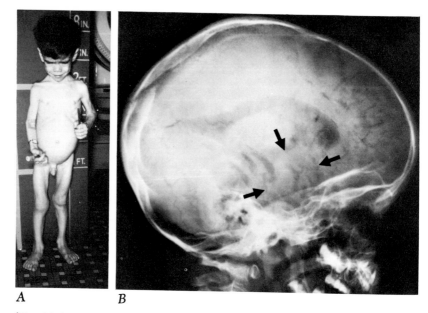

Fig. 10-4. A, 3-year-old boy with diencephalic syndrome. Notice profound emaciation with total loss of subcutaneous fat (courtesy of Dr. J. D. Smith). B, pneumoencephalogram showing obliteration of the anterior part of the third ventricle by a mass in the hypothalamus.

unsatisfactory. Partial removal, with or without a shunting procedure, to relieve obstructive hydrocephalus followed by radiation therapy is the treatment of choice. Ten years' survival after onset of symptoms has not been unusual. In the late stages of the disease many patients with diencephalic syndrome have undergone a gradual transition to obesity. This phenomenon could be explained in the untreated patient by extension of the process to adjacent areas of the hypothalamus, and in treated patients by destruction of the same areas at the time of surgery or as a result of radiation therapy.

Tumors of the Pineal Gland

One-third of tumors of the pineal gland occur during childhood. The signs and symptoms produced by these tumors are those of any midline mass and are the result of compression of neighboring structures such as the aqueduct of Sylvius, producing obstructive hydrocephalus, or compression of the superior colliculi, causing paralysis of upward gaze (Parinaud syndrome). Forward invasion into the hypothalamus may produce precocious puberty. Bilateral pyramidal tract signs and ataxia of the trunk and legs are common physical findings.

Tumors of the pineal gland are of four histologic types: (1) pinealomas, (2) pineoblastomas, (3) teratomas, and (4) germinomas. Pineal teratomas frequently contain calcium that can be demonstrated in plain roentgenograms of the skull. The location of these tumors makes surgical removal extremely difficult, if not impossible. Obstructive hydrocephalus can be treated by a shunting procedure. Tumors of the pineal gland are only slightly sensitive to radiation therapy.

Tumors of the Cerebral Hemispheres

In childhood, tumors of the cerebral hemispheres constitute approximately 5 to 10 percent of all intracranial neoplasms. The most common tumors of the cerebral hemispheres in children are astrocytomas, ependymomas, and oligodendrogliomas. Tumors in this location may attain an enormous size before causing symptoms. The signs and symptoms of tumors of the cerebral hemispheres are primarily related to their location and consist of focal, jacksonian, or generalized seizures, progressive hemiparesis, sensory deficit, or homonymous hemianopia on the side opposite the lesion. Eventually signs and symptoms of increased intracranial pressure develop. Focal seizures, especially in young children, are in most instances not a manifestation of tumors of the cerebral hemispheres. Persistent localized headaches may be the presenting complaint of tumors in this location. Any child with this symptom should be listened to and carefully examined; his complaint is usually significant.

Intracerebral calcification occurs frequently in oligodendrogliomas (40 percent) and less commonly in astrocytomas (12 percent) and ependymomas (5 percent). However, since astrocytomas are much more common supratentorial tumors than ependymomas or oligodendrogliomas, the presence of intracerebral calcification in a child with signs and symptoms of a hemispheric tumor makes an astrocytoma the more likely diagnostic possibility.

Diagnostic studies in patients suspected of having a tumor in this location include x-rays of the skull, which may show spreading of the sutures in young children, other roentgenographic signs of increased intracranial pressure in older ones, or intracerebral calcification (Fig. 10-5); electroencephalography, which may reveal a slow-wave focus on the side of the lesion; and brain scanning, which may demonstrate an area of increased uptake of radioisotope. Air-contrast studies and angiography may show evidence of hydrocephalus or distortion of the ventricular system and displacement of vessels or midline structures away from the side of the lesion (Fig. 10-6). Long-term prognosis following surgery and/or radiation therapy depends primarily on the degree of malignancy of the tumor.

Intraventricular tumors like choroid plexus papillomas occur usually

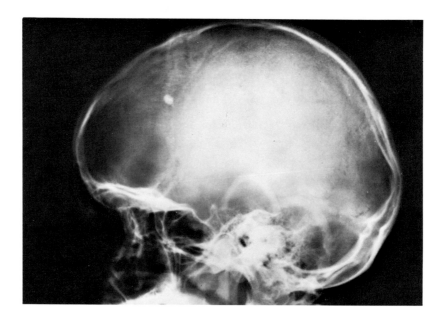

Fig. 10-5. Lateral view of skull showing calcification in left frontoparietal astrocytoma in a 12-year-old boy with a one-year history of right focal seizures.

in the fourth ventricle, where they cause symptoms similar to those seen with ependymomas, but may also occur in the lateral ventricles, where they produce signs and symptoms of increased intracranial pressure. Colloid cysts of the third ventricle are rare tumors in children. They arise from the anterior part of the ventricle, causing signs and symptoms of increased intracranial pressure by obstruction of the cerebrospinal fluid at the level of the foramen of Monro. A diagnosis of intraventricular tumor can be made by air-contrast study, which reveals a mass or a filling defect in one of the ventricles or dilatation of one or both lateral ventricles. Metastatic tumors, which constitute a large percentage of cerebral tumors in adults (primarily carcinoma of the breast and lungs), are, with the exception of leukemia, extremely rare in children.

HYDROCEPHALUS

By definition increased intracranial pressure is a sine qua non of hydrocephalus in infancy and childhood (see Chapter 11).

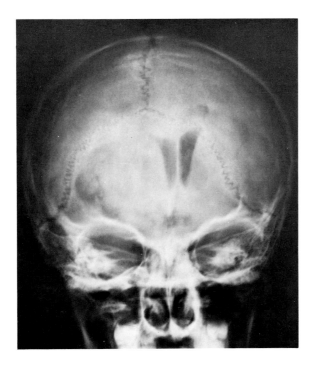

Fig. 10-6. Pneumoencephalogram in a 10-year-old boy showing displacement to the left of the anterior horns of the lateral ventricles by an astrocytoma of the right frontal lobe.

INTRACRANIAL HEMORRHAGE

Increased intracranial pressure is an almost constant feature of gross intracranial bleeding (subarachnoid hemorrhage, extradural, subdural, or intracerebral hematoma) (see Chapter 9).

BRAIN ABSCESS

Microorganisms may gain access to the brain by direct introduction following compound fractures of the skull or other severe head injuries, by direct extension from a purulent otitis media, mastoiditis, or sinusitis, and by the hematogenous route as the result of septicemia, bacterial endocarditis, lung abscesses, or other infections. Brain abscesses occur in approximately 3 percent of patients with cyanotic congenital heart disease with a right-to-left shunt. This complication is seen almost exclusively in patients older than 2 years. When microorganisms reach the brain by the hematogenous route, multiple abscesses may develop.

Brain abscesses occurring by direct extension from an infected focus in the middle ear or mastoid are usually located within the temporal lobe or the cerebellum or in the frontal lobe when the infection extends from the paranasal sinuses. Brain abscesses are usually caused by *Staphylococcus albus* or *aureus,* alpha-hemolytic streptococcus, or pneumococcus, although any of the common pyogenic bacteria may be found. As in any other organ of the body, once the microorganisms reach the brain an inflammatory reaction takes place.

The clinicopathologic course of a brain abscess can be divided into three stages. During the first stage, there is a localized cerebritis or focal inflammatory reaction clinically manifested by fever, malaise, headache, stiff neck, or seizures. There is leukocytosis and an elevated sedimentation rate. During the second stage the area of cerebritis is slowly surrounded by a capsule consisting of three layers—an inner layer of collagenous connective-tissue fibers, a middle layer rich in capillaries and fibroblasts, and an external layer of connective tissue containing vessels and phagocytes. During this stage the initial symptoms usually decrease in severity or may disappear altogether. The abscess continues to enlarge, and eventually the first manifestations of increased intracranial pressure or focal neurologic deficit herald the onset of the third stage of decompensation with signs and symptoms such as headache, nausea and vomiting, papilledema and sixth-nerve palsy, or focal neurologic deficit depending on the location of the abscess: hemiparesis, hemiplegia, and an extensor plantar response (Babinski sign) when the motor areas are involved; mental confusion and behavioral disturbances with abscesses of the frontal lobe; hemianopia and aphasia with involvement of the temporal and parieto-occipital lobes; and ipsilateral ataxia of the limbs and nystagmus with the gross component to the side of the lesion and the fine to the opposite side when the abscess is located in the cerebellum. Subsequently, the abscess, acting as any expanding intracranial mass, causes progressive increase in intracranial pressure with uncal and brain stem herniation. Occasionally a brain abscess will rupture into the ventricles. This complication is followed by meningitis and abrupt clinical deterioration.

A diagnosis of brain abscess should be considered in any child with chronic ear infection, cyanotic congenital heart disease, or any chronic suppurative process, who develops signs of focal neurologic deficit or signs of increased intracranial pressure. Roentgenograms of the skull may show signs of increased pressure (separation of sutures and bulging fontanelle in infants, and demineralization of the sella turcica and clinoid processes in older children). Brain scanning, electroencephalography, and angiography may be helpful in the localization of the abscess by demonstrating an area of increased isotope uptake, a persistent slow-wave focus, or displacement of cerebral blood vessels. Examination of the cerebrospinal fluid at any stage may show an increased pressure and the changes seen in aseptic meningitis (lymphocytic pleo-cytosis, a normal glucose level, and a moderate elevation of the protein level).

The treatment of a brain abscess is similar to that of bacterial menin-gitis of unknown etiology. Once the abscess is accurately localized by one or more of the previously mentioned diagnostic studies, it should be aspirated and drained. Prophylactic anticonvulsant therapy is recom-mended to prevent the occurrence of seizures, especially in abscesses located in the frontal or temporal lobes.

The differential diagnosis during the first stage of focal cerebral in-flammatory reaction includes encephalitis of viral origin and aseptic or purulent meningitis. When decompensation has occurred a brain ab-scess may resemble a number of other intracranial space-occupying lesions, such as chronic subdural hematomas and brain tumors, which produce increased intracranial pressure and focal neurologic deficit.

VENOUS SINUS THROMBOSIS

Thrombosis of one or more of the large intracranial venous sinuses may cause increased intracranial pressure.

Sagittal Sinus Thrombosis

Thrombosis of the superior sagittal sinus is not uncommonly seen at autopsy in infants with severe diarrhea and dehydration. Isolated thrombosis of the superior sagittal sinus causes signs and symptoms of increased intracranial pressure. If the thrombosis extends to involve the superior cerebral veins draining into the sinus, a hemorrhagic infarction of cortical and subcortical white matter may occur. The main condi-tions leading to thrombosis of the superior sagittal sinus are infections of the skull and facial sinuses, epidural or subdural abscesses, and ex-tension of thrombosis from a lateral sinus. Nonseptic sinus thrombosis in infancy is usually secondary to severe dehydration or marasmus.

Signs and symptoms of sagittal sinus thrombosis are fever, irritability, headache, and papilledema. There may be local signs such as tension of the anterior fontanelle in infants and dilatation and tortuosity of scalp veins. Focal or generalized seizures, hemiplegia, hemianopia, or aphasia may occur if retrograde infarction of brain tissue develops. A definite diagnosis can only be established by angiography. The progno-sis of thrombosis of the sagittal sinus is generally poor and correlates directly with the underlying pathology as well as the severity of associ-ated brain damage. The treatment of the septic type is by antibiotics; except for symptomatic treatment no therapy is available for nonseptic thrombosis.

Lateral Sinus Thrombosis

Thrombosis of the lateral or transverse sinus is almost always secondary to chronic mastoiditis or chronic otitis media. If the dominant sinus (the right in most people) is thrombosed, signs and symptoms of increased intracranial pressure are prominent (drowsiness, headache, nausea, vomiting, and papilledema). Examination of the cerebrospinal fluid reveals increased pressure, a lymphocytic pleocytosis, a moderate elevation óf the protein and a normal glucose level. Approximately 50 percent of patients develop septicemia. A diagnosis of thrombosis of the lateral sinus should be suspected in patients with acute or chronic otitis media or mastoiditis and signs and symptoms of increased intracranial pressure. The most important differential diagnosis in patients with this combination of symptoms is brain abscess. In contrast to patients with a brain abscess, focal neurologic signs are rare in patients with lateral sinus thrombosis. Laboratory procedures such as the electroencephalogram, brain scan, and angiogram may be of help in the differential diagnosis between these two conditions. The treatment of lateral sinus thrombosis is the administration of antibiotics and surgical drainage.

Thrombosis of the cavernous sinus causes proptosis; it may also cause an aseptic meningitis but is not a cause of increased intracranial pressure (see Chapter 7).

PSEUDOTUMOR CEREBRI

In recent years a syndrome referred to as *pseudotumor cerebri* has been reported in association with disorders such as hypervitaminosis A, prolonged steroid therapy, sudden withdrawal of steroids in patients with nephrosis, and in pubertal and obese girls. Pseudotumor cerebri affects females three times as frequently as males. The clinical picture consists of intermittent headaches, nausea and vomiting, blurred or double vision, and dizziness. Papilledema in the absence of focal or lateralizing neurologic signs is the hallmark of this disorder. Unilateral or bilateral sixth-nerve palsy, secondary to increased intracranial pressure, is seen in about 50 to 70 percent of patients. Roentgenograms of the skull may show signs of increased intracranial pressure, and the electroencephalogram may show generalized slowing. An enlarged blind spot consistent with the degree and duration of papilledema can be demonstrated by visual-field examination with the tangent screen. Contrast studies (ventriculogram, pneumoencephalogram, and arteriograms) are normal. Except for increased pressure, examination of the cerebrospinal fluid is normal.

The diagnosis of pseudotumor cerebri is one of elimination and by definition can be made only when focal or lateralizing signs including plantar responses (Babinski sign) are absent. The presence of a space-occupying lesion such as a tumor, chronic subdural hematoma, abscess, etc., should be ruled out by careful neurologic examination and ancillary diagnostic studies (brain scan, electroencephalogram, echoencephalogram) and contrast studies.

Symptoms of increased intracranial pressure can be alleviated by repeated lumbar punctures. If there is any reason to believe that vision is in danger subtemporal decompression may be indicated. Treatment with steroids is effective in relieving increased intracranial pressure. Pseudotumor cerebri is in all but exceptional instances a self-limited disease. Papilledema may persist for weeks or months. Prognosis for life and preservation of vision is excellent.

TOXIC ENCEPHALOPATHY

Increased intracranial pressure is the hallmark of toxic encephalopathy (acute brain swelling, Reye's syndrome) (see Chapter 9).

CRANIOSYNOSTOSIS

Craniosynostosis is a congenital anomaly of the skull characterized by premature closure of one or more cranial sutures. In premature closure of the sagittal suture growth takes place almost exclusively in the anteroposterior diameter (Fig. 10-7) and the head becomes abnormally shaped (scaphocephaly). If one or both coronal sutures close prematurely the skull grows primarily in its transverse diameter, resulting in marked brachycephaly (Fig. 10-8); the orbit and anterior and middle fossae are usually malformed and shortened, producing proptosis due to shallow orbits and occasionally optic atrophy even in the absence of increased intracranial pressure. Increased intracranial pressure may occur if two or more cranial sutures close prematurely (Fig. 10-9). Surgery is indicated in these cases to prevent this as well as other serious neurologic complications. If only a single suture is involved, surgery is in general recommended for cosmetic purposes alone. Since this type of surgery carries a very low mortality rate but a significant morbidity, some clinicians feel that the decision to operate on an infant with premature closure of a single suture, the sagittal in most instances, should be made by the parents and not by the pediatrician or neurosurgeon.

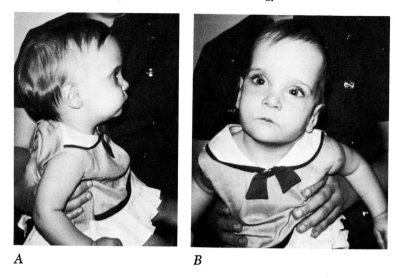

A   B

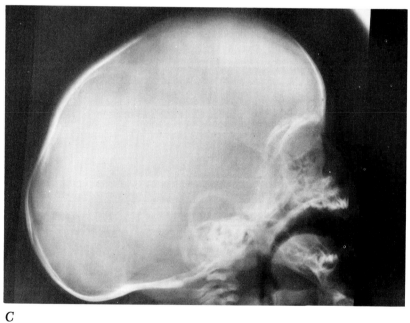

C

Fig. 10-7. A, B, 8-month-old infant with premature closure of the sagittal suture. Notice elongation of the head in the anteroposterior diameter. C, skull x-ray of same patient at 5 months of age. Normal psychomotor development and no evidence of neurologic deficit.

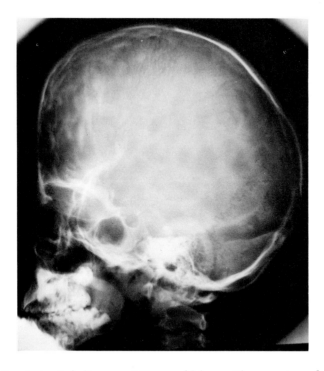

Fig. 10-8. Lateral skull x-ray of 7-year-old boy with premature closure of both coronal sutures. Tall and wide skull with small anteroposterior diameter. No neurologic deficit and normal psychomotor development.

LEUKEMIA OF THE CENTRAL NERVOUS SYSTEM

Involvement of the central nervous system by leukemia in children has increased since the advent of effective antileukemic therapy. The main complications of central nervous system leukemia are intracranial hemorrhages, a common cause of death in acute as well as chronic forms, and leukemic infiltration of the brain, spinal cord, meninges, and nerve roots. The patient with meningeal leukemia with or without infiltration of the brain substance usually presents with progressive headache, nausea, and vomiting. Other signs of increased intracranial pressure may be present, such as unilateral or bilateral sixth-nerve palsy or ataxia. Examination of the cerebrospinal fluid usually shows an elevated pressure, a decreased or normal glucose level, an elevated protein content, and pleocytosis. Malignant cells can rarely be demonstrated. Most cases of central nervous system leukemia occur when the patient is in hematologic remission. The cause of increased intracranial pressure may be due to cerebral edema secondary to leukemic infiltration of

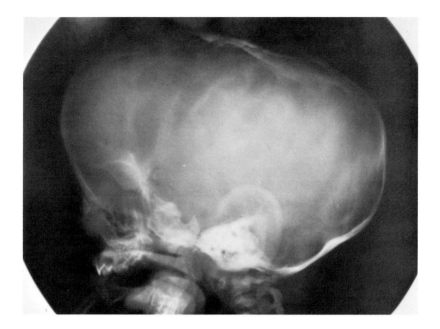

Fig. 10-9.   Lateral skull x-ray of 3-month-old infant with premature closure of all major cranial sutures.

the brain substance or to communicating hydrocephalus due to infiltration of the arachnoid at the base of the brain or over the convexity of the brain.

MISCELLANEOUS CONDITIONS

Increased intracranial pressure and papilledema may also occasionally occur in a number of other disorders.
See listing in Chapter 6, page 92.

REFERENCES

Bailey, P., Buchanan, D. N., and Bucy, P. C.   *Intracranial Tumors of Infancy and Childhood.* Chicago: University of Chicago Press, 1939.
Brown, J. R.   Cerebellar tumors in children. *Mayo Clin. Proc.* 42:511, 1967.
Cuneo, H. M., and Rand, C. W.   *Brain Tumors of Childhood.* Springfield, Ill.: Thomas, 1952.
Feldman, M. H., and Schlezinger, N. S.   Benign intracranial hypertension associated with hypervitaminosis A. *Arch. Neurol.* 22:1, 1970.

Ford, F. M. *Diseases of the Nervous System in Infancy, Childhood and Adolescence* (5th ed.). Springfield, Ill.: Thomas, 1966.

Greer, M. Benign intracranial hypertension (pseudotumor cerebri). *Pediat. Clin. N. Amer.* 14:819, 1967.

Hemple, D. J., et al. Craniosynostosis involving the sagittal suture only: Guilt by association. *J. Pediat.* 58:342, 1961.

Hubert, L. Thrombosis of the lateral sinus. *J.A.M.A.* 117:1409, 1941.

Loeser, E., and Scheinberg, L. Brain abscesses: A review of 99 cases. *Neurology* 7:601, 1957.

Lysak, W. R., and Svien, H. L. Long term follow-up on patients with diagnosis of pseudotumor cerebri. *J. Neurosurg.* 25:284, 1966.

Merrit, H. H. *A Textbook of Neurology* (4th ed.). Philadelphia: Lea & Febiger, 1967.

Russell, A. A diencephalic syndrome of emaciation in infancy and childhood. *Arch. Dis. Child.* 26:274, 1951.

Russell, D. S., and Rubinstein, L. J. *Pathology of Tumors of the Nervous System* (2nd ed.). Baltimore: Williams & Wilkins, 1963.

Shilito, J., Jr., and Matson, D. D. Craniosynostosis: Review of 519 surgical patients. *Pediatrics* 41:829, 1968.

Yang, D. C., et al. Thrombosis of the superior longitudinal sinus during infancy. *J. Pediat.* 74:570, 1969.

11
Macrocephaly and Microcephaly

THE GROWTH of the skull is intimately linked to that of the brain; the bones of the cranial vault need the outward pressure of the developing brain in order to achieve a normal growth. Both the brain and the skull grow rapidly during the first two years of life. The head circumference, which appears to be a good index of brain size, increases from an average of 35 cm. at birth to 46 cm. by one year of age, and to 49 cm. by the end of the second year. During the next three years the head circumference will increase only an additional 1.5 cm. By the end of the fifth year, the brain and the skull have already attained over 90 percent of their adult size.

The craniofacial ratio is at birth 3:1; it is 2:1 by two years and subsequently continues to decrease slowly to reach an adult ratio of 3:2 by ten years. Both head circumference and craniofacial ratio are affected in patients with large or small heads; only the former, however, can be easily and accurately determined without skull x-rays and is thereby of more practical importance.

The infant or young child with an abnormally large head or with a head which appears to be growing at an abnormal rate often represents a difficult diagnostic problem. The common practice of not measuring head circumference as a routine office procedure during well-baby examinations is a formidable handicap for the physician who is asked to evaluate a child who has an unusually large head or a head which may be growing too rapidly. Since no previous points of reference are available, it is difficult to determine whether the child happens to have a large head or whether the head is growing at an abnormal rate. Nevertheless, in a large percentage of children with large heads other signs may be present (large anterior fontanelle, dilated scalp veins, frontal bossing, setting-sun sign, or localized or diffuse increase in glowing on the skull on transillumination) which facilitate a diagnosis or provide indications for a more extensive diagnostic investigation. When these signs are lacking, however, the situation may be confusing, especially if the child has a normal psychomotor development and the neurologic examination reveals no abnormalities.

It is necessary to emphasize that the circumference of the head does not correlate well with that of the chest. If the height of an infant is at the fiftieth percentile and both the chest and head circumference at the ninety-seventh percentile, the odds are that the large head is probably due to some sort of intracranial pathology. On the other hand, tall infants have a head circumference which is, in most instances, proportional to their body size. For example, if the height of an infant is at the seventy-fifth percentile, the head circumference may be between the seventy-fifth and ninety-seventh percentile. The parents of these infants are usually also tall, and at least one of them has a large head. Occasionally a child is seen with a head that is unusually large in comparison with the rest of the body but which over a period of months or years follows a normal growth curve. If no abnormal neurologic signs or symptoms are present and roentgenograms of the skull show no evidence of spreading of the sutures or other signs of increased intracranial pressure, serial measurements of the head circumference at periodic intervals are all that is indicated. In a period of two or three months the physician will be able in most cases to determine the pattern of growth of the infant's head. The previous considerations serve to point out the need of measuring the head circumference in all infants as part of their routine physical checkups. The procedure takes only a few seconds and can be done by the nurse at the time the height and weight are determined.

HYDROCEPHALUS

In infancy hydrocephalus is by far the most common cause of macrocephaly. Sometimes a diagnosis of hydrocephalus can be made only after serial measurements of the head circumference over a period of several weeks or months in a child whose head initially appears to be only slightly large. In the great majority of cases, however, a diagnosis can be made by simple inspection. The heads of these children have a typical hydrocephalic configuration, with frontal bossing, orbital prominence, and dilated scalp veins. The anterior fontanelle may or may not bulge or be tense. In severe cases the setting-sun sign is usually present (Fig. 11-1).

The great majority of cases of hydrocephalus occur during the first few months of life at a time when the cranial sutures can easily spread and thereby compensate for the increased pressure within the cranial cavity. Owing to the ability of the infant's skull to accommodate an expanding brain, papilledema is rarely if ever seen during this age pe-

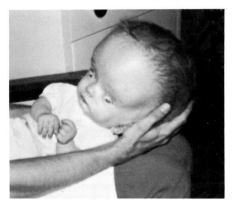

Fig. 11-1.   7-month-old infant with hydrocephalus. Large head, dilated scalp veins, and setting-sun sign.

riod. Optic atrophy, on the other hand, is not an uncommon complication of infantile hydrocephalus.

Hydrocephalus may be secondary to overproduction of cerebrospinal fluid, obstruction to normal flow, or deficient absorption of the cerebrospinal fluid; the result is an accumulation of fluid under increased pressure. The cerebrospinal fluid is produced in the walls of the ventricles of the brain and in the choroid plexus. After its exit from the foramina of Luschka and Magendie in the fourth ventricle the cerebrospinal fluid reaches the subarachnoid spaces over the convexity of the brain, where it is reabsorbed into the dural sinuses by way of the arachnoid villi.

Pathologically, two types of hydrocephalus can be distinguished: obstructive (noncommunicating) and nonobstructive (communicating). Strictly speaking, all varieties of hydrocephalus are due to an obstruction, functional or anatomic, at a certain point in the cerebrospinal fluid pathways.

The incidence of hydrocephalus in early infancy is 2 to 3 per 1000 live births. Overproduction of cerebrospinal fluid, a rare cause of hydrocephalus, is seen in association with choroid plexus papillomas. The most important etiologies of obstructive hydrocephalus are congenital stenosis, forking, and gliosis of the aqueduct of Sylvius (Fig. 11-2). Occasionally a septum is present at the caudal end of the aqueduct causing obstruction. A similar type of hydrocephalus in which the aqueduct is compressed from the outside is seen as a common complication in infants with an aneurysm of the vein of Galen.

Hydrocephalus occurs frequently in patients with meningomyelocele and is in this case almost always due to an associated Arnold-Chiari malformation. This congenital abnormality consists of a downward displacement of the brain stem and cerebellar tonsils into the cervical

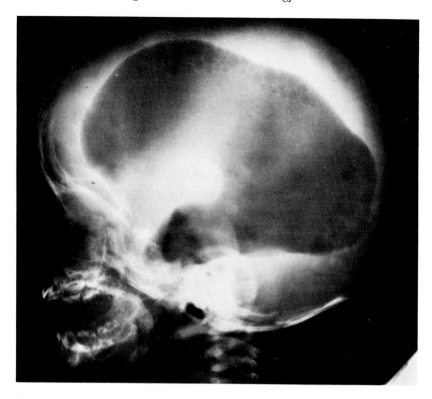

Fig. 11-2. Lateral view of ventriculogram in 6-month-old infant with obstructive hydrocephalus due to stenosis of the aqueduct of Sylvius. Tremendously dilated ventricular system beyond the point of obstruction.

spinal canal, a stretched-out fourth ventricle, and adhesions between the medulla and the cerebellar tonsils. The cerebellar lobes may be of normal size or small (Fig. 11-3). If the meningomyelocele is located higher than the first or second lumbar vertebra, an Arnold-Chiari malformation is almost invariably present. However, only about 50 to 75 percent of these patients will develop obstructive hydrocephalus, usually during the first three months of life. Beyond infancy, obstructive hydrocephalus may be caused by tumors of the brain, especially by those of the third ventricle or the posterior fossa, and by reactive inflammatory stenosis of the aqueduct or adhesions at the base of the brain following meningitis or subarachnoid bleeding.

Nonobstructive hydrocephalus may be idiopathic or secondary to malabsorption of the cerebrospinal fluid as a consequence of postmeningitic adhesions or other causes over the convexity of the brain.

Transillumination of the head may show an abnormal glowing in severe cases. In general, however, this is of little help, since no areas of

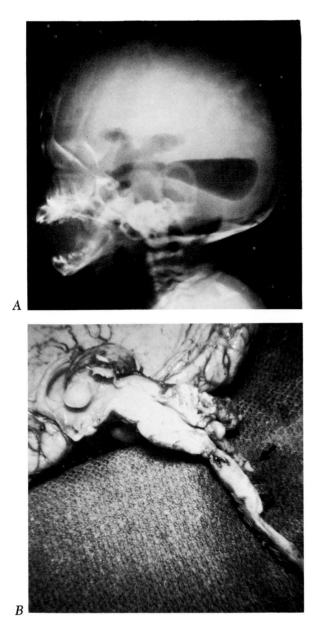

Fig. 11-3. A, lateral view of ventriculogram in 1-month-old infant with Arnold-Chiari malformation and hydrocephalus. Fourth ventricle is below the level of the foramen magnum. B, autopsy specimen in patient with hydrocephalus and Arnold-Chiari malformation. There is elongation of fourth ventricle and caudal displacement of medulla and portion of cerebellum into the spinal canal (arrow). Notice also hypoplastic cerebellum.

abnormal glowing can be demonstrated unless the cerebral mantle is less than 1 cm. in thickness. Skull x-rays may show spreading of the sutures in infants and signs of increased intracranial pressure such as demineralization or erosion of the sella turcica in older children. The electroencephalogram may be normal or may show diffuse, nonspecific abnormalities. The echoencephalogram may reveal displacement of the lateral walls of the third ventricle. During infancy the differential diagnosis is in general limited to subdural hematoma, which can be ruled out by bilateral subdural punctures. If these are negative a needle is inserted into one of the lateral ventricles and a ventriculogram performed. This procedure will demonstrate the patency and size of the ventricular system as well as possible displacement of the midline structures by a subdural hematoma not detected by subdural puncture, a brain tumor, a porencephalic cyst, or some other type of space-occupying lesion.

The treatment of hydrocephalus is surgical and consists of shunting the CSF from one of the lateral ventricles to the cisterna magna (Torkildsen ventriculocisternal shunt) or to a site outside the central nervous system, most commonly the right auricle and the pleural or peritoneal cavity. Procedures such as third-ventriculostomy and choroid plexotomy are no longer in use. The different shunting devices (one-way plastic catheter) often need to be revised because of obstruction at either end of the catheter. Nowadays the most popular and effective shunting procedure is the ventriculoatrial shunt. The complications encountered with this type of shunt include occlusion of the catheter, thrombosis of the superior vena cava or thrombus formation within the right auricle, pulmonary embolism, bacterial endocarditis, septicemia, and meningitis.

Encouraging results have been reported with acetazolamide (Diamox) in the treatment of infants with chronic, slowly progressive, communicating hydrocephalus. In about 45 percent of patients the hydrocephalus becomes spontaneously arrested during the first two years of life and in 57 percent of these the IQ is 75 or above. Despite frequent complications, surgical treatment of infantile hydrocephalus is justified in the great majority of patients. Morbidity, mortality, and prognosis for future psychomotor development are better in treated than in nontreated patients.

CHRONIC SUBDURAL HEMATOMA

Chronic subdural hematoma is the second commonest cause of an abnormally large head in infancy and early childhood (Fig. 11-4). A head with a hydrocephalic configuration is sometimes seen in infants or

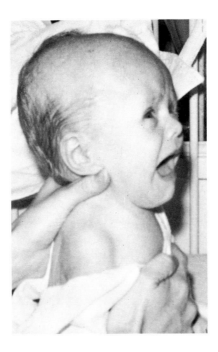

Fig. 11-4.   6-week-old infant with chronic subdural hematoma and an abnormally large head (head circumference 42 cm.).

young children with chronic subdural hematoma. The superficial location of the fluid in this condition facilitates transmission of light and the demonstration of areas of abnormal glowing of the skull. Thus, a positive transillumination of the head is seen with greater frequency in patients with chronic subdural hematoma than in those with hydrocephalus. Skull x-rays may show separation of the sutures. The electroencephalogram may show an amplitude asymmetry or a slow-wave focus on the side of the lesion, and the brain scan may demonstrate an area of increased uptake of radioactive material in the area of the hematoma. Subdural taps are diagnostic and therapeutic (see Chapter 9).

PORENCEPHALIC CYST

Occasionally a large porencephalic cyst may produce an abnormal growth of the head. Areas of increased glowing of the skull can be demonstrated in the great majority of cases. Severe neurologic deficit is present in most infants with large porencephalic cysts.

BRAIN TUMORS

Brain tumors are not a common cause of progressive enlargement of the head in infancy. In rare instances contrast studies will reveal the presence of a deep midline tumor producing hydrocephalus in a child suspected of having chronic subdural hematoma or hydrocephalus.

MEGALENCEPHALY

Megalencephaly is a rare condition in which the brain is unusually large, in some instances weighing as much as 2800 gm. In most cases of megalencephaly there are severe associated structural brain anomalies. Individuals of average or exceptional intelligence occasionally may have an unusually large brain. On the other hand, true megalencephaly is always associated with severe degrees of mental subnormality. The configuration of the head in these patients resembles that of a normal head rather than that of hydrocephalus or chronic subdural hematoma. Skull x-rays show no evidence of increased intracranial pressure, and contrast studies (ventriculography or pneumoencephalography) reveal a normal-sized or small ventricular system with no evidence of obstruction.

DEGENERATIVE DISEASES OF THE CENTRAL NERVOUS SYSTEM

A number of degenerative diseases of the central nervous system may cause an abnormal enlargement of the head.

Tay-Sachs Disease

Enlargement of the head secondary to an abnormal accumulation of gangliosides in cerebral neurons is common during the third stage of this condition (see Chapter 16). Signs or symptoms of increased intracranial pressure do not occur, and other characteristic signs are present (seizures, hypertonia, increased reflexes, cortical or peripheral blindness, and a cherry-red spot in the macula).

Spongy Degeneration of the White Matter (Canavan's Disease)

This condition was formerly included in the group of leukodystrophies. The disease begins between the ages of 3 and 9 months and occurs most frequently in children of Jewish heritage. There is progressive dementia and initial hypotonia followed by spasticity and blindness. In most cases there is progressive enlargement of the head with separation of cranial sutures. At autopsy there is diffuse demyelination and small cystic spaces in the white matter of the cerebral hemispheres and to a lesser extent the cerebellum.

Sulfatide Lipidosis

Enlargement of the head is a not uncommon physical finding in patients with sulfatide lipidosis (metachromatic leukodystrophy) (see Chapter 16).

Generalized Gangliosidosis

In this condition there is accumulation of ganglioside in brain, liver, and spleen. The phenotype and bony abnormalities which are present since birth are similar to those of Hurler's syndrome. Patients with generalized gangliosidosis have a large, dolichocephalic head.

CEREBRAL GIGANTISM

Cerebral gigantism is a condition characterized by excessive somatic growth during the first few years of life, acromegalic features, and a nonprogressive cerebral disorder with mental retardation. Patients with this disorder have a large and abnormal brain with a head of normal configuration which bears a linear relationship with facial structures and body height. Children with cerebral gigantism are large at birth and continue to grow at an accelerated rate for the first few years of life. They have large hands and feet, a prominent forehead and a large jaw, high arched palate, and heavy supraorbital ridges (Fig. 11-5). The pneumoencephalogram reveals varying degrees of ventricular dilatation without evidence of a block or increased cerebrospinal fluid pressure in about 75 percent of cases. Bone age is characteristically advanced in relation to chronologic age. The accelerated growth seen in patients with cerebral gigantism is probably due to hypothalamic dysfunction. Levels of circulating growth hormone are normal.

MACROCEPHALY, CUTANEOUS HEMANGIOMAS, AND PSEUDOPAPILLEDEMA (RILEY-SMITH SYNDROME)

Riley-Smith syndrome is a rare familial disorder inherited as a dominant trait and characterized by macrocephaly, cutaneous hemangiomas, and pseudopapilledema (Fig. 11-6). Macrocephaly may be present

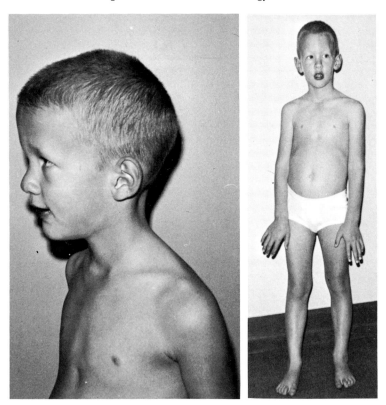

Fig. 11-5. 7-year-old boy with cerebral gigantism. Tall stature (3 standard deviations above the mean for his age), and large head, hands, and feet. Advanced bone age and moderate psychomotor retardation.

since birth. The skin abnormalities appear from birth to 5 years of age. Pneumoencephalography in these patients shows a normal ventricular system.

HEMOLYTIC ANEMIAS

Occasionally severe hemolytic anemias (sickle-cell and Cooley's anemias) may produce a marked degree of thickening of the calvaria and enlargement of the head without an increase in size of intracranial structures.

OSTEITIS DEFORMANS (JUVENILE PAGET'S DISEASE)

Paget's disease (osteitis deformans) is a chronic progressive disturbance in bone metabolism characterized by softening and later on thickening and deformity of the skull and long bones. The disease is rare

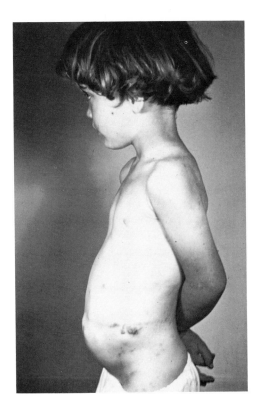

Fig. 11-6. 5-year-old girl with macrocephaly (head circumference 57 cm.)
and cutaneous hemangiomas over the abdominal wall. (From Riley, H. D.,
Jr., and Smith, W. R., *Pediatrics* 26:293, 1960)

under the age of twenty. Deafness is a common early symptom, and
optic atrophy is sometimes observed. Serum calcium is normal, phosphorus is normal or slightly elevated, and serum alkaline phosphatase is
elevated. Roentgenographic changes are characteristic.

MUCOPOLYSACCHARIDOSES

Hurler's Syndrome (Mucopolysaccharidosis I)

Patients with Hurler's syndrome have a head which is disproportion-
ately large in comparison with the facial structures. A prominent ridge
along the sagittal suture is often present. The facial and body appearance of patients with Hurler's syndrome is characteristic, with thick
lips, a depressed nasal bridge, prominent forehead, broad hands, short
and stubby fingers, contractures of the hips, knees, and elbows, a pro-

tuberant abdomen, hepatosplenomegaly, thick skin, hirsutism, and corneal clouding. Skull x-rays may show hyperostosis and an enlarged sella turcica (boot or shoe-shaped sella). Hurler's syndrome is characterized biochemically by an increased excretion of chondroitin sulfate B and heparitin sulfate in the urine.

Hunter's Syndrome (Mucopolysaccharidosis II)

Hunter's syndrome is an X-linked recessive disorder of mucopolysaccharide metabolism characterized by clinical features similar to, although less severe than, those seen in patients with Hurler's syndrome. Patients with this condition also excrete increased amounts of chondroitin sulfate B and heparitin sulfate in the urine. Mental retardation is a fairly constant feature of both Hurler's and Hunter's syndromes. A large head is not a feature in patients with Sanfilippo syndrome (mucopolysaccharidosis III), Morquio's disease (mucopolysaccharidosis IV), or Scheie's disease (mucopolysaccharidosis V).

ACHONDROPLASIA

A relatively large head is the rule in achondroplasia. In addition, the incidence of hydrocephalus is higher in this disorder than in the general population or among patients with other syndromes in which skeletal malformations are a prominent feature.

CHONDRODYSTROPHIA CALCIFICANS CONGENITA

A large head is sometimes seen in patients with chondrodystrophia calcificans congenita, a syndrome characterized by stippled epiphyses, contractures, bony abnormalities, bilateral cataracts, optic atrophy, saddle nose, and skin abnormalities.

FAMILIAL METAPHYSEAL DYSPLASIA (PYLE'S DISEASE)

Familial metaphyseal dysplasia is a condition characterized by macrocephaly, hypertelorism, a prominent glabella, and cranial nerve abnormalities secondary to obstruction of cranial foramina.

MICROCEPHALY

The size of the head, as any other biologic parameter, varies within a wide range of normal values. Tall individuals may have small heads and short ones large heads. Generally, and within certain limits, however, there is a linear relationship between body height and head size. A small head is not incompatible with average intelligence. Anatole France, French writer and Nobel laureate, is said to have had a brain which weighed only 1040 gm. Individuals with a head circumference below two standard deviations (less than third percentile in standard charts of head growth) are almost always of subnormal intelligence. Arbitrarily, true microcephaly is defined as a head circumference of minus three or less standard deviations below the mean for a certain age. Microcephaly is invariably accompanied by mental subnormality.

Microcephaly can be divided into (1) primary, or genetically determined, and (2) secondary to various etiologies such as congenital infections, birth trauma, intrauterine radiation, severe neonatal anoxia, repeated and severe episodes of hypoglycemia in early infancy, or a large number of developmental anomalies of the central nervous system. In patients with primary microcephaly there is a remarkable discrepancy between mental and motor development. In spite of severe mental retardation many of these infants reach the milestones of motor development at an average age (Fig. 11-7). The configuration of the head in patients with primary microcephaly is characterized by a receding forehead and a furrowed scalp, the small head contrasting markedly with

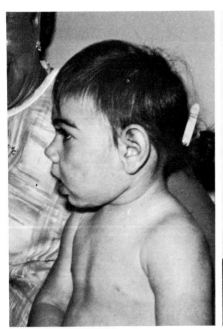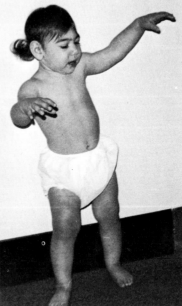

Fig. 11-7. 12-month-old infant with primary microcephaly (head circumference 40 cm.) and severe mental retardation. Motor development, however, is normal for her age.

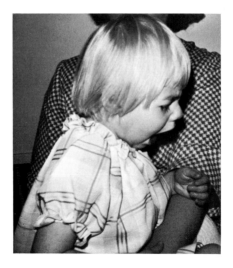

Fig. 11-8. 5-year-old girl with secondary microcephaly due to neonatal meningitis. Head circumference 46 cm. Severe psychomotor retardation.

the normal size of the facial structures, a relatively prominent nose, and large ears.

In secondary microcephaly the head has a normal configuration (Fig. 11-8). Below is a list of some conditions which may produce or are often associated with secondary microcephaly.

SECONDARY MICROCEPHALY

INFECTIONS

Congenital cytomegalic inclusion
  body disease
Congenital toxoplasmosis
Rubella embryopathy
Neonatal meningitis

METABOLIC ABNORMALITIES

Phenylketonuria
Maple syrup urine disease
Severe neonatal hypoglycemia

CHROMOSOME ABNORMALITIES

Trisomy 21 (mongolism)
Trisomy 13-15
Trisomy 18
Cri-du-chat syndrome

DEVELOPMENTAL ABNORMALITIES

Bird-headed dwarf (Virchow-
  Seckel)
Cebocephaly
Cyclopia
Happy-puppet syndrome
Marinesco-Sjögren syndrome
Neurodegenerative disease with
  monilethrix (kinky-hair disease)
Hallerman-Streiff syndrome
Rubinstein-Taybi syndrome
Smith-Lemli-Opitz syndrome

MISCELLANEOUS CONDITIONS

Birth trauma
Severe perinatal anoxia
Infantile spasms
Craniosynostoses (all sutures)

REFERENCES

Gellis, S. S., and Feingold, M. *Atlas of Mental Retardation Syndromes.* U. S. Department of Health, Education and Welfare, 1968.

Laurence, K. M. The natural history of hydrocephalus. *Lancet* 2:1152, 1958.

Martin, H. P. Microcephaly and mental retardation. *Amer. J. Dis. Child.* 119:128, 1970.

McDonald, R. Large heads in small children: Notes on the causes of increased head circumference. *Clin. Pediat.* (Phila.) 6:47, 1967.

O'Connel, E. J., et al. Head circumference, mental retardation, and growth failure. *Pediatrics* 36:62, 1965.

Ott, J. E., and Robinson, A. Cerebral gigantism. *Amer. J. Dis. Child.* 117:357, 1969.

Paine, R. S. Hydrocephalus. *Pediat. Clin. N. Amer.* 14:779, 1967.

Riley, H. D., Jr., and Smith, W. R. Macrocephaly, pseudopapilledema and multiple hemangiomata: A previously undescribed heredofamilial syndrome. *Pediatrics* 26:293, 1960.

Schain, R. J. Carbonic anhydrase inhibitors in chronic infantile hydrocephalus. *Amer. J. Dis. Child.* 117:621, 1969.

Smith, D. W. *Recognizable Patterns of Human Malformation: Genetic, Embryologic and Clinical Aspects.* Philadelphia: Saunders, 1970.

Sotos, J. F., et al. Cerebral gigantism in childhood. *New Eng. J. Med.* 271:109, 1964.

12
Headache

HEADACHE is one of the most common of all presenting complaints. Headache may result from stimulation, traction, or pressure on any of the pain-sensitive structures of the head such as the trigeminal, glossopharyngeal, vagal, and upper cervical nerves; the large arteries at the base of the brain and their major branches; the dura mater at the base of the skull; the cranial sinuses and afferent veins; the arteries of the dura mater; and some extracranial structures such as the scalp, muscles, and arteries. The brain proper, choroid plexus, pia-arachnoid, parts of the dura, and the skull are insensitive to pain.

Headache in children is nowadays a frequent complaint and somehow has replaced abdominal pain as an instrument of attracting attention; it is often used by the child in an effort to manipulate his environment. In many instances, however, headache is a significant and genuine complaint. Therefore, the physician should be familiar with the fairly typical characteristics of some of the most common causes of organic headache in childhood. Any child complaining of persisting or recurrent paroxysmal attacks of headache should be listened to carefully, and a detailed history of his complaints should be taken and a thorough general and neurologic examination performed. Important points in the history of a child with headache are (1) mode of onset, (2) duration, (3) location, (4) precipitating and aggravating factors, (5) prodromata, (6) character, (7) associated signs and symptoms, (8) alleviating factors, and (9) the family history.

TRACTION HEADACHES

These headaches are the result of traction on intracranial pain-sensitive structures by conditions such as hydrocephalus, brain tumor, intracranial hematoma, intracranial aneurysm, cerebral abscess, and pseudotumor cerebri, and following lumbar puncture. With the only exception of postlumbar-puncture headache and the headache of cerebral aneurysm, in all the other previously mentioned conditions increased intracranial pressure is also an important, although not indispensable, etiologic factor.

It is difficult to state with any degree of accuracy whether hydrocephalic infants experience headache. However, many of them exhibit marked irritability which disappears or improves following a ventriculogram or a shunting procedure.

The headache of brain tumors has an aching, steady character and is seldom rhythmic or throbbing as are vascular headaches. The headache is usually intermittent and of moderate severity in contrast to the very severe pain of trigeminal neuralgia, subarachnoid hemorrhage, encephalitis, or meningitis. The headache of brain tumors is sometimes more severe in the early morning and in the erect position. These two features, however, are the exception rather than the rule.

Increased intracranial pressure does not seem to be an essential etiologic factor of headaches due to brain tumors. Headaches may occur in patients with brain tumors and increased intracranial pressure as well as in patients with brain tumors and no increased intracranial pressure. In some patients with pseudotumor cerebri, for example, the headache is of mild or moderate intensity and sometimes absent, even in the presence of very high and prolonged increased intracranial pressure.

The headache is said to overlie brain tumors in about one-third of cases. In the absence of papilledema, circumscribed headache appears to be of localizing value.

Headache is not a common initial complaint in supratentorial tumors and is seldom the first symptom in tumors of the posterior fossa, although eventually it occurs in all patients at some stage in the natural course of the disease.

Headache following lumbar puncture appears to be related to traction by the brain on pain-sensitive structures. This traction mechanism is facilitated by dilatation of some of these structures as well as by a temporary increase in brain volume. Lumbar puncture is almost always followed by prolonged secondary leakage of cerebrospinal fluid through the dural hole in the lumbar sac. Lumbar-puncture headache can be alleviated by the intrathecal injection of saline solution or by changing the patient's position from the erect to the horizontal and can be increased by bilateral jugular vein compression.

VASCULAR HEADACHE OF MIGRAINE TYPE

Migraine is a paroxysmal disorder characterized by recurrent headache with or without associated visual, gastrointestinal, or autonomic nervous system disturbances. The headaches are often preceded by visual phenomena such as scintillating scotomas or visual-field defects, paresthesias, speech difficulties, and rarely hemiparesis. Other common associated clinical features are nausea, vomiting, irritability, photophobia, constipation, diarrhea, abdominal distention, vertigo, tremor, pallor, excessive sweating, and a feeling of extreme malaise (sick headache).

The underlying pathophysiology of migraine is unknown. In the initial stage of an attack there is vasoconstriction of cerebral arteries primarily involving the branches of the external carotid artery. This is followed by a second phase of vasodilatation which initiates the attack of headache. Vasodilatation is followed by a third phase of edema. During the latter phase the headache may become dull and steady, vomiting is frequent, and the patient may complain of dryness of the mouth and excessive sweating or chilliness.

The incidence of migraine headache in schoolchildren has been estimated to be around 4 percent. Vascular headaches occur much more frequently in children than is generally recognized. Often in an older child with migraine headache the physician is able to elicit a history of recurrent episodes of unexplained crying and irritability since early childhood. A history of migraine headaches can be elicited in other family members in the great majority of patients. In contrast to adults, a history of visual disturbances such as scintillating scotomas, hemianopia, or blurred vision is seldom elicited in children. The recurrent attacks of headache are usually unilateral at the onset but become generalized after one or two hours. They may occur at any time of the day and characteristically occur against a background of relative well-being. Nausea, vomiting, irritability, and photophobia are frequent accompanying symptoms. At the onset of each attack the headache is usually localized to one side of the head, but either side may be involved initially in different episodes. During the attack these children try to avoid noises, bright lights, and almost invariably "sleep off their headaches." The attacks of migraine may last from one or two hours to one or two days. Not infrequently after symptoms have subsided the scalp is tender in the area where the headache began. Children suffering from migraine headaches are usually bright and tend to have a rigid and compulsive personality. The great majority of children with migraine seem to benefit from continuous treatment with Dilantin and an analgesic such as aspirin at the time of the headache. If attacks are unusually severe an ergotamine preparation can be given in the form of suppositories or sublingual tablets (see Appendix 2).

The outlook for children with migraine headaches is relatively good. In a series of 92 cases followed for periods of up to 15 years and in which several different types of treatment were used, Hinrichs and Keith in 1965 found that 80 percent of children were completely free (33 percent) or were considerably improved (47 percent). Twenty percent were not benefited by any form of therapy.

Ophthalmoplegia is a rare complication of migraine headache. In the typical case of ophthalmoplegic migraine approximately 6 to 24 hours after the onset of an attack there is a partial or complete third-nerve palsy on the same side where the headache began (Fig. 12-1). Rarely the sixth (abducens) cranial nerve is affected. The ophthalmoplegia as a rule subsides completely in a matter of a few days to one to two weeks. However, after repeated episodes the deficit may become permanent in the form of a partial or complete third-nerve paralysis.

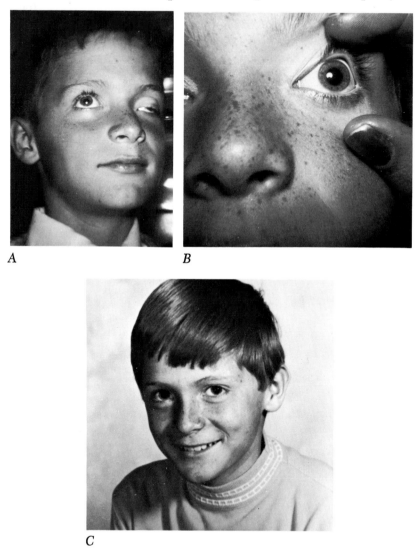

A   B

C

Fig. 12-1. Ophthalmoplegic migraine. A, B, 11-year-old boy with sudden onset of third cranial nerve paralysis 24 hours following attack of migraine headache. C, complete recovery one month later. (*Amer. J. Dis. Child.* 122: 237, 1971).

A large and slowly reacting pupil may be the only sequela. Patients with ophthalmoplegic migraine should be treated with an ergotamine preparation shortly after the onset of subsequent episodes if permanent neurologic sequelae are to be prevented. Ergotamine tartrate 0.5 mg. by rectum early in the course of the headache may be effective in a child of school age, whereas in a preschool child 0.3 mg. would seem sufficient.

Any patient with recurrent episodes of unilateral, localized, steady, or throbbing type of headache should have careful auscultation of the skull for bruits. The presenting complaint in a patient with an arteriovenous malformation may be recurrent episodes of localized headache indistinguishable from vascular headaches. The recurrent episodes of vascular headaches which occasionally occur in patients with arteriovenous malformations always begin on the same side of the lesion in contrast to migraine in which either side may be initially affected. Electroencephalography and brain scanning are important tools in the diagnosis of arteriovenous malformations. The electroencephalogram may show localized dysrhythmias or a slow-wave focus on the side of the lesion, and the brain scan may demonstrate an area of increased uptake of radioisotope.

Paroxysmal episodes of headache, usually associated with abdominal pain, also occur as a manifestation of seizure activity (epileptic equivalent). These patients frequently have electroencephalographic abnormalities and respond to treatment with Dilantin, phenobarbital, or Diamox.

HEADACHE DUE TO CRANIAL INFLAMMATION

Headache is a common initial symptom in intracranial inflammatory conditions such as encephalitis or meningitis.

MUSCLE CONTRACTION HEADACHE
(TENSION HEADACHE)

Sustained contraction of skeletal muscle of the head and neck occurs in tense, apprehensive, and anxious people. The headache is steady in nature, of moderate severity, and variously described as a feeling of tightness, pressure, or a band around the head. Muscle contraction headache is rare in childhood.

HEADACHE DUE TO DISEASES OF THE EAR, NOSE, AND EYES

Chronic intermittent headache associated with diseases of the nose, ears, and paranasal sinuses is rare in children.

Optic or retrobulbar neuritis may produce sudden onset of pain in or around the eye. In this condition the eyeglobe is tender to palpation, and varying degrees of visual loss are uniformly present. Funduscopic examination reveals swelling of the optic nerve which is indistinguishable from papilledema due to increased intracranial pressure. Loss of vision, however, is rarely seen with papilledema and is a constant finding in optic or retrobulbar neuritis.

Refractive errors, disturbances of extraocular muscle equilibrium, and increased intraocular pressure (glaucoma) may also cause headache. In these instances the pain radiates to the area of the skull supplied by the ophthalmic branch of the trigeminal nerve.

POSTTRAUMATIC HEADACHE

Posttraumatic headache is seldom seen in children. Following moderately severe head injuries many children will exhibit personality changes, mood disturbances, behavioral problems, and learning difficulties.

HEADACHE SECONDARY TO SYSTEMIC DISORDERS

Headaches associated with fever of any cause, poisoning, hypoxemia, and postictal states are probably due to distention of cerebral and pial vessels. Their mechanism resembles that of the headache which follows the administration of histamine.

MISCELLANEOUS CONDITIONS

Persistent, localized occipital headache is a symptom of basilar impression. The pain in this condition is probably due to compression or stretching of the roots of the second and third cervical nerves. A diagnosis of basilar impression is based on the presence of signs of lower cranial nerve involvement, nystagmus, ataxia, or pyramidal tract signs in a patient with typical head configuration and a short neck. The diagnosis can be confirmed by plain skull and cervical roentgenograms or by tomograms of the upper cervical spine and foramen magnum which demonstrate upward displacement of the odontoid process of the axis (see Chapter 3).

Trigeminal neuralgia (tic douloureux) is a disorder of function of the sensory division of the fifth cranial nerve characterized by paroxysmal attacks of pain in the distribution of one of its branches. Trigeminal neuralgia is essentially a disease of middle life, although it has also been reported in children under the age of 10 years. The pain of trigeminal neuralgia is of very short duration, is severe, and usually occurs in rapid bursts over a period of several minutes or longer.

REFERENCES

Bille, B.   Migraine in school-children. *Acta Paediat.* Suppl. 136, 1962.

Classification of headache.   Ad hoc committee on classification of headache, National Institute of Neurological Diseases and Blindness. *J.A.M.A.* 179:717, 1962.

Friedman, A. P., et al.   Ophthalmoplegic migraine. *Trans. Amer. Neurol. Ass.* 86:169, 1961.

Hinrichs, W. L., and Keith, H. M.   Migraine in childhood: Follow-up report. *Mayo Clin. Proc.* 40:593, 1965.

Van Pelt, W., and Andermann, F.   On early onset of ophthalmoplegic migraine. *Amer. J. Dis. Child.* 107:628, 1964.

Wolff, H. G.   *Headache and Other Head Pain.* New York: Oxford University Press, 1963.

13

Abdominal Pain of Central Nervous System Origin

A NUMBER of disorders affecting the central and peripheral nervous system or related structures may cause abdominal pain. It is important that the clinician be aware that some diseases of the central or peripheral nervous system may initially and sometimes for a prolonged period of time cause abdominal pain before localizing or other diagnostic signs or symptoms appear.

TUMORS OF THE SPINAL CORD

Not infrequently the presenting complaint of a patient with a spinal cord tumor is recurrent abdominal pain. In some series of intraspinal neoplasms up to 10 percent of patients have undergone negative exploratory laparotomies. For this reason it is recommended that examination of the CSF and x-rays of the entire spine be done in any child with recurrent episodes of abdominal pain of unknown etiology. Intraspinal neoplasms in children are as a general rule slowly growing tumors. Elevated protein level in the CSF is found in the great majority of cases.

ACUTE INTERMITTENT PORPHYRIA

Acute intermittent porphyria classically has been associated with the triad of convulsions, abdominal pain, and psychosis. Even though this is an inborn error of metabolism and is present since birth, symptoms do not appear until adolescence or early adulthood. The diagnosis of acute intermittent porphyria can be confirmed by the demonstration of elevated porphyrin precursors during an attack (porphobilinogen and delta-aminolevulinic acid) in the urine or increased porphobilinogen during remissions.

HERPES ZOSTER

Herpes zoster is a vesiculobullous skin eruption due to involvement of the sensory ganglia. Herpes zoster in children is usually a self-limited and benign disease. Complications are rare. Postherpetic neuralgia does not occur in children. A mild meningeal reaction may occur in some cases. If the infection involves the lower thoracic (T_{8-12}) or the first lumbar ganglia, abdominal pain may be the presenting complaint (Fig. 13-1). With the appearance, one or two weeks after the onset of pain, of the typical vesiculobullous lesions which follow a dermatome distribution, the diagnosis becomes obvious. Treatment of herpes zoster in children is limited to the care of skin lesions. Rarely, there may be involvement of the facial or trigeminal nerves. Encephalomyelitis secondary to herpes zoster, a not-uncommon complication in adults, is extremely rare in children.

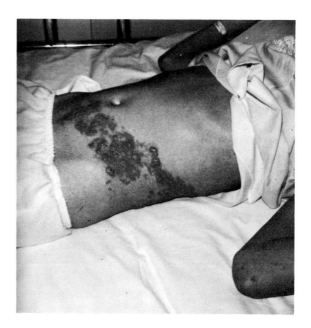

Fig. 13-1. Herpes zoster in 14-year-old girl involving lower thoracic dermatomes. Abdominal pain preceded the appearance of the typical cutaneous lesions by one week.

LEAD POISONING

Abdominal colic associated with nausea, vomiting, and constipation or bloody diarrhea is seen in adults with chronic lead poisoning but is rarely if ever a feature of plumbism in children.

ABDOMINAL EPILEPSY (EPILEPTIC EQUIVALENT)

Recurrent episodes of severe abdominal pain with or without nausea or vomiting, or vasomotor or other autonomic disturbances, may occur as the result of epileptogenic cerebral discharges. A diagnosis of abdominal epilepsy is one of elimination and can be made only after ruling out intestinal or other causes of recurrent abdominal pain. Helpful features in the diagnosis are a family history of epilepsy, the sudden onset and termination of the attacks, the presence of electroencephalographic abnormalities, and the improvement or complete cessation of attacks following anticonvulsant therapy.

INTERVERTEBRAL DISC INFECTION

Infection of an intervertebral disc is secondary to bacterial seeding from a focus elsewhere in the body. The diagnosis of intervertebral disc infection is a difficult one to make in the early stages of the disease. The original infection has usually subsided by the time symptoms referable to the spine become apparent. Initial symptoms are low-grade fever, malaise, localized back and abdominal pain, and reflex spasms of the paraspinal muscles. The back pain is aggravated by flexion of the thoracolumbar spine, flexion of the neck, or extension of the legs and hips. The patient with an intervertebral disc infection prefers to lie quietly on his back and if too young to complain will cry when the parent or physician attempts to disturb this position of comfort. Children with intervertebral disc infection often have pain in the lower abdominal quadrants or flanks. The sedimentation rate is usually elevated and a moderate leukocytosis may or may not be present.

Owing to the marked stiffness of the back a diagnosis of meningitis is frequently suspected early in the course of the disease, and a lumbar puncture is performed. Following the normal results of the cerebrospinal fluid examination a diagnosis of osteomyelitis is usually entertained and the patient treated with antibiotics and bedrest. Because of this presumptive diagnosis, roentgenographic examinations of the spine are in most cases performed at frequent intervals. One or two

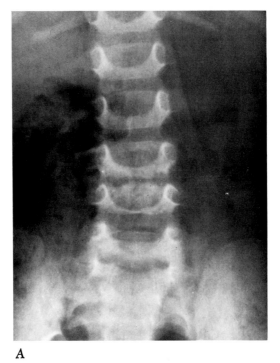

A

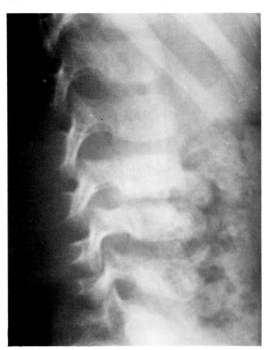

B

weeks after the onset of symptoms narrowing of the affected intervertebral space can be demonstrated and the true nature of the process becomes apparent (Fig. 13-2). In addition to narrowing of the involved intervertebral space there may be erosion of the adjacent vertebral endplates. Eventually bridging of the disc space by new bone formation occurs.

The treatment of intervertebral disc infection consists of prolonged immobilization of the spine by bedrest with or without a cast or corset. Treatment with antibiotics does not seem to influence the natural course of the disease.

REFERENCES

Lascari, A. D., et al.   Intervertebral disk infection in children. *J. Pediat.* 70:751, 1967.

Milone, F. P., et al.   Infections of the intervertebral disk in children. *J.A.M.A.* 181:1092, 1962.

Winkelmann, R. K., and Perry, H. O.   Herpes zoster in children. *J.A.M.A.* 171:876, 1959.

Fig. 13-2.   Intervertebral disc infection in a 5-year-old boy. Anteroposterior (A) and lateral (B) views of the lumbar spine show narrowing of the intervertebral space between L_3 and L_4. Onset of symptoms one month prior to evaluation with stiffness of the back, pain in the lower abdominal quadrants, and intermittent low-grade fever.

14
Skin Abnormalities and the Central Nervous System (Neurocutaneous Syndromes)

IT HAS BEEN SAID that the skin is an external mirror of the nervous system. This is not surprising since both skin and nervous system originate from the same germinal layer. There are few developmental anomalies of the central nervous system not associated with some sort of skin abnormality. Van der Hoeve (1920) found in a patient with tuberous sclerosis associated tumors of the optic disc and the retina which he called *phakomas*. The same author proposed to include both tuberous sclerosis and neurofibromatosis under the name *phakomatoses*. Subsequently this term was used to describe four syndromes having in common peripheral lesions and central nervous system manifestations (tuberous sclerosis, neurofibromatosis, Sturge-Weber syndrome and von Hippel-Lindau disease). In recent years a large number of new clinical entities or syndromes have been reported and added to the original list. It would seem that the alternative term *neurocutaneous syndrome* is probably much more appropriate and logical, since only patients with tuberous sclerosis, one of the four original diseases included under the category of phakomatoses, have retinal tumors or phakomas.

NEUROFIBROMATOSIS
(VON RECKLINGHAUSEN'S DISEASE)

Neurofibromatosis is the most common neurocutaneous syndrome with an incidence of 1 in 3000 births. This condition is characterized by lesions of the skin and subcutaneous tissues (café-au-lait spots and subcutaneous lymphangiomas, hemangiomas, and lipomas) and by multiple fibromas of the peripheral nerves, which may range in number from a few to several hundred. Neurofibromatosis is a familial disease transmitted as an autosomal dominant trait. Males are affected twice as often as females. The cutaneous manifestations are commonly present since childhood; however, they may be easily overlooked if a careful examination of the entire body surface is not performed. It is generally accepted that five or more café-au-lait spots should be considered a sign of neurofibrosis until proved otherwise (Fig. 14-1). It is not uncommon, on the other hand, to find patients with only one or two large café-au-lait spots who subsequently develop other typical signs of the disease.

Involvement of the central nervous system occurs in about 50 percent of cases. Neurologic symptoms may appear at any age from the first to the sixth decade. The most common manifestations of involvement of the central nervous system are those produced by associated gliomas of the optic nerve or optic chiasma, astrocytomas, acoustic neuromas, multiple intracranial tumors, or intraspinal nerve tumors. Intraspinal tumors are multiple in about one-third of cases and occur most commonly in the cervical and lower thoracic regions, producing pain and neurologic deficit due to nerve root or spinal cord compression. Involvement of

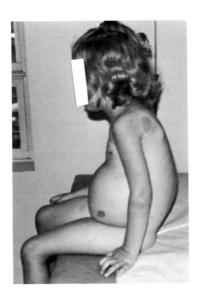

Fig. 14-1. 4-year-old girl with café-au-lait spots since early infancy as the only manifestation of neurofibromatosis. Between 2 and 4 years of age developed progressive abdominal enlargement secondary to a huge paravertebral neurofibroma.

the brachial plexus can cause severe disability due to pain, weakness, or both. Plexiform neuromas with associated overgrowth of the skin and other tissues (elephantiasis) may be the source of much pain as well as disfigurement. Peripheral nerve or intraspinal involvement is distinctly uncommon in childhood. Malignant degeneration of neurofibromas occur in less than 5 percent of cases. The widely quoted figure of 13 to 16 percent is probably much too high. Additional neurologic manifestations of neurofibromatosis are seizures and mental retardation which are present in 10 percent of patients. Skeletal abnormalities occur in a small number of cases and pheochromocytomas in 5 percent of patients with neurofibromatosis.

TUBEROUS SCLEROSIS

Tuberous sclerosis has been traditionally associated with the triad of epilepsy, mental retardation, and adenoma sebaceum. Tuberous sclerosis is inherited as a dominant trait, but it appears that there is a high mutation rate of the responsible gene. Its incidence is equal in both sexes. Approximately 60 percent of patients with tuberous sclerosis are mentally retarded and 40 percent are of average intelligence. Mentally retarded patients with tuberous sclerosis almost invariably have seizures.

Adenoma sebaceum is pathognomonic of tuberous sclerosis; it is present in over 80 percent of patients and usually develops in the first 5 years of life, more commonly from the second to the fifth birthday (Fig. 14-2). Fifty-three percent of patients with tuberous sclerosis have retinal tumors or phakomas (Fig. 14-3). Roentgenographic evidence of intracranial calcification is found in 51 percent of patients (Fig. 14-4) and areas of increased density (sclerosis) in the calvarium in 40 percent of patients with intracranial calcification. Occasionally areas of skull sclerosis are present in the absence of intracranial calcification. Pathologically, cortical tubers and many small sclerotic nodules projecting into the ventricles are seen (Fig. 14-5). These subependymal masses can be demonstrated during life by contrast studies.

Tuberous sclerosis is a multifocal disease despite the occasional finding of monosymptomatic clinical forms. Tumors of the kidneys (angioleiomyomas) occur in 80 percent of patients. Tumors of the heart and spleen and cystic tumors of the lungs are occasionally found. The most frequent signs and symptoms of tuberous sclerosis in order of frequency are: (1) seizures, (2) adenoma sebaceum, (3) mental retardation, (4) phakomas, (5) intracranial calcification, and (6) shagreen patches of the skin, usually found in the lumbar area. Other skin lesions include periungual fibromas of toes or fingers, achromic patches of the skin,

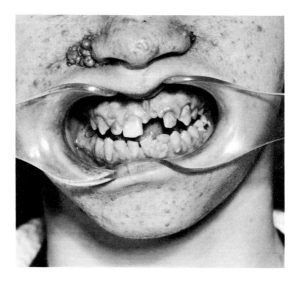

Fig. 14-2.   14-year-old boy with adenoma sebaceum and gingival fibroma.
(From J. C. Lagos and M. R. Gomez, *Mayo Clin. Proc.* 42:26, 1967)

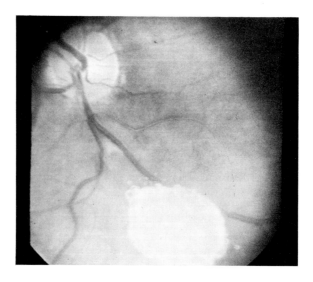

Fig. 14-3.   Retinal phakoma in patient with tuberous sclerosis. These glial
tumors are more often located in the periphery of the optic discs. (From
J. C. Lagos and M. R. Gomez, *Mayo Clin. Proc.* 42:26, 1967)

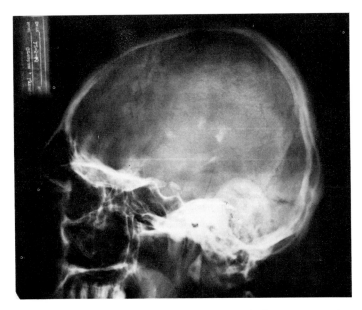

Fig. 14-4. Lateral view showing intracerebral calcification in patient with tuberous sclerosis. With few exceptions, intracranial calcification in tuberous sclerosis is confined to the central regions of the brain in and around the basal ganglia, as in this patient.

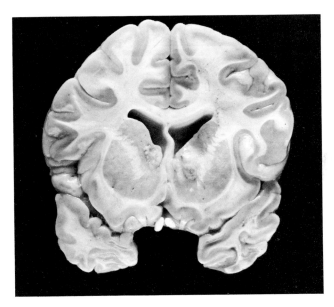

Fig. 14-5. Cortical tubers and subependymal nodules projecting into the ventricles. (From J. C. Lagos and M. R. Gomez, *Mayo Clin. Proc.* 42:26, 1967)

subcutaneous nodules, areas of skin hyperpigmentation, and café-au-lait spots. The combination of massive myoclonic seizures of early infancy (infantile spasms) and achromic patches of the skin appears to be the earliest sign of tuberous sclerosis. Tuberous sclerosis is often a progressive disease. Mental deterioration may occur even in patients whose seizures are well controlled by anticonvulsant drugs.

STURGE-WEBER SYNDROME (ENCEPHALOTRIGEMINAL ANGIOMATOSIS)

Sturge-Weber syndrome, or encephalotrigeminal angiomatosis, is characterized clinically by a nevus flammeus (port-wine stain) involving the skin of the face in the distribution of the trigeminal nerve (Fig. 14-6A) and pathologically by an ipsilateral vascular anomaly involving the pia mater and the occipital or parieto-occipital regions of the brain. Occasionally the skin of the neck, anterior trunk, or arms is also involved. If the upper lid is affected, involvement of the choroid may occur. Periodic ophthalmologic examinations should be performed in these patients to detect at an early stage and prevent the development of glaucoma. Intracranial calcification occurs in the outer layers of the involved cerebral cortex and can be demonstrated by roentgenographic examination of the skull as serpiginous double contour lines which follow the folds of the gyri (Fig. 14-6B). Contralateral hemiplegia, focal or generalized seizures and mental retardation occur in a significant number of patients with Sturge-Weber syndrome.

ATAXIA-TELANGIECTASIA (LOUIS-BAR SYNDROME)

Ataxia-telangiectasia is a syndrome inherited as an autosomal recessive and characterized by progressive cerebellar ataxia, recurrent sinopulmonary infections, and telangiectasia of the bulbar conjunctiva, ears, neck, antecubital fossa, wrists, and knees (Fig. 14-7). Other cutaneous manifestations are an atrophic skin, white macules, and premature graying of hair. Mental retardation is a common associated clinical feature. Patients with ataxia-telangiectasia have an abnormal immune mechanism. This deficiency is manifested by low or absent IgA in the serum, decreased peripheral lymphoid tissue, lymphopenia, impaired skin homograft rejection, and immaturity of the thymus. Patients with ataxia-telangiectasia have a high incidence of lymphoreticular malignancies.

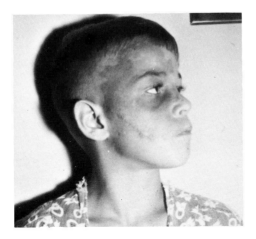

Fig. 14-6A. Port-wine stain (nevus flammeus) in 13-year-old boy with Sturge-Weber syndrome.

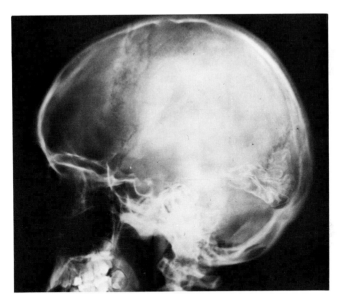

Fig. 14-6B. Lateral view showing the typical serpiginous double contour lines of calcification in the occipital region in patient with Sturge-Weber syndrome.

Fig. 14-7. Telangiectasia of the bulbar conjunctiva in 12-year-old boy with ataxia-telangiectasia.

VON HIPPEL-LINDAU DISEASE (CEREBELLORETINAL ANGIOMATOSIS)

Von Hippel, in 1904, described retinal angiomatosis. In 1926 Lindau established the relationship between angiomas of the retina and cerebellum. Von Hippel-Lindau disease, or cerebelloretinal angiomatosis, is a disorder transmittted as an autosomal dominant trait. The retinal changes begin as a benign asymptomatic nest of angiomatous tissue and may involve one or both eyes. As the retinal lesion grows it becomes round, elevated, and whitish-red (Fig. 14-8). Characteristically, the arteriole and vein that feed and drain the tumor enlarge. The retinal lesions are usually asymptomatic during childhood. In adulthood

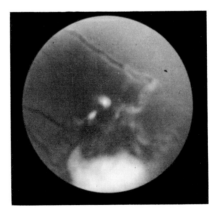

Fig. 14-8. Angiomatous malformation of the retina in patient with von Hippel-Lindau disease. (Courtesy of Dr. James Wise)

they may be a cause of retinal detachment, retinal hemorrhages, glaucoma, and loss of vision.

The cerebellar angiomas, as any other posterior fossa tumors, may produce focal signs of cerebellar dysfunction with or without signs and symptoms of increased intracranial pressure. Variations in pressure due to hemorrhages or spontaneous changes in pressure within the cystic mass can produce a fluctuant clinical course. Tumors of the kidney and pancreas are common associated findings. Histologically, the tumors of the kidney resemble hypernephromas but are usually benign. Polycythemia secondary to the production of erythropoietin by the cerebellar lesion is a common laboratory finding. The cerebellar tumor can usually be removed in toto and a complete cure accomplished. The diagosis of von Hippel-Lindau disease is made on the basis of the typical retinal legions, signs of cerebellar dysfunction, and a positive family history.

WYBURN-MASON SYNDROME

Angiomas of the retina may also occur in association with angiomas of the brain stem (Wyburn-Mason syndrome) or the cervical or lumbosacral enlargement of the spinal cord. A syringomyelic cavity is often encountered at the same level of the lesion, giving rise to the usual signs of syringomyelia (dissociated sensory loss and muscular atrophy).

WAARDENBURG SYNDROME

Waardenburg syndrome is a dominantly inherited disorder clinically manifested by a white forelock, lateral displacement of the medial canthi, bushy eyebrows, premature graying of the eyebrows and eyelashes, congenital sensory hearing loss, and heterochromia iridis.

INCONTINENTIA PIGMENTI
(BLOCH-SULZBERGER SYNDROME)

Incontinentia pigmenti is a hereditary disorder characterized by bizarre cutaneous lesions in the form of pigmented macules (flecks, whorls, streaks, flowery or spidery patterns) and a number of other developmental abnormalities (Fig. 14-9). Females are more frequently affected than males. The disease begins shortly after birth. Initially inflammatory lesions in the form of vesicles and bullae appear in lines or patches. These early cutaneous lesions may wax and wane over a period of weeks or months, but eventually become pigmented, pro-

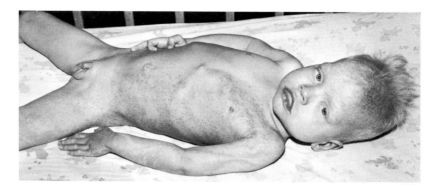

Fig. 14-9.   3-year-old severely retarded boy with typical widespread skin lesions of incontinentia pigmenti.

ducing the typical macules. Other cutaneous lesions are nail deformities and alopecia. Neurologic manifestations include psychomotor retardation, seizures, microcephaly, atonic diplegia, and hemiparesis. Other developmental anomalies are malformed teeth, absent retinal pigment, supernumerary ears, congenital heart disease, and glaucoma.

ACANTHOSIS NIGRICANS

The infantile form of acanthosis nigricans is characterized by hyperpigmentation of the skin, papillary hypertrophy, and verrucous lesions (Fig. 14-10). The hyperpigmentation of the skin primarily involves the axillae, neck, and external genitalia, although it may spread widely. Mental subnormality is a frequent associated clinical finding. Seizures occur with higher frequency than in the general population.

HARTNUP DISEASE

Hartnup disease is an inborn error of tryptophan metabolism characterized by recurrent episodes of cerebellar ataxia and a pellegra-like rash on the exposed parts of the body.

SJÖGREN-LARSSON SYNDROME

Sjögren-Larsson syndrome consists of congenital ichthyosis, spastic diplegia, and severe mental retardation.

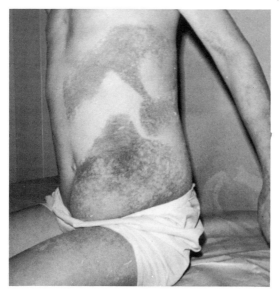

Fig. 14-10. Extensive cutaneous lesions of acanthosis nigricans in 8-year-old boy with severe psychomotor retardation.

NEVOID-BASAL-CELL CARCINOMA SYNDROME

This is an inherited disorder transmitted as a dominant trait and characterized by generalized basal-cell carcinomas and mild to moderate mental retardation which is present in about 25 percent of cases (Fig. 14-11). Other clinical features include congenital hydrocephalus, cataracts, premature calcification of falx cerebri and the dura mater, and an abnormal size or shape of the sella turcica. Less frequent abnormalities are dental cysts, prognathism, frontal bossing, and vertebral and rib anomalies.

XERODERMA PIGMENTOSUM

Xeroderma pigmentosum is a recessively inherited disorder with onset in infancy and childhood. Cutaneous lesions evolve from erythematous and hyperpigmented lesions to atrophy of the skin, telangiectasis, and eventually carcinomatous degeneration. There are atrophic areas of skin, verrucosities, ulcerations, and scars. Neurologic manifestations, which are present in about 15 to 20 percent of patients, include mental retardation, seizures, deafness, spastic paralysis, and speech disturbances.

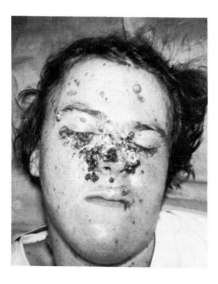

Fig. 14-11. 16-year-old girl with multiple nevoid-basal-cell carcinomas. (Courtesy of Dr. R. L. Olson)

MISCELLANEOUS DISORDERS

CLINICAL ENTITIES	MAJOR CLINICAL FEATURES
Feuerstein-Mims syndrome	Linear nevus sebaceus, seizures, and mental retardation
Hallerman-Streiff syndrome	Dwarfism, craniofacial dysplasia, mental retardation, microphthalmia, congenital cataracts, hypotrichosis and localized areas of alopecia, and atrophic skin
Neurodegenerative disease with monilethrix	Severe mental retardation, seizures, and coarse, kinky, sparse scalp hair

REFERENCES

Boder, E., and Sedgwick, R. P.   Ataxia-telangiectasia: A review of 101 cases. *Little Club Clinics on Developmental Medicine* 8:110, 1963.

Canale, D., et al.   Neurologic manifestations of von Recklinghausen's disease of the nervous system. *Confin. Neurol.* 24:359, 1964.

Carney, R. G.   Incontinentia pigmenti. *Arch. Dermat.* 64:126, 1951.

Chao, D. H.   Congenital neurocutaneous syndromes in childhood: I. Neurofibromatosis. II. Tuberous sclerosis. III. Sturge-Weber disease. *J. Pediat.* 55:189, 447, 635, 1959.

Christoferson, L. A., et al.   Von Hippel-Lindau's disease. *J.A.M.A.* 178:280, 1961.

Eisen, A. H., et al. Immunologic deficiency in ataxia telangiectasia. *New Eng. J. Med.* 272:18, 1965.

Falkinburg, L. W., et al.   Sturge-Weber-Dimitri disease. *Pediatrics* 22:319, 1958.

Feuerstein, R. C., and Mims, L. C.   Linear nevus sebaceus of face with convulsions and mental retardation. *Amer. J. Dis. Child.* 104:675, 1962.

Gorlin, R. J., et al.   Multiple basal-cell nevi syndrome. *Cancer* 18:89, 1965.

Jackson, R., and Nigam, S.   Incontinentia pigmenti: A report of three cases in one family. *Pediatrics* 30:433, 1962.

Lagos, J. C., et al.   Tuberous sclerosis: Neuroroentgenologic observations. *Amer. J. Roentgen.* 104:171, 1968.

Lagos, J. C., and Gomez, M. R.   Tuberous sclerosis: Reappraisal of a clinical entity. *Mayo Clin. Proc.* 42:26, 1967.

Reed, W. B.   Xeroderma pigmentosum with neurologic complications. *Arch. Dermat.* 91:224, 1965.

Rugel, S. J., and Keates, E. U.   Waardenburg's syndrome in six generations of one family. *Amer. J. Dis. Child.* 109:579, 1965.

Warin, R. P., and Wolske, M. M.   Juvenile acanthosis nigricans in twins with spastic paraparesis. *Proc. Roy. Soc. Med.* 56:303, 1963.

15
Nonprogressive Psychomotor Retardation

PSYCHOMOTOR RETARDATION is probably the most common neurologic disorder affecting man. Mental retardation not only is a medical problem but also carries important social and economic implications. The rapid advances in technology made by civilized countries in the past 50 years has contributed, to a great extent, to enlarging the gap between individuals with different intellectual endowments. A significant percentage of patients with mental subnormality are the product of complicated pregnancies or difficult deliveries. This is one general area in which a slow but progressive decline in morbidity should be expected in future years. Another large group of patients with severe psychomotor retardation are the product of known or unknown inherited disorders, most of them transmitted as an autosomal recessive character. The treatment of these disorders, including those in which a biochemical abnormality has been defined, remains highly unsatisfactory. From a didactic and diagnostic standpoint psychomotor retardation can be classified in two broad categories according to whether the responsible cerebral defect is static or progressive.

Many cases of nonprogressive psychomotor retardation are due to hereditary disorders or developmental defects of the central nervous system or are secondary to environmental factors operating upon the fetus during its early development, the period of transition to extrauterine life, or the early years of development. The list on page 243 includes a number of conditions that can be diagnosed by simple inspection and may be associated with nonprogressive mental retardation. The frequency and severity of mental retardation vary with different entities. In some of them, such as familiar microcephaly, megalencephaly, congenital cytomegalic inclusion disease, Marinesco-Sjögren syndrome, and most of the chromosomal aberrations, mental retardation is the rule and it is usually of a severe degree. In others, such as achondroplasia, craniosynostosis, Pierre Robin syndrome, and cleido-cranial dysostosis, mental retardation is not a constant feature and when present is often mild or moderate.

Children with nonprogressive psychomotor retardation far outnumber those with progressive retardation. The great majority of clinical entities included in the listing (p. 243) have distinctive features on the basis of which the clinician can make a diagnosis. Yet, with few exceptions, such as hydrocephalus and mongolism, the rest are all relatively uncommon disorders. It has been estimated that in about 40 percent of mentally retarded children an etiologic diagnosis cannot be made on clinical grounds and at autopsy no clear-cut cerebral pathology can be demonstrated. These are usually children with an IQ between 50 and 80 (educable) who do not exhibit gross neurologic defects. Some workers have postulated that the retardation in many of these children is secondary to sociocultural deprivation or lack of education, whereas others feel that multiple factors are involved, many of them of congenital origin. In the remaining 60 percent of mentally retarded children the cause is maldevelopment of the central nervous system in approximately 45 percent; some kind of environmental injury to the brain occurring during intrauterine life, the perinatal period, or later in life in 20 percent; and inborn errors of metabolism or chromosomal defects in 35 percent. Patients of the latter group are as a rule severely handicapped both from a mental (IQ below 50) and motor standpoint and frequently exhibit gross neurologic abnormalities.

A diagnosis of mental retardation is sometimes difficult to make during the first six months of life. Unless gross developmental anomalies are present, mental retardation is not suspected until the infant fails to reach certain well-known milestones of motor development such as sitting without support, pulling up to stand, or walking. Milestones of motor and mental development are usually equally impaired in these patients. Motor milestones, however, have a greater range of normal variation than mental milestones. It is not uncommon, for example, to see a child of normal intelligence who does not walk until the age of 18 months; it is rare, on the other hand, to see a child with normal intelligence who does not smile before the age of 2 months, one who in the absence of physical handicap does not adopt a position of welcome anticipation to the mother's presence by the age of 4 months, or an infant older than 6 months who does not cry when left alone with the examiner. By the same token, the physician should be alerted to the possibility of mental retardation or hearing deficit if a child does not say his first meaningful word by 18 months of age.

If a young child has failed to reach the milestones of motor development at the expected ages but his mental development appears to be normal, the possibility of a lesion of the lower motor neuron, such as a congenital myopathy, congenital muscular dystrophy, spinal muscular

NONPROGRESSIVE PSYCHOMOTOR RETARDATION

HEREDITARY AND DEVELOPMENTAL ANOMALIES

Familial microcephaly
Absent corpus callosum
Hydrocephalus
Hydranencephaly
Megalencephaly
Cerebral gigantism
Familial dysautonomia (Riley-Day syndrome)
Sturge-Weber syndrome
Ataxia-telangiectasia
Neurofibromatosis
Waardenburg syndrome
Nevoid-basal-cell carcinoma syndrome
Incontinentia pigmenti
Feuerstein-Mims syndrome
Sjögren-Larsson syndrome
Achondroplasia
Chondroectodermal dysphasia (Ellis-van Creveld syndrome)
Arachnodactyly (Marfan's syndrome)
Familial metaphyseal dysplasia (Pyle's disease)
Rubinstein-Taybi syndrome
Treacher Collins syndrome
Pierre Robin syndrome
Crouzon's disease (craniofacial dysostosis)
Apert's disease (acrocephalosyndactyly)
Craniosynostosis
Cleidocranial dysostosis
Osteogenesis imperfecta
Osteopetrosis
Cyclopia
Cebocephaly
Hallerman-Streiff syndrome
Möbius syndrome
Laurence-Moon-Biedl syndrome
Leprechaunism
Marinesco-Sjögren syndrome
Cerebrohepatorenal syndrome
Oculocerebrorenal syndrome (Lowe's syndrome)
Oral-facial-digital syndrome
Otopalatodigital syndrome
Smith-Lemli-Opitz syndrome
Prader-Willi syndrome
Oculo-auriculovertebral dysplasia
Progeria (Hutchinson-Gilford syndrome)
Neurodegenerative disease with monilethrix
Myotonic dystrophy
Cornelia de Lange syndrome

CHROMOSOMAL ABNORMALITIES

Trisomy 13–15
Trisomy 18
Trisomy 21 (mongolism)
Ring chromosome 18
Deletion 18
Cri-du-chat syndrome
Turner's syndrome
Klinefelter's syndrome

INFECTIONS OF THE CENTRAL NERVOUS SYSTEM

Prenatal
Cytomegalic inclusion body disease
Toxoplasmosis
Syphilis
Rubella embryopathy
Postnatal
Bacterial meningitis
Tuberculous meningitis
Encephalitis
Postpertussis encephalopathy
Postinfectious encephalomyelitis

METABOLIC AND TOXIC DISORDERS AND CEREBRAL ANOXIA

Kernicterus (Bilirubin encephalopathy)
Cretinism
Hypoglycemic encephalopathy
Lead poisoning
Carbon monoxide poisoning
Infantile hypercalcemia
Severe cerebral anoxia of any cause

TRAUMA AND CEREBROVASCULAR ACCIDENTS

Severe head trauma
Subdural hematoma
Intracerebral hemorrhage
Acute infantile hemiplegia

atrophy, or myasthenia gravis should be entertained and ruled out by appropriate studies (electromyogram, Tensilon test, serum enzyme determinations, and muscle biopsy). Severe hypotonia or muscle weakness of cerebral origin is almost invariably associated with other manifestations of central nervous system dysfunction. An important point in the differential diagnosis is the absence or presence of muscle stretch reflexes. Infants with delayed motor development due to diseases of the lower motor neuron have markedly decreased or absent muscle stretch reflexes in contrast to those with weakness of cerebral origin, in whom they are almost always present.

Delayed speech development, a common presenting complaint in children with suspected mental retardation, may be due to hearing loss, to specific motor problems affecting the vocal apparatus, to mental retardation, congenital aphasia, or infantile autism. Hearing loss need not amount to total deafness to be a cause of speech retardation. A child with a high-frequency hearing loss, for example, will be unable to reproduce speech sounds even if he is able to respond to sounds of low frequency such as those produced by the usual tuning fork (156 cycles per second), the ringing of a bell, or the noise produced by the dropping of a heavy object on the floor. Sounds of high frequency, such as whistling or the crackling of a piece of paper presented to the child from out of his field of vision, are much more reliable tests than the traditional office tests of hearing acuity. Mental retardation, unless of a severe degree, is seldom a cause of complete mutism. Most mentally retarded children learn single words by 2 to 3 years of age and are able to make two- or three-word sentences by 5 years. Speech in many of these children is used in a demanding or repetitious and meaningless way rather than as a means of communication. Children of average achievement in nonverbal areas may have delayed speech development as the result of dysarthria or incoordination of the muscles of phonation. This is often seen in patients with the spastic variety of cerebral palsy; other motor problems which may cause delayed speech development are dyspraxia or ataxia of the oropharyngeal muscles. Motor problems affecting the vocal apparatus may occur as an isolated phenomenon in patients with no other apparent neurologic abnormalities.

The child with infantile autism has a normal motor development but is unable from the very beginning of life to relate to people and appears to live in a world of his own. Despite an intelligent appearance of the child, communication by facial expression, gesture, and other forms of language is severely restricted. As an infant he does not develop a smile by 2 months of age and fails to assume the posture of welcome anticipation to the approach of his mother that usually develops by 4 months. As the child grows older he is aloof and exhibits an obsessive need for preservation of sameness. Later on, he has a vacant stare, ignores his parents and other children, and seems preoccupied with inanimate objects.

Children with congenital aphasia are unable to understand and to use language in the absence of hearing loss, motor deficit, intellectual impairment, or emotional disturbances. The language deficit in children with congenital aphasia may be chiefly receptive or expressive. In most cases, however, a mixed deficit is present. The aphasic child can be differentiated from the deaf child by his ability to hear and respond to nonlanguage sounds.

The investigation of children in whom an etiologic diagnosis of mental retardation cannot be made on the basis of well-defined physical abnormalities should include a detailed history of the pregnancy (infection, trauma, bleeding, exposure to radiation), labor and delivery, family history, and a complete general and neurologic examination. Laboratory tests, seldom rewarding, include skull x-rays, determination of PBI and bone age (for cretinism), urinary screening tests for inborn errors of metabolism, and in selected cases 24-hour determination of urinary amino-acids and chromosome analysis. The electroencephalogram may be normal or may show nonspecific abnormalities; it is seldom of any diagnostic value. In most instances the differentiation between nonprogressive and progressive psychomotor retardation is easy. The child with nonprogressive retardation fails to reach the milestones of motor and social development at the expected age but makes progress at a slow but steady pace. On the other hand, the child with progressive mental retardation usually develops normally up to a certain age and then exhibits motor or mental deterioration or both. He loses already acquired motor or mental abilities and more often than not develops additional neurologic signs and symptoms. Progressive loss of already acquired motor abilities in the absence of deterioration of social development almost always indicates a lesion of the neuromuscular apparatus.

Parents of mentally retarded children are often poorly informed or have serious misconceptions regarding the severity of the problem. If the physician is asked or wishes to give an opinion as to the degree of retardation, this estimate should be made in terms of developmental quotient and not in months or years. Time and again we see parents who are genuinely convinced that their child is 6 or 12 months behind in his psychomotor development when in fact he may have a developmental quotient of 50 or less. For example, a 12-month-old infant who is functioning at a 3- or 6-month level of psychomotor development is not 9 or 6 months "behind" as compared to a normal 12-month-old infant, but three-fourths or one-half of his life behind, so that when he reaches the age of 12 years chances are that his mental age will be 3 or 6 years and not 11 years and 3 months or 11½ years.

REFERENCES

Brown, J. R., et al.   Disorders of communication. *Pediat. Clin. N. Amer.*
    14:725, 1967.
Gellis, S. S., and Feingold, M.   *Atlas of Mental Retardation Syndromes.*
    U. S. Department of Health, Education and Welfare, 1968.
Grossman, H. J. (Ed.).   Mental retardation. *Pediat. Clin. N. Amer.* 15:819,
    1968.
Smith, D. W.   *Recognizable Patterns of Human Malformation: Genetic,
    Embryologic and Clinical Aspects.* Philadelphia: Saunders, 1970.

16
Progressive Psychomotor Retardation

THE NUMBER of known disorders causing progressive psychomotor retardation has increased considerably during the past decade. This increase has been due almost exclusively to the discovery of new inborn errors of metabolism, especially those involving amino acids. In general, disorders which may cause progressive psychomotor retardation are classified according to the pathologic characteristics of the degenerative process (e.g., leukodystrophies) or to etiology when known, for example, inborn errors of amino acid or carbohydrate metabolism, and some of the lipidoses. In keeping with the practical diagnostic approach of classification used throughout this book, progressive psychomotor retardation will be discussed according to usual age of onset and divided into three main groups: starting shortly after birth, during the first 2 years of life, and after the age of 2. Needless to say, some overlapping is unavoidable with any classification based on age alone. Nevertheless, until all the progressive diseases affecting the central nervous system of children can be defined in biochemical or other more precise terms, we believe that this is a useful guide in the differential diagnosis.

Progressive psychomotor retardation beginning soon after birth is almost always secondary to inborn errors of amino acid or carbohydrate metabolism. Where the mode of inheritance is known, these diseases are transmitted as autosomal recessive traits. These conditions cannot be differentiated on clinical grounds alone. The clinical picture is uniformly one of severe progressive psychomotor retardation with few, if any, distinctive features on which the clinician can base an educated diagnostic guess. The only way to arrive at a diagnosis in most of these disorders is by routine screening tests and by quantitative determination of metabolites in body fluids (blood, urine, or cerebrospinal fluid). The lack of distinguishing or pathognomonic clinical features does not need to disturb the clinician inasmuch as most case reports, particularly those involving inborn errors of amino-acid metabolism, have been fortuitous and unexpected findings during mass screening of patients with progressive mental retardation of unknown etiology.

Progressive psychomotor retardation with onset between 3 months and 2 years includes some degenerative diseases of the central nervous system, but for the most part conditions with an underlying biochemical defect that results in the accumulation in the central nervous system of an abnormal or normal cerebral compound (lipidoses) or conditions characterized by degeneration of the white and gray matter as a consequence of a dystrophic process (leukodystrophies) which in all likelihood is also due to a biochemical abnormality that produces diffuse demyelination, gliosis, and neuronal degeneration.

Progressive psychomotor deterioration with onset after the age of 2 years comprises a more heterogenous group of conditions. They are either examples of well-defined biochemical abnormalities such as Wilson's disease; are the result of a destructive process by exogenous or endogenous factors exerting their deleterious effects on an already well-formed myelin (e.g., Schilder's disease); they are secondary to direct invasion of the central nervous system by a virus (e.g., subacute sclerosing panencephalitis) or to an immune reaction to it; or are due to an inherited degenerative process of the central nervous system of unknown etiology (e.g., Huntington's chorea).

PROGRESSIVE PSYCHOMOTOR RETARDATION STARTING SHORTLY AFTER BIRTH

Phenylketonuria

Phenylketonuria (PKU) is the prototype of diseases caused by absence or decreased activity of a single enzyme. Phenylketonuria was first described by Fölling in 1934. The common denominator in the patients reported by Fölling was mental deficiency and the excretion of phenylpyruvic acid in the urine. The basic defect in PKU is an absence or decreased activity of the liver enzyme phenylalanine hydroxylase, which converts phenylalanine to tyrosine, with resulting accumulation of phenylalanine in the blood. PKU is a disorder inherited as an autosomal recessive trait. Major clinical features are mental subnormality, hyperkinesis, tremors, microcephaly, a dirty-blond hair and blue eyes, a peculiar muddy odor, eczema, hyperactive reflexes, major motor and massive myoclonic seizures of early infancy, and EEG abnormalities. Most individuals with PKU are mentally subnormal, but a few with normal intelligence have been described. In general, mental retardation is more pronounced than motor retardation.

Pathologic examination of the brain of patients with PKU reveals deficient myelin formation and decreased content of brain cerebrosides and cholesterol. A diagnosis of PKU may be suspected by the finding of a positive ferric chloride or Phenistix test in the urine and confirmed by the presence of high levels of serum phenylalanine. Urinary screening tests (ferric chloride and Phenistix) give a relatively high degree of false negative results and therefore blood tests are recommended. Serum phenylalanine levels above 15 mg./100 ml. with tyrosine levels less than 5 mg./100 ml. are generally indicative of phenylketonuria. Serum phenylalanine levels between 5 and 15 mg./100 ml. with tyrosine levels of less than 5 mg./100 ml. may represent an atypical form of phenylketonuria or delayed development of phenylalanine hydroxylase. Elevated levels of both phenylalanine (5 to 15 mg./100 ml.) and tyrosine (above 5 mg./100 ml.) may be seen in premature infants, in babies of phenylketonuric mothers, in tyrosinosis and galactosemia, and in congenital hepatic or renal dysfunction.

The exact mechanism by which high blood levels of phenylalanine leads to mental deterioration is unknown. Mental deterioration can be prevented to a large extent if a diet low in phenylalanine is instituted early in life before irreversible damage to the maturing central nervous system has occurred. During treatment serum phenylalanine levels should be maintained between 3–7 mg./100 ml. The maintenance of these levels necessitates constant dietary supervision and periodic determinations of serum levels of phenylalanine as well as adjustments in the diet as the child grows older. If suboptimal levels of this essential amino acid are provided, marked and serious side effects may occur such as growth arrest, refractory anemia, hypoglycemia, and unexpected death. Protein malnutrition in early life may produce irreversible damage to the developing brain. It is possible that a diet markedly deficient in phenylalanine, an essential amino acid, may be an additional cause of mental deterioration in some patients with PKU.

Pyridoxine Dependency

Pyridoxine dependency becomes manifest in the neonatal period by major motor seizures which are refractory to conventional anticonvulsant therapy but which cease promptly after the IM or IV administration of pyridoxine. Pyridoxine dependency is a preventable cause of progressive severe brain damage. In the untreated patient death ensues usually within a few weeks after birth. The exact mechanism by which some children require more vitamin B_6 to carry on adequately some of their metabolic processes remains unknown. Patients with pyridoxine dependency need approximately 5 to 10 times the average daily requirement.

Maple Syrup Urine Disease (Branched-Chain Keto-Aciduria)

Maple syrup urine disease is due to an inborn error of the metabolism of the branched-chain amino acids valine, leucine, and isoleucine, characterized biochemically by a deficiency in the oxidative decarboxylation of the respective alpha-keto-acids leading to an accumulation of both the keto-acids and their respective amino acids in the blood and urine. Maple syrup urine disease becomes manifest early in infancy by intractable major motor seizures and signs and symptoms of rapid cerebral deterioration. There is anorexia, vomiting, and increasing hypertonicity. The urine and wet diapers of these babies have a strong maple syrup odor. Rapidly progressive cerebral damage occurs if the patient is not treated early with a diet low in valine, leucine, and isoleucine. A presumptive diagnosis can be made by the finding of a positive 2,4-dinitrophenylhydrazine test in the urine. A definite diagnosis can be made by quantitative chromatography of plasma and urine.

Hypersarcosinemia

Sarcosine is an intermediate metabolite between dimethylglycine and glycine in the 1-carbon cycle. Normal blood levels are less than 1 mg./100 ml. The biochemical defect in hypersarcosinemia is probably a deficiency or decreased activity of the enzyme sarcosine dehydrogenase. Hypersarcosinemia is clinically manifested by hypertonicity, generalized tremor, inability to swallow, and profound psychomotor retardation since early infancy. Increased levels of sarcosine are found in the blood and the brain.

Carnosinemia

Carnosinemia appears to be due to a deficiency in the activity of the enzyme carnosinase which hydrolyzes carnosine to alanine and histidine. Carnosine (beta-alanyl-histidine) levels in the urine and serum are increased. Clinically carnosinemia is manifested by generalized grand mal and myoclonic seizures from early infancy and progressive psychomotor deterioration.

Hyperlysinemia

Hyperlysinemia (increased levels of lysine in the serum and overflow renal lysinuria) is clinically characterized by convulsions in early infancy, muscle hypotonia, and severe psychomotor retardation. The cause of this inborn error of metabolism is unknown.

Hyperbeta-Alaninemia

Hyperbeta-alaninemia in association with beta-amino-aciduria and delta-aminobutyric-aciduria is an abnormal biochemical constellation clinically manifested by lethargy, somnolence, and major motor seizures starting shortly after birth. Microcephaly and severe psychomotor retardation are associated findings.

Galactosemia

Galactosemia is due to an inborn error of carbohydrate metabolism characterized biochemically by congenital absence of the enzyme galactose 1-phosphate-uridyl-transferase which is necessary to convert galactose 1-phosphate to glucose 1-phosphate. Ingested galactose (milk) is not converted into glucose and it accumulates in many body tissues. Clinical features of galactosemia includes jaundice during the newborn period, feeding difficulties, hepatosplenomegaly, hypoglycemic convulsions, and cataracts which may develop as early as two months of age. Mental deterioration is a prominent part of the clinical picture. A diagnosis of galactosemia can be suspected if reducing substances are found in the urine. Galactose gives a positive reaction with Benedict reagent in urinary concentrations exceeding 100 mg./100 ml. If the Benedict test is positive and the Clinistix (with glucose oxidase and specific for glucose) is negative, it may be assumed that the reducing substance in the urine is galactose. A definite diagnosis of galactosemia can be made by determination of the enzyme activity in erythrocytes or by paper chromatography of urine which permits demonstration of abnormal amounts of galactose not detectable by the Benedict reagent. The treatment of galactosemia consists in the administration of a galactose-free diet. If treatment is started early in infancy, marked improvement in the clinical picture may occur.

Homocystinuria

Homocystinuria, a disorder of the metabolism of the sulfur-containing amino acids, is probably, after phenylketonuria, the most common inborn error of metabolism causing mental retardation. Age of onset of mental deterioration in reported cases has varied from early infancy to as late as 4½ years of age. A few patients with normal intelligence have been described. Homocystinuria is transmitted as an autosomal recessive trait. Homocystine, an intermediate in the metabolism of methionine, is not a normal constituent of body fluids. An abnormal accumulation of this substance results as a consequence of an absence or decreased activity of the enzyme cystathionine synthetase, which combines homocysteine with serine to form cystathionine. Free homocysteine is then converted into homocystine which accumulates in tissue and body fluids.

Patients with homocystinuria bear a striking resemblance in their body configuration to those with Marfan's syndrome (tall stature and long slim limbs) as well as in the incidence of dislocated lenses, a common feature of both disorders. Additional clinical findings in patients with homocystinuria include a fine, fair, and sparse hair, blue eyes, malar flush, and livedo reticularis of the extremities, pes cavus, and genu valgum. More than 50 percent of patients have seizures. Patients with homocystinuria have a strong tendency to develop arterial and venous thrombosis of major vessels; pulmonary emboli, renal artery thrombosis, and cerebral thrombosis are common complications. The diagnosis can be suspected on clinical grounds alone or by the finding of a positive cyanidenitroprusside test in the urine. A definite diagnosis can be made by quantitative analysis of homocystine in urine, plasma, or cerebrospinal fluid. Treatment with a diet low in methionine has not been successful.

PROGRESSIVE PSYCHOMOTOR RETARDATION STARTING IN FIRST TWO YEARS

Amaurotic Family Idiocy

The amaurotic family idiocies are a group of diseases characterized by progressive psychomotor deterioration and blindness. There are five generally accepted varieties of amaurotic family idiocy: a rare congenital form (Norman-Wood); an infantile form (Tay-Sachs); a late infantile form (Bielschowsky-Jansky); a juvenile form (Batten); and an adult form (Kufs). This classification is essentially a clinical one based upon the age of onset, the ethnic background, and the ophthalmoscopic picture.

TAY-SACHS DISEASE. Tay-Sachs disease (infantile amaurotic family idiocy) is an inherited disorder of ganglioside metabolism characterized by progressive psychomotor deterioration and blindness. Tay-Sachs disease has been reported from every continent and in most ethnic groups, but about 90 percent of affected children are of Jewish heritage. The disease is transmitted as an autosomal recessive trait; penetrance seems to be nearly complete; and both sexes are equally affected. The carrier state in the Jewish population in New York City is about 1:30 compared to a carrier's rate of about 1:300 in a non-Jewish American. The disease is most common in Jews from the Lithuanian and Polish provinces of Korno and Grodo. The significant pathologic changes in Tay-Sachs disease are restricted to the central nervous system where ganglion cells are overloaded with gangliosides (100 to 300 times normal cerebral concentration). Over 90 percent of the accumulated material is a monosialoganglioside lacking the terminal molecule of galactose present in most gangliosides in normal brain; in addition, in Tay-Sachs disease there is a greatly increased amount of cerebral neutral amino glycolipids. The biochemical defect in Tay-Sachs disease appears to be a deficiency or absence of hexosaminidase A, an enzyme that participates in the breakdown of the particular ganglioside which accumulates in this disorder.

The clinical course of Tay-Sachs disease has been divided into several phases correlated with certain pathologic changes which are observed as patients with this disease survive beyond 15 months of age. During Phase 1, between 3 and 14 months of life, there is loss of already acquired motor abilities, progressive muscle weakness, hypotonia, hyperacusis (exaggerated startle response to sounds), progressive peripheral blindness, and growth retardation. A cherry-red spot in the macula is seen in 90 percent of patients (Fig. 16-1). Lipid vacuoles may be seen in lymphocytes. The pneumoencephalogram during this period shows diffuse cerebral atrophy and secondary ventricular dilatation. At autopsy the brain shows mild to moderate atrophy. During Phase 2, between 15 and 24 months, hypotonia increases in severity; there are occasional convulsive seizures and episodes of extensor rigidity; the pupils respond sluggishly to light; there is muscle atrophy; and the head enlarges. The pneumoencephalogram during this phase shows a decrease of the formerly demonstrable ventricular enlargement. At autopsy the size of the brain is normal or moderately increased. After 24 months (Phase 3), except for an occasional seizure, the child is immobile; there is marked muscle atrophy, emaciation, and increasing dementia. Physical examination may reveal hypo- or hypertonia and decreased or increased muscle stretch reflexes, lack of response to any form of visual or tactile stimuli, and progressive enlargement of the head secondary to increase in the size of the brain. The pneumoencephalogram during this phase shows a diminution in the size of the lateral ventricles.

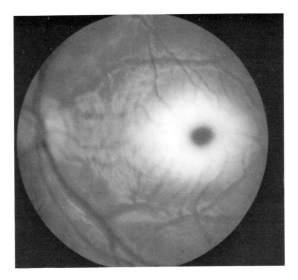

Fig. 16-1.   Cherry-red spot in macula of 8-month-old infant with Tay-Sachs disease.

An abnormal laughter is a common symptom of Tay-Sachs disease. The episodes of laughter appear at about 10 months of age, and usually precede the appearance of seizures. This pathologic laughter is felt to be a seizure phenomenon arising from subcortical structures. A definite diagnosis can be made in most patients with Tay-Sachs disease on the basis of the typical clinical picture or by rectal biopsy and the demonstration of lipid-laden neurons in myenteric plexus. Prognosis is poor, and the great majority of patients die in a decerebrate and vegetative state before the age of 5 years.

Hyperuricemia, Athetosis, and Self-mutilation

Lesch and Nyhan, in 1964, described a syndrome occurring only in males and characterized by behavioral aberrations in the form of self-mutilation, a movement disorder of the choreoathetoid variety, psychomotor retardation, and elevated uric acid levels in the blood and urine. Other neurologic signs include swallowing difficulties, spasticity, dystonic posturing, torsion spasms, and opisthotonos. The disease becomes manifest usually during the first six months of life. Uricosuric agents such as probenecid or allopurinol are of questionable value in the treatment of this disorder; they lower the serum levels of uric acid to normal levels but appear to exert little influence on the organic brain syndrome.

Subacute Necrotizing Encephalomyelitis

Subacute necrotizing encephalomyelitis is a disease of the central nervous system with onset usually under the age of 2 years and characterized pathologically by lesions in the basal ganglia and periaqueductal gray matter and clinically by progressive psychomotor deterioration. In most cases symptoms begin early in infancy and consist of feeding difficulties, vomiting, a feeble cry, progressive muscle hypotonia and weakness, normal or increased muscle stretch reflexes, and respiratory difficulties in the form of asthma-like attacks or sighing respirations. Nystagmus and peculiar jerky eye movements occur in a large percentage of patients. Initially, spasticity may be present in some patients, but hypotonia with normal muscle stretch reflexes is a more common finding. With the exception of atonic diplegia this particular combination of signs is rarely found in any other neurologic condition of early childhood. At autopsy, there are symmetrical lesions in the basal ganglia and brain stem characterized by marked vascular overgrowth, loss of oligodendroglia, demyelination, and spongy changes. The pathologic features are similar to those of Wernicke's encephalopathy of adults with the exception that in subacute necrotizing encephalomyelitis the mamillary bodies are rarely involved and hemorrhages are absent or are minimal. The lesions are usually of variable age and have a predilection for the gray matter of the brain stem around the aqueduct and the floor of the fourth ventricle. Similar histologic changes can also be seen in the medulla, cerebellum, thalamus, hypothalamus, optic nerves, optic chiasma, cerebral cortex, and white matter. The disease runs a subacute course, with death ensuing in most cases within 1 to 3 years after onset of symptoms.

Leukodystrophies

The term *leukodystrophy* was introduced by Bielschowsky and Henneberg in 1928 to designate a progressive, familial disease of the central nervous system characterized pathologically by diffuse demyelination of the cerebral white matter. The leukodystrophies are genetically determined inborn errors of metabolism in which the primary abnormality appears to be a disturbance of myelin formation. In the past a basic difference was thought to exist between the leukodystrophies and the central nervous system lipidoses, in which there is an accumulation of specific lipids in neurons. It is now recognized, however, that at least in one of the leukodystrophies, the metachromatic type, there is not only degeneration but also an accumulation of sulfatides in the white matter. While all the leukodystrophies are probably the result of genetically determined enzymatic defects, sulfatide lipidosis, or metachromatic leukodystrophy, is the only one in which a specific chemical abnormality has been clearly defined.

SULFATIDE LIPIDOSIS (METACHROMATIC LEUKODYSTROPHY). Sulfatide lipidosis is a progressive degenerative disease of the central and peripheral nervous system of early childhood. Although a rare condition, it is the most common form of leukodystrophy. Alzheimer, in 1910, reported the finding of metachromatic granules in the central nervous system of a patient with diffuse sclerosis. Austin and co-workers in 1957 first demonstrated the presence of metachromatic granules in the urine of patients with this condition. Since then a diagnosis of sulfatide lipidosis has been possible during life by the demonstration of metachromatic granules in fresh voided urine specimens or the demonstration of metachromatic material in sural nerve biopsy (Fig. 16-2). Patients with sulfatide lipidosis have decreased or absent arylsulfatase A. This can be demonstrated in the urine and provides a relatively simple diagnostic test.

There are now recognized three forms of sulfatide lipidosis—a late infantile form with onset before 30 months, a juvenile form with onset between 4 and 16 years, and an adult form with onset after age 16. Sulfatide lipidosis is a genetically determined disease transmitted in an autosomal recessive manner. A common feature in reported cases has been the relative constancy of age of onset in a single sibship. The

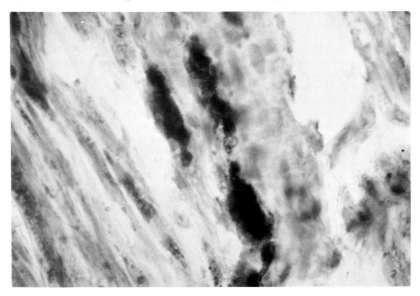

Fig. 16-2.   Sural nerve biopsy in patient with sulfatide lipidosis, showing clumps of metachromatic material.

clinical course of the infantile form is invariably characterized by a normal early psychomotor development up to the age of 12 to 18 months. The first clinical manifestations consist usually of some kind of locomotor difficulties. Initially there may be weakness and hyper- or hypotonicity of the legs, ataxia, or spastic paralysis. Muscle stretch reflexes may be decreased or increased according to the degree of involvement of the central and peripheral nervous systems. Seizure activity in a variety of forms has been noted in the majority of patients. Involvement of peripheral nerves can be documented by nerve conduction velocity studies even in patients with signs of an upper motor neuron lesion, such as spasticity and increased muscle stretch or pathologic reflexes.

Patients with sulfatide lipidosis manifest speech regression, progressive swallowing difficulties, and weakness of all extremities. Seizures occur in 50 percent and optic atrophy in about one-third of patients. Oculomotor palsies and nystagmus are also common signs. An extensor plantar response (Babinski sign) is observed in the late stages of the disease in about two-thirds of cases. Enlargement of the head is not uncommon. Examination of the cerebrospinal fluid reveals an increase in protein levels from 100 mg. to 200 mg./100 ml. from the early stages. Skull x-rays are normal. The electroencephalogram may show evidence of seizure activity or diffuse, nonspecific changes. The disease runs a subacute or chronic course with death within five months to 10 years after onset of symptoms. In the final stages of the disease patients with

Fig. 16-3. Fraternal twins 4 years of age with sulfatide lipidosis. Onset of symptoms in both patients at the age of 20 months with signs of peripheral neuropathy, followed by a partial left third cranial nerve palsy in one and nystagmus in the other. Elevated cerebrospinal fluid protein and metachromatic material in sural nerve biopsy in both patients (Fig. 16-2). The course of the disease was characterized by progressive psychomotor deterioration, spastic quadriparesis, optic atrophy, and swallowing difficulties.

sulfatide lipidosis lie in a state of decerebrate or decorticate rigidity and are totally unresponsive to visual or auditory stimuli (Fig. 16-3). At autopsy there is diffuse demyelination with loss of axis cylinders, metachromatic material irregularly distributed, and an abnormal accumulation of sulfatide in the central and peripheral nervous system. Metachromatic material as well as an abnormal storage of sulfatide can be found in the kidneys, gallbladder, and liver.

KRABBE'S LEUKODYSTROPHY. Krabbe's (globoid cell) leukodystrophy is characterized clinically by a normal psychomotor development up to the age of 4 to 6 months followed by progressive deterioration. Inheritance is as an autosomal recessive trait. Pathologically, Krabbe's leukodystrophy is characterized by demyelination of the centrum ovale, cerebellum, and brain stem. In addition, and as a distinctive pathologic feature, large multinucleated histiocytes (globoid cells) containing increased amounts of galactocerebrosides are found around precapillary vessels. In most patients hypotonia is present initially and this is followed by progressive spasticity and an extensor plantar response (Babinski sign). Brief generalized tonic seizures and an exaggerated startle response are frequent signs. There may be optic atrophy or cortical blindness. A reduced head size is noticeable in the child surviving the longest. The electroencephalogram usually shows diffuse slow waves of high voltage. Examination of the cerebrospinal fluid reveals in most cases an elevation of the protein levels. Slow nerve conduction velocity in motor fibers has been demonstrated in some patients with peripheral nerve involvement.

The metabolic defect of Krabbe's leukodystrophy appears to be a decreased activity of or absent galactocerebroside beta-galactosidase. The average duration of the disease is approximately 10 months.

PELIZAEUS-MERZBACHER LEUKODYSTROPHY (CHRONIC INFANTILE CERE-
BRAL SCLEROSIS). Pelizaeus-Merzbacher leukodystrophy is a sex-linked inherited condition with onset in the first year of life and which runs a chronic course of several years' duration. The initial symptoms in this type of leukodystrophy are nystagmus, tremor of the head, and oscillations of the eyes. This is followed by delay in psychomotor development and spastic weakness, choreoid, athetoid, or other involuntary movements, intention tremor, scanning speech, and ataxia. Muscle stretch reflexes are increased and plantar responses are extensor (Babinski sign). Optic atrophy is rarely a feature of this type of leukodystrophy. Examination of the cerebrospinal fluid shows no abnormalities.

Spongy Degeneration of the White Matter (Canavan's Disease)

Spongy degeneration of the white matter, formerly classified as a leukodystrophy, is now recognized as a separate entity. The onset of symptoms is usually between the third and ninth months of age. Its incidence is higher in infants of Jewish heritage. The clinical picture consists of initial hypotonia followed by spasticity, progressive dementia, blindness, and sometimes deafness. Moderate or severe enlargement of the head with separation of cranial sutures occurs in most cases. Except for increased pressure, examination of the cerebrospinal fluid is normal. This condition can be suspected during life on clinical grounds but a definite diagnosis made only by brain biopsy. Spongy degeneration of the white matter runs a subacute course, with death occurring within 6 to 24 months after the onset of symptoms. At autopsy the brain is large. There is an excess of subarachnoid fluid; the convolutions may be flattened and the gyri large. Histologically there is demyelination of the white matter and multiple cystic spaces in the white matter of the cerebral hemispheres and cerebellum.

Gaucher's Disease

Gaucher's disease is due to an inborn error of lipid metabolism characterized biochemically by the accumulation of glucocerebroside in the reticuloendothelial cells of spleen, liver, and bone marrow, due to a decreased activity or absence of the enzyme glucocerebrosidase. Two forms of Gaucher's disease are recognized, an infantile and an adult form. The infantile form is characterized clinically by severe neurologic deficit beginning early in infancy. There is generalized hypertonia, opisthotonos, rigidity, dysphagia, laryngeal spasms, and profound and progressive mental and physical deterioration. Splenomegaly, which occurs first, and later hepatomegaly are constant features.

The chronic form of Gaucher's disease has a more insidious onset. The most common initial sign is splenomegaly, which is followed by liver enlargement. Involvement of the central nervous system is rare in this form. A diagnosis of Gaucher's disease can be made by demonstrating typical foam cells by bone marrow examination. Prognosis is poor in the infantile form, death occurring in most patients before the age of 2 years.

Niemann-Pick Disease

Niemann-Pick disease is caused by an inborn error of lipid metabolism characterized by an abnormal accumulation of sphingomyelin in various organs. The disease occurs most commonly in Jews and is inherited as an autosomal recessive trait, although many sporadic cases have been reported. The basic defect in this condition appears to be a deficiency of sphingomyelinase, an enzyme which hydrolyzes sphingomyelin. Niemann-Pick disease may become manifest at any time from birth to the end of the first year of life. Physical and mental deterioration is accompanied by enlargement of the liver and spleen. Involvement of the central nervous system is manifested by progressive spasticity, blindness, and deafness. A cherry-red spot in the macula is present in about 60 percent of patients. Death usually occurs before the third year of life. At autopsy, the liver, spleen, lungs, bone marrow, and lymph nodes show the typical foam or Niemann-Pick cells. The abnormal accumulation of lipids in foam cells consists of phospholipids, chiefly sphingomyelin and lecithin. A characteristic pathologic change in the central nervous system of patients with Niemann-Pick disease is a distention or ballooning of the large neurons almost identical to that which occurs in patients with Tay-Sachs disease. A diagnosis can be made during life by bone marrow examination.

Generalized Gangliosidosis

Generalized gangliosidosis is due to an inborn error of glycolipid metabolism characterized by the deposition of gangliosides in many body tissues. In this condition, a monosialoganglioside normally present in the brain accumulates in the central nervous system and viscera. In addition, mucopolysaccharides (keratosulfate and sialomucopolysaccharide) are also stored in abnormal amounts in viscera. The defect responsible for this abnormal accumulation appears to be the result of a deficiency of beta-galactosidase, an enzyme which participates in the catabolism of both gangliosides and mucopolysaccharides.

Patients with generalized gangliosidosis manifest psychomotor retardation since early infancy. The clinical picture is characterized by hypotonia, facial and peripheral edema, frontal bossing, large and low-set ears, wide upper lips, gum hypertrophy, liver enlargement, and a cherry-red spot in the macula which is present in about 50 percent of cases. Splenomegaly develops in about 80 percent of cases by 6 months of age. Clinical features similar to those found in Hurler's syndrome are usually present (characteristic facies, broad hands and short, stubby fingers, and hypoplastic beaked vertebral bodies and lumbar kyphosis), although these changes are seen at an earlier age in generalized gangliosidosis. From this description it is apparent that the phenotype of generalized gangliosidosis has features common to both Hurler's syndrome and Tay-Sachs disease. In contrast to patients with Hurler's syndrome, however, those with generalized gangliosidosis excrete normal or only slightly elevated amounts of mucopolysaccharides in the urine.

Mucopolysaccharidoses

The mucopolysaccharidoses are a group of diseases characterized by the accumulation of mucopolysaccharides in many organs of the body and clinically by a variety of abnormalities of morphology and function of affected systems. According to mode of inheritance, phenotypic characteristics, and type of biochemical abnormality, several syndromes are recognized. Mental retardation is not always progressive. Some patients may have normal intellect.

HURLER'S SYNDROME (MUCOPOLYSACCHARIDOSIS I).   Hurler's syndrome represents the prototype of the mucopolysaccharidoses. Hurler's syndrome is inherited as an autosomal recessive trait. The chief clinical manifestations are psychomotor retardation, kyphosis, restriction of joint extension most prominent at the elbows, hepatomegaly, cloudy corneas, an enlarged head especially in its anteroposterior diameter, hirsutism, broad hands and stubby fingers, and a characteristic facies due to a wide nose, a flat nasal bridge, thickened lips, and a large tongue. Children with Hurler's syndrome exhibit an apelike posture with limbs flexed and clawlike hands. Roentgenographic abnormalities seen in patients with Hurler's syndrome are premature closure of cranial sutures (especially the sagittal), a spurred appearance of the first and second lumbar vertebrae, and an ovoid configuration of vertebral bodies. The bones of the extremities have a massive appearance and the metacarpals a sugar-loaf configuration.

Patients with Hurler's syndrome excrete abnormal amounts of chondroitin sulfate B and heparitin sulfate in the urine.

HUNTER'S SYNDROME (MUCOPOLYSACCHARIDOSIS II).   Hunter's syndrome is inherited as a sex-linked recessive trait and occurs only in boys. Clinical features of Hunter's syndrome are a fairly normal early development followed by psychomotor retardation by the second year of life; a typical appearance consisting of an abnormal posture due to restriction of joint movement, especially elbows and knees, a flat nasal bridge with a broad base, a large head with a prominent sagittal suture, large tongue and thickened lips, hirsutism, occasional kyphosis, atypical retinitis pigmentosa, and coarse eyebrows and eyelashes. In most cases there is progressive sensorineural deafness. Corneas are normal.

Roentgenographic abnormalities are similar but less pronounced than those seen in patients with Hurler's syndrome. Common symptoms of these two syndromes are frequent upper respiratory infections, inguinal and umbilical hernias, and nasal discharge and noisy breathing. Patients with Hunter's syndrome also excrete abnormal amounts of chondroitin sulfate B and heparitin sulfate in the urine.

SANFILIPPO SYNDROME (MUCOPOLYSACCHARIDOSIS III). Patients with this form of mucopolysaccharidosis exhibit severe progressive psychomotor retardation and present few of the clinical and roentgenographic features which characterize the Hurler-Hunter phenotype. Patients with Sanfilippo syndrome excrete excessive amounts of heparitin sulfate in the urine. Inheritance is as an autosomal recessive trait.

Disorders of Glycogen Metabolism

AGLYCOGENOSIS (GLYCOGEN SYNTHETASE DEFICIENCY). Aglycogenosis is a disorder characterized by a deficit of the readily available liver glycogen found in normal individuals due to a deficiency in glycogen synthetase. Hypoglycemic seizures since early infancy are frequent in patients with aglycogenosis, and consequently the risk of progressive severe psychomotor retardation is high. Treatment consists of frequent feedings. Prolonged continuous or intermittent treatment with ACTH may be helpful in the prevention of hypoglycemic attacks.

GLYCOGEN STORAGE DISEASE II. The glycogenoses are inherited disorders of carbohydrate metabolism characterized by an abnormal accumulation of glycogen in different body organs. Type II glycogenosis (Pompe's disease) is a disorder inherited as an autosomal recessive trait and is defined biochemically by the absence of the lysosomal enzyme acid maltase (alpha-1, 4-glucosidase) which results in a widespread accumulation of glycogen. Infants with Pompe's disease develop normally until the age of 2 to 3 months, when they develop progressive hypotonia and muscle weakness, swallowing difficulties, exertional dyspnea, and cardiomegaly. The tongue is frequently enlarged. The muscle weakness steadily progresses to an almost complete flaccid paralysis in spite of an apparent normal muscle bulk. Death occurs in the majority of patients before the end of the first year of life as a result of respiratory infection or cardiac failure. Because of some of its clinical features such as a large tongue, hypotonia, and severe muscle weakness this condition may be mistaken for cretinism or for spinal muscular atrophy. Type II glycogenosis can be differentiated from cretinism by thyroid function studies and from spinal muscular atrophy by the dull appearance of the patients, the absence of fasciculations of the tongue, and by the electromyogram, which shows myopathic instead of neurogenic changes. The diagnosis can be established by muscle biopsy, which shows a large amount of glycogen, or by the demonstration of low or absent acid maltase activity in muscle or liver. Patients with glycogenosis I (glucose 6-phosphatase deficiency, von Gierke's disease), glycogenosis III (amylo-1, 6-glucosidase deficiency, Forbes' disease), and glycogenosis VI (liver glycogen phosphorylase deficiency, Hers' disease), may have frequent episodes of hypoglycemia without the usual associated neurologic symptoms. Mental retardation is not a feature of these disorders of carbohydrate metabolism.

Tuberous Sclerosis

Tuberous sclerosis is a heredofamilial disease manifested by a great variety of lesions in different organs of the body. Traditionally tuberous sclerosis has been associated with the triad of adenoma sebaceum, mental retardation, and seizures. Mental subnormality is present in about 60 percent of patients with tuberous sclerosis. Standard textbooks still state that the great majority of patients with tuberous sclerosis are low-grade imbeciles who require institutional care. A large number of patients with tuberous sclerosis and normal intelligence are simply not diagnosed because they are not mentally retarded or because their only complaint may be a seizure disorder which is well controlled by conventional anticonvulsant therapy. In some patients with tuberous sclerosis, however, mental deterioration may progress over many years regardless of the spontaneous or therapeutic control of seizures. It is likely that as some of these patients advance in age the convulsive threshold rises while integrative functions of the central nervous system deteriorate (see also Chapter 14).

PROGRESSIVE PSYCHOMOTOR RETARDATION STARTING AFTER TWO YEARS

Late Infantile Amaurotic Idiocy

Late infantile amaurotic family idiocy (LIAI) differs from Tay-Sachs disease and from the juvenile form in several respects. LIAI is a disorder inherited as an autosomal recessive. There is no racial predilection. The onset of symptoms is between 2 and 4 years of age, although in rare instances it has been reported in infancy and occasionally after age 5, so that age alone does not appear to be an absolute differentiating feature. The initial manifestations in patients with LIAI are progressive loss of intellectual capacity and speech regression. Major motor and myoclonic seizures are common.

Neurologic examination reveals a cerebellar type of ataxia and some degree of extrapyramidal rigidity. The maculae may show a yellowish-gray color. Occasionally a cherry-red spot is seen. Late signs of the disease are idiocy, inability to walk, and generalized hypotonia. The electroencephalogram may show an abnormal tracing with spikes, polyspikes, and 2-per-second atypical spikes and waves. Other laboratory studies are normal. The disease runs a subchronic course, with an average duration of four years. Pathologic changes consist of atrophy of the brain and spinal cord. As in Tay-Sachs disease there is accumulation of lipid material in swollen ganglion cells. This material appears to be a ganglioside different from that found in Tay-Sachs disease.

Juvenile Amaurotic Idiocy

Juvenile amaurotic idiocy has its onset between the ages of 5 and 7 years. The disease is inherited as an autosomal recessive trait. There is no racial predilection. The first clinical manifestations are mental deterioration and decrease in visual acuity. Loss of vision progresses rapidly to complete blindness in a matter of a few years. Ophthalmoscopic examination during the first stages reveals a pale spot in the macula surrounded by dark brown spots. These abnormalities may disappear at a later age when optic atrophy becomes prominent. The mental changes are also progressive and usually appear simultaneously with visual ones. Additional neurologic findings include abnormalities of posture, athetosis, hypertonicity, and increased muscle stretch reflexes. Major motor seizures occur in most cases. Examination of the cerebrospinal fluid may show an elevation of protein levels. Electroencephalographic abnormalities are invariably present but do not differ from those encountered in other diseases associated with seizures and progressive cerebral degeneration.

Pathologic changes are similar to those found in Tay-Sachs disease; the ganglion cells, however, are enlarged only in selected areas. As in Tay-Sachs disease the stored material appears to be a glycolipid containing neuraminic acid. However, the total content of gangliosides in the brain of these patients is not increased as in those with Tay-Sachs disease.

Familial Myoclonic Epilepsy

Familial myoclonic epilepsy is a clinicopathologic entity inherited as an autosomal recessive and characterized initially by grand mal seizures, followed in a period of a few months to 2 to 6 years by myoclonus and progressive mental deterioration. Myoclonic epilepsy has its onset usually during late childhood or adolescence. Additional symptoms are speech deterioration and gait and upper limb ataxia. During the late stages of the disease myoclonus may occur almost continuously, and it is often precipitated by noise. Laboratory investigations, including examination of the cerebrospinal fluid, are normal. The pneumo-encephalogram may show ventricular dilatation without evidence of obstruction. The electroencephalogram is always abnormal and is characterized by a background of slow activity on which there are superimposed spikes, polyspikes and waves, and spike-wave complexes, any of which may occur focally or in bilateral synchronous bursts. Pathologically diffuse degenerative changes are present in the brain. Lafora (1911) and Gluck (1912) described typical inclusion bodies in the nerve cells of the dentate nuclei, basal ganglia, and cerebral cortex. These intracytoplasmic bodies contain acid mucopolysaccharides and neutral saccharide-containing compounds. Death occurs in patients with familial myoclonic epilepsy usually within 4 to 19 years after onset of symptoms.

Juvenile Form of Sulfatide Lipidosis

The juvenile form of sulfatide lipidosis (metachromatic leukodystrophy) has its onset between 4 and 6 years of age and is characterized initially by visual disturbances and intellectual deterioration. Differential diagnosis at this age includes the late infantile and juvenile forms of amaurotic family idiocy and Schilder's disease. An adult form of sulfatide lipidosis with onset of symptoms after the age of 16 has also been described. In the latter form psychiatric disturbances dominate the clinical picture.

Schilder's Disease

Schilder's disease (diffuse cerebral sclerosis) is a disease of the central nervous system characterized pathologically by extensive and sharply demarcated areas of demyelination of the cerebral hemispheres. In approximately half the cases the disease has its onset between the ages of 5 and 10 years. Some investigators have suggested that Schilder's disease may be an acute or subchronic form of multiple sclerosis. The clinical picture of Schilder's disease may fall into one of four types: (1) a progressive form with mental difficulties, pyramidal tract signs, blindness, and deafness; (2) a polysclerotic variety in which the disease progresses by successive bursts as in classical multiple sclerosis of the adult; (3) a pseudotumoral form with signs and symptoms of increased intracranial pressure and papilledema as in Schilder's original case; and (4) a form with predominantly psychiatric symptoms.

As a general rule Schilder's disease appears in the so-called progressive variety with mental difficulties, signs of increased intracranial pressure, pyramidal tract signs, and cortical blindness and deafness. The disease runs a subchronic course with death occurring within three years after onset of symptoms in about 50 percent of cases. At autopsy some patients with Schilder's disease have concentric areas of uneven cerebral demyelination (Balo's encephalitis periaxialis concentrica). There is no reason to believe that this is a separate clinicopathologic entity, but rather that it represents a variant of Schilder's diffuse sclerosis.

Progressive Cerebral Poliodystrophy (Alper's Disease)

Progressive cerebral poliodystrophy is a disease characterized by degeneration of the cerebral gray matter with relative preservation of the white matter. Clinical features are an onset in middle childhood, with progressive mental deterioration, spasticity, myoclonic and major motor seizures, ataxia, choreoathetosis, and death within four years after onset of symptoms. A diagnosis during life can be made only by cerebral biopsy.

Subacute Sclerosing Panencephalitis

Subacute sclerosing panencephalitis (SSPE) is a disease of childhood and early adulthood characterized by demyelination, sclerosis, and inflammatory exudates in the white matter of the cerebral hemispheres and the presence of intranuclear type A inclusion bodies in many cortical neurons.

Dawson in 1933 described a case of lethargic encephalitis with cellular inclusions in affected areas of the cerebral cortex. He believed that this represented a distinct pathologic entity, which he subsequently called "inclusion body encephalitis," and postulated it was probably due to a viral infection of the central nervous system. Since then numerous investigators attempted but failed to prove a viral etiology. In recent years overwhelming evidence has been accumulated implicating measles virus as the etiologic agent of SSPE.

Pathologically the presence of inclusion bodies in cortical neurons is the most prominent feature in acute cases, while chronic ones show more demyelination, sclerosis, and inflammatory changes. The disease occurs preferentially in children or young adults between the ages of 4 and 20 years. Males are affected twice as often as females.

The clinical course of SSPE in its most common form can be divided into three more or less stereotyped stages. *First stage:* Onset is usually insidious in the form of intellectual deterioration or psychologic disturbances. These may become manifest in poor school performance, erratic behavior, or mental dullness. An occasional generalized seizure may occur. *Second stage:* Personality changes are followed by involuntary movements of the face, limbs, or trunk. Within weeks or months mental deterioration progresses rapidly and the child becomes totally disoriented and is unresponsive to visual stimuli (cortical blindness). *Third stage:* During the last phase of the disease the child is in a vegetative state and is unresponsive to visual or auditory stimuli. Eventually he is bedfast and assumes a position of decortication which is interrupted at frequent intervals (4 to 12 times per minute) by sudden myoclonic jerks of the extremities.

Subacute sclerosing panencephalitis does not always occur in this classic form. Its onset may be abrupt with generalized convulsions, visual disturbances, and myoclonic jerks; occasionally its course is marked by remissions and exacerbations. During the first and second stages there are characteristic electroencephalographic changes in the form of repetitive cerebral discharges of high-amplitude slow-wave biphasic complexes. The form of the complexes, however, varies from patient to patient and often in the same patient at different times. The periodic EEG discharges occur synchronously with the myoclonic jerks. During the final stages of the disease these periodic complexes become less distinct or disappear altogether. Although characteristic of SSPE this EEG pattern is not present in all patients. Examination of the cerebrospinal fluid during the second and third stages reveals normal or moderately elevated protein levels and an elevation of its gamma globulin fraction in almost all patients. In about one-third of cases serum gamma globulins are also elevated.

In the great majority of patients the disease runs a subacute (2 to 9 months in young children) or subchronic course (1 or more years) in young adults. A course characterized by remissions and exacerbations, as well as nonfatal cases, has also been recorded. Treatment of SSPE with antiviral agents, steroids, or immunosuppressive agents has not proved successful.

Heller's Infantile Dementia

Heller, in 1908, described as a distinct clinical entity a disease characterized by the onset of progressive dementia between the ages of 2 and 4. The subject of his report manifested speech regression and his behavior became infantile. Complete dementia developed within a few years. General and neurologic examinations were normal, and there were no locomotor difficulties, ataxia, eye abnormalities, or changes in muscle stretch or abnormal reflexes. Autopsy findings in a few other reported cases have been inconclusive. We have seen one patient with a clinical picture similar to that described by Heller in a girl 6 years of age who developed normally up to the age of 2 and then over a period of two years gradually lost her speech and developed a slowly progressive dementia. Neurologic examination was normal and multiple laboratory investigations to uncover possible metabolic or known degenerative diseases of the central nervous system yielded negative results. Differential diagnosis includes childhood schizophrenia as well as a number of degenerative diseases of the central nervous system.

Pigmentary Degeneration of the Globus Pallidus (Hallervorden-Spatz Disease)

Pigmentary degeneration of the globus pallidus is a rare familial disease of the basal ganglia characterized by deposition of a greenish blue or brown pigment in the globus pallidus and clinically by stiffness of the extremities, dysarthria, optic atrophy, retinitis pigmentosa, extensor plantar responses (Babinski sign), and progressive dementia. The disease has its onset at about 10 years of age and runs a progressive course with death in 5 to 20 years.

Wilson's Disease

See Chapter 5.

Huntington's Chorea

See Chapter 5.

REFERENCES

Aronson, S. M., et al.   A genetic profile of infantile amaurotic family idiocy. *Amer. J. Dis. Child.* 98:50, 1959.

Austin, J. H.   Metachromatic form of diffuse cerebral sclerosis: I. Diagnosis during life by urine sediment examination. *Neurology* 7:415, 1957.

Austin, J., et al.   Studies in globoid (Krabbe) leukodystrophy (G.L.D.): V. Controlled enzymatic studies in ten human cases. *Arch. Neurol.* 23:502, 1970.

Bejsovec, M., et al.   Familial intrauterine convulsions in pyridoxine dependency. *Arch. Dis. Child.* 42:201, 1967.

Berry, H. K., et al.   Diagnosis and treatment: Interpretation of results of blood screening studies for detection of phenylketonuria. *Pediatrics* 37:102, 1966.

Berry, H. K., et al.   Treatment of phenylketonuria. *Amer. J. Dis. Child.* 113:2, 1967.

Cardiff, R. D.   A histochemical and electron microscopic study of skeletal muscle in a case of Pompe's disease (glycogenosis II). *Pediatrics* 37:249, 1966.

Chen, T. T., et al.   Subacute sclerosing panencephalitis: Propagation of measles virus from brain biopsy in tissue culture. *Science* 163:1193, 1969.

Dawson, J. R.   Cellular inclusions in cerebral lesions of lethargic encephalitis. *Amer. J. Path.* 9:7, 1933.

Dunn, H. G., et al.   Homocystinuria. *Neurology* 16:407, 1966.

Dunn, H. G., et al.   The neuropathy of Krabbe's infantile cerebral sclerosis (globoid cell leucodystrophy). *Brain* 92:329, 1969.

Efron, M. L. Aminoaciduria. *New Eng. J. Med.* 272:1058, 1107, 1965.

Gerritsen, T., and Waisman, H. A. Hypersarcosinemia: An inborn error of metabolism. *New Eng. J. Med.* 275:66, 1966.

Ghadimi, H., et al. Hyperlisenemia associated with retardation. *New Eng. J. Med.* 273:723, 1965.

Greenhouse, A. H., and Schneck, S. A. Subacute necrotizing encephalomyelopathy: A reappraisal of the thiamine deficiency hypothesis. *Neurology* 18:1, 1968.

Hsia, D. Y., et al. Gaucher's disease: Report of two cases in father and son and review of the literature. *New Eng. J. Med.* 261:164, 1959.

Kamoshita, S., et al. Infantile Niemann-Pick disease. *Amer. J. Dis. Child.* 117:379, 1969.

Kanof, A., et al. Clinical progression of amaurotic family idiocy. *Amer. J. Dis. Child.* 97:656, 1959.

Leroy, J. G., and Crocker, A. C. Clinical definition of the Hurler-Hunter phenotypes. *Amer. J. Dis. Child.* 112:518, 1966.

Lonsdale, D., and Barber, D. H. Maple syrup urine disease: Report of a case, with a pedigree. *New Eng. J. Med.* 271:1338, 1964.

Michener, W. M. Hyperuricemia and mental retardation with athetosis and self-mutilation. *Amer. J. Dis. Child.* 113:195, 1967.

O'Brien, J. Generalized gangliosidosis. *J. Pediat.* 75:167, 1969.

Perry, T. L., et al. Carnosinemia: A new metabolic disorder associated with neurologic disease and mental defect. *New Eng. J. Med.* 277:1219, 1967.

Resnick, J. S., et al. Subacute sclerosing panencephalitis: Spontaneous improvement in a patient with elevated measles antibody in blood and spinal fluid. *New Eng. J. Med.* 279:126, 1968.

Robinson, F., et al. Necrotizing encephalomyelopathy of childhood. *Neurology* 17:472, 1967.

Rosenberg, A. L., et al. Hyperuricemia and neurologic deficits: A family study. *New Eng. J. Med.* 282:992, 1970.

Schettler, G. (Ed.). *Lipids and Lipidoses.* Berlin: Springer, 1967.

Scriver, C. R., et al. Hyper-beta-alaninemia associated with beta-aminoaciduria and delta-aminobutyricaciduria, somnolence and seizures. *New Eng. J. Med.* 274:635, 1966.

Sever, J. L., and Zeman, W. (Eds.). Measles virus and subacute sclerosing panencephalitis. *Neurology* 18 (Suppl.):1, 1968.

Smith, H. L., et al. Type II glycogenosis: Report of a case with four-year survival and absence of acid maltase associated with an abnormal glycogen. *Amer. J. Dis. Child.* 111:475, 1966.

Thomas, R. P., et al. Homocystinuria and ectopia lentis in Negro family. *J.A.M.A.* 198:560, 1966.

Waldinger, C., and Berg, R. B. Signs of pyridoxine dependency manifest at birth in siblings. *Pediatrics* 32:161, 1963.

Westall, R. G. Dietary treatment of maple syrup urine disease. *Amer. J. Dis. Child.* 113:58, 1967.

Yudell, A., et al. The neuropathy of sulfatide lipidosis (metachromatic leukodystrophy). *Neurology* 17:103, 1967.

17

Neurologic Syndromes Associated with Chromosomal Abnormalities

IT WAS NOT until 1956 that the correct number of 46 chromosomes in man was definitively established, 22 pairs of autosomes and 2 sex chromosomes (Fig. 17-1). In 1960 the current system of nomenclature of the human chromosomes was devised. The two primary features used in the identification of individual chromosomes are the relative length and the centromere position. There are seven groups of autosomal chromosomes, each consisting of two to seven pairs. The A group contains three pairs of large chromosomes with nearly metacentric centromeres. The next group (B), in order of decreasing length, consists of two pairs of medium-sized chromosomes with submetacentric centromeres. Chromosomes of the C group (6–12) and the X chromosome are very similar. They have submetacentric centromeres and form a very distinctive group. Chromosomes 13, 14, and 15 form the group D of long acrocentrics. These chromosomes have a long arm and a very small short arm. Chromosomes 16, 17, and 18, or group E, are small chromosomes with submetacentric centromeres. The two chromosomes 19 and 20 (group F) are short and metacentric and are very similar to one another. The last, or G group (21 and 22), consists of two short acrocentric chromosomes. The Y chromosome is at first glance similar to numbers 21 and 22; however, it is usually somewhat larger and has a more nearly terminal centromere.

With the exception of some highly differentiated cells (e.g., neurons) all the cells of the body are potentially able to divide into two essentially similar cells. Somatic cells divide only by mitosis, the result being

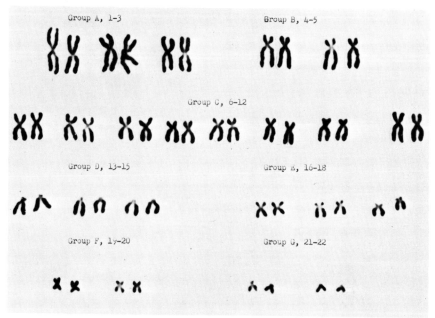

A

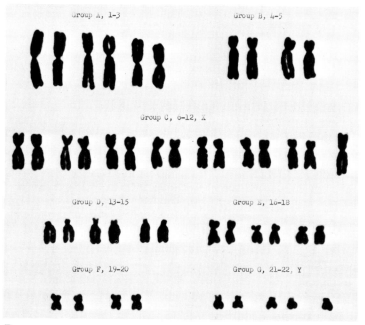

B

Fig. 17-1.   *A*, karyotype of normal female (46 XX). *B*, karyotype of normal
male (46 XY). (Courtesy of Dr. J. R. Seely)

an equal distribution of genetic material to the two daughter cells, each with 46 chromosomes. During gametogenesis germ cells divide by meiosis, a process in which the original number of 46 chromosomes is reduced to 23 chromosomes (reduction division). Meiosis is at least twice as complex as mitosis. It is not surprising then that during its course chromosomal mistakes may occur, resulting in an unequal distribution of chromosomes or of chromosomal material.

Minor chromosomal abnormalities occur in apparently healthy men and women. Experimental work has shown that viruses may produce changes in the chromosomes. The deleterious effect of viruses on genetic material has been confirmed in the case of the congenital rubella syndrome. Chromosomal abnormalities have been found also in a number of viral infections. It has been suggested that the virus of hepatitis may play a role in the production of Down's syndrome, the chromosomes of the ovum being affected by the virus before or about the time of conception. Chromosome studies carried out in spontaneous human abortions have demonstrated a great variety of abnormalities (trisomies, monosomies, and polyploids). Altered immunity has also been invoked as a possible etiologic mechanism. In recent years a large number of new syndromes consisting of patients with psychomotor retardation and multiple congenital anomalies have been reported. However, only a few of them have been associated with specific structural changes of a particular chromosome or group of chromosomes.

DOWN'S SYNDROME (MONGOLISM)

The basic defect in this syndrome remained an enigma until 1959 when Lejeune and co-workers in France observed that patients with Down's syndrome had 47 chromosomes instead of the normal number of 46 (Fig. 17-2). An extra acrocentric chromosome belonging to the number 21 group is present, producing trisomy 21. This is caused by a mistake (nondisjunction) in the reduction division that forms the ovum or sperm from which the child develops. In approximately 1 of 500 to 600 conceptions the 21 chromosomes fail to separate so that one daughter cell has two chromosomes, the other none. This type of abnormality accounts for about 95 percent of cases. A less common cause of trisomy 21 is that in which the extra chromosome 21 is translocated to the short arm of a chromosome of group D or G. The first type of mistake is a developmental aberration; the second may be a familial abnormality transmitted to the child by the mother or the father who, although phenotypically normal, may be a balanced translocation carrier. When one of these individuals produces ova or spermatozoa some of them will contain two 21 chromosomes, others will have none. From the union of

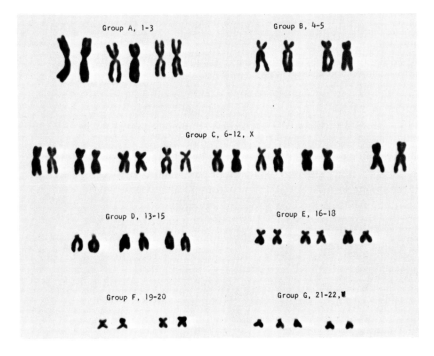

Fig. 17-2. Karyotype of a patient with Down's syndrome, showing trisomy of chromosome 21. (Courtesy of Dr. J. R. Seely)

such an individual with a chromosomally normal partner, four outcomes are possible—a nonviable zygote, a child with translocation form of trisomy 21, a phenotypically normal child who will be a balanced translocation carrier, or a normal child. Chromosome analysis should be done in parents of patients with this type of trisomy 21 to determine whether they are carriers of the translocation. If one of the parents is a carrier all siblings of an affected child should also be tested.

Another uncommon cause of Down's syndrome is 21/21 translocation in one of the parents. A conception in this case may result only in a nonviable zygote or a child with trisomy 21. In some patients with trisomy 21 the clinical manifestations are less pronounced. This is usually due to mosaicism, a form of trisomy 21 which results from mitotic nondisjunction during the early stages in the development of the embryo. These patients have two lines of cells with a chromosome count of 47 or 46. Both lines are usually represented in the same tissue.

The incidence of Down's syndrome increases with maternal age, from about 1:1500 births at age 20 to 1:50 at age 45. A diagnosis of Down's syndrome can usually be made by simple inspection (Fig. 17-3). One of the cardinal signs in trisomy 21 is muscular hypotonia. This

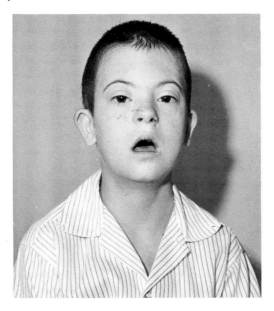

Fig. 17-3. 10-year-old boy with Down's syndrome. Typical mongoloid facies: epicanthal folds, mongoloid slant of eyes, and large tongue. (Courtesy of Dr. J. R. Seely)

is especially marked during the first year of life and tends to improve with advancing age. When an infant with Down's syndrome is held in ventral suspension the trunk and the limbs collapse over the examiner's hand. The normal response, arching of the spine and flexion of the arms and legs, does not take place. The Moro, plantar, and grasp reflexes persist much longer in infants with Down's syndrome than in normal infants. Muscle strength is usually normal in older children with Down's syndrome. There are no focal neurologic signs. Mental subnormality is the rule, with the great majority of patients having an IQ between 25 and 50.

No distinctive neuropathological changes have been demonstrated in the central nervous system of patients with Down's syndrome. The brain is small and round, with an almost vertical occipital contour. The brain stem, medulla, and cerebellum are small in relation to the rest of the brain. In about 50 percent of patients both superior temporal gyri are narrow (Fig. 17-4). Many microscopic abnormalities are found in the brain. These are nonspecific and are also present in patients with moderate to severe mental retardation due to other etiologies. The most striking microscopic features are a paucity of cells in the cerebral cortex, poor myelination of the gray and white matter, and marked fibrillary gliosis of the central white matter.

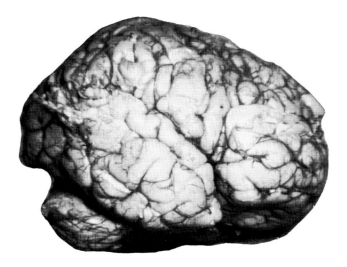

Fig. 17-4. Brain of patient with Down's syndrome showing narrow superior temporal gyrus and small cerebellum.

Skeletal malformations are present in all patients. The head is brachycephalic, the face and the occiput are flat, and the hands are short and broad. Pelvic abnormalities occur in more than 90 percent of patients and consist of small acetabular angles, large ilia, and elongated ischia (Fig. 17-5). These can be demonstrated from early infancy by x-rays of the pelvis and may be helpful in making a diagnosis in doubtful cases. A radially curved little finger (clinodactyly) is present in most patients with Down's syndrome. This skeletal abnormality is due to hypoplasia of the middle phalanx and is seldom prominent early in life but becomes more noticeable with advancing age. A flexion crease of the little finger is seen in one-third and a transverse (simian) palmar crease in about one-half of cases (Fig. 17-6).

Ocular signs are very prominent. The most common ocular abnormalities are slanting eyes (40 to 80 percent), epicanthal folds (20 to 80 percent), Brushfield spots (15 to 90 percent), and hypoplasia of the iris (30 to 40 percent). Brushfield spots are whitish or light-colored nodules located in the periphery of the iris and consist of condensations of connective tissue of the anterior part of the iris. These spots differ only in the number and size but not in structure or appearance from similar spots seen in normal individuals. Hypoplasia of the iris is clinically manifested by a dark peripheral discoloration of the iris; it is due to thinning of the periphery of the iris at the junction of the middle and outer thirds, the dark posterior epithelium becoming thus more apparent.

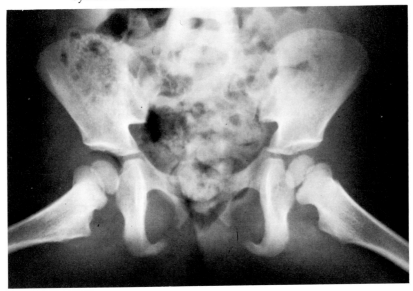

Fig. 17-5. X-ray of the pelvis in 3-year-old child with Down's syndrome demonstrating small acetabular angles and long ischia.

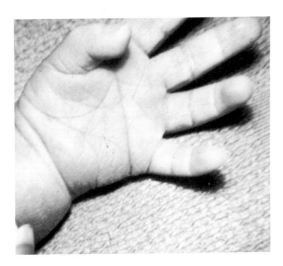

Fig. 17-6. Transverse (simian) crease in patient with Down's syndrome.

Congenital malformations of the heart occur in about half of patients. The most common defects are, in order of frequency, ventricular septal defect, atrial septal defect, and patent ductus arteriosus. Malformations of the gastrointestinal tract include a large or fissured tongue, esophageal atresia, congenital stenosis of the colon, imperforate anus or annular pancreas, and congenital atresia or stenosis of the duodenum.

ANTIMONGOLISM

Lejeune in 1964 and Reisman and associates in 1966 described two patients with a chromosomal count of 45 and a minute fragment interpreted as being a deleted 21 chromosome. These patients had the following features in common: (1) hypertonia; (2) antimongoloid slant of the eyes; (3) mental retardation; (4) a prominent nasal bridge; (5) micrognathia; and (6) a normal iliac and acetabular index. Since this is almost the exact mirror image of mongolism it was given the name *antimongoloid syndrome*.

TRISOMY 13–15

Patau and co-workers in 1960 described an infant with multiple congenital anomalies associated with an extra chromosome in the 13–15 or D group (Fig. 17-7). The incidence of trisomy 13–15 is approximately 1:5000 liveborn infants. The anomalies found in this syndrome are severe and include anophthalmia, cleft lip and cleft palate, polydactyly and flexion contractures of the fingers, ventricular septal defect, patent

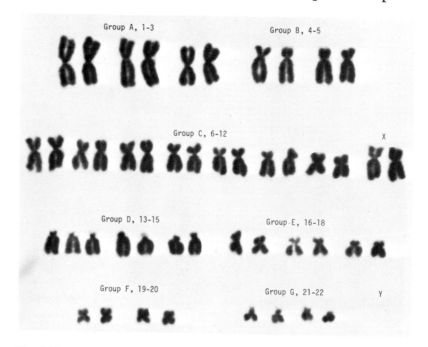

Fig. 17-7. Karyotype of patient with trisomy 13–15. An extra chromosome is present in the 13–15 group. (Courtesy of Dr. J. R. Seely)

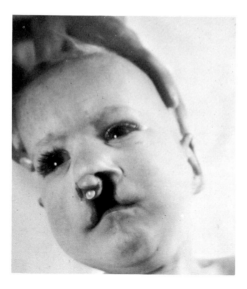

Fig. 17-8.   16-month-old infant with trisomy 13–15 showing characteristic midline defects. Right cornea larger than left one and cataract in left eye.

ductus arteriosus, and malformations of the gastrointestinal tract and kidneys (Fig. 17-8). Ocular defects appear to be an almost constant finding in this syndrome. These include microphthalmos, cataracts, uveal tract colobomas, retinal dysplasias, optic atrophy, and defective angle development. Patients with trisomy 13–15 have severe psychomotor retardation, often exhibit a moderate degree of spasticity, and are frequently subject to myoclonic seizures. Autopsy in these patients has shown that all have developmental abnormalities of the brain arising from anomalous differentiation of facial and telencephalic structures. However, the cerebral malformations seen in trisomy 13–15 vary greatly in extent. Some cases have shown fused frontal lobes and single ventricules, while in others only abnormalities of the olfactory nerves and lobes have been observed. Although arhinencephaly and related malformations are considered to be typical of trisomy 13–15, they have also been found in children with normal karyotypes. The great majority of patients with trisomy 13–15 reported in the literature have died within the first few months of life. Most patients have a count of 47 chromosomes, with an extra chromosome for the D group. In some patients the chromosome count is normal (46), with the extra chromosome translocated into one of the chromosomes of the 13–15 group. Chromosome studies in the parents of these patients have shown that some of them may be carriers of a translocated 13–15 chromosome with a chromosome count of 45 instead of the normal 46.

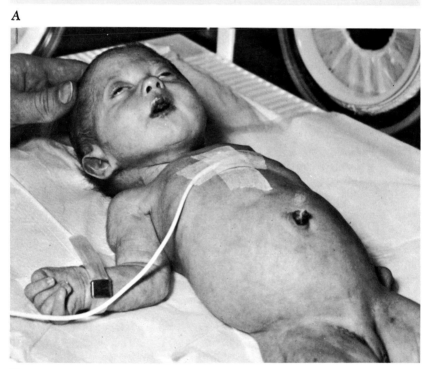

Group A, 1-3   Group B, 4-5

Group C, 6-12   X

Group D, 13-15   Group E, 16-18

Group F, 19-20   Group G, 21-22   Y

A

B

C

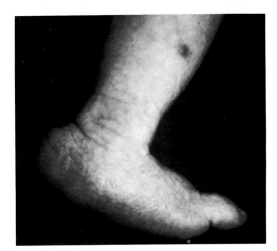

Fig. 17-9.   A, karyotype of patient with trisomy 18. An extra chromosome is present in the 18 group. *B*, 1-month-old infant with trisomy 18. Notice malformed and low-set ears, micrognathia, and abnormal posturing of fingers. *C*, rocker-bottom foot in patient with trisomy 18. (Courtesy of Dr. J. R. Seely)

TRISOMY 18

Edwards in 1960 gave the first detailed description of a patient with multiple congenital anomalies due to nondisjunction of one of the chromosomes in the 18 group (Fig. 17-9A). The number of cases of trisomy 18 so far reported is well over 200. It has been estimated that the incidence of this syndrome is approximately 1:3000 births. The ratio of affected females to males is about 3:1. Severe psychomotor retardation and failure to thrive since early infancy are constant findings (Fig. 17-9B). Because of poor sucking and swallowing difficulties these infants often have to be gavage-fed. Their cry is weak and their ears are malformed and set low and back. Skeletal abnormalities include a small head with a prominent occiput, small mandible, small pelvis, short sternum, and rocker-bottom feet (Fig. 17-9C). The majority of patients have anomalies of the hand, with the index finger overlapping the third finger. More than 80 percent of reported patients with trisomy 18 have died before one year of age.

DELETION 18

Patients with partial deletion of the long arm of chromosome 18 have mental retardation, microcephaly, skin dimples over the acromion, and a peculiar facies characterized by midfacial hypoplasia and a prominent antihelix and antitragus. Additional features include epicanthal folds, cleft lip and cleft palate, various types of congenital heart disease, long hands, short first metacarpal with proximal thumb, visual problems, and conductive hearing loss.

RING CHROMOSOME 18

This chromosomal abnormality results from breakage and fusion of the arms of chromosome 18 resulting in a circular structure. Clinical features include mental retardation, microcephaly, epicanthal folds, antimongoloid slant, deafness, micrognathia, and a number of other congenital abnormalities.

CRI-DU-CHAT SYNDROME

Lejeune and co-workers described in 1964 a new clinical syndrome associated with partial deletion of the short arm of chromosome 5. The common features in these cases were craniofacial deformity with microcephaly, moon face, and hypertelorism, with oblique palpebral fissures and low implantation of essentially normal ears, pronounced mental deficiency, a peculiar shrill and plaintive cry, simulating the mewing of a cat, characteristic dermatoglyphic anomalies, and deletion of about half the length of the short arm of one of the 5-chromosomes (Fig. 17-10). The characteristic cat cry in these children appears to be related to supraglottic anomalies and a hypoplastic larynx.

KLINEFELTER'S SYNDROME

Klinefelter's syndrome combines a series of gonadal anomalies. The only constant feature which develops at puberty is testicular atrophy and azoospermia. Common clinical findings are a eunuchoid body build and gynecomastia. The most common chromosomal aberration of Klinefelter's syndrome is the presence of 47 chromosomes with a karyotype of XXY. Other chromosomal variants have been reported such as XXXY, XXXXY, and XXXYY, as well as occasional mosaicism. Buccal smears in these patients show positive sex chromosome bodies equal in number to the number of X chromosomes minus one. The incidence of Klinefelter's syndrome is in the order of 1:500 in the general population

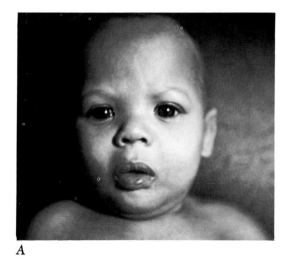

Fig. 17-10. A, 7-month-old infant with cri-du-chat syndrome: microcephaly, moon face, hypertelorism, and severe psychomotor retardation. *B*, karyotype of same patient showing deletion of the short arm of one chromosome 5. (Courtesy of Dr. J. R. Seely)

and about 1:100 in the mentally retarded. It has been suggested that the mental defect in these patients is proportional to the number of supernumerary X chromosomes. The number of patients reported with karyotypes other than the classic XXY is, however, too small to be of significant statistical value.

TURNER'S SYNDROME

Turner's syndrome consists of primary amenorrhea, aplastic ovaries without follicles, underdeveloped breasts, short stature, cubitus valgus, and webbing and/or shortening of the neck. Additional findings include epicanthal folds, a broad bridge of the nose, congenital heart disease, especially coarctation of the aorta and pulmonic stenosis, wide-spaced nipples, and clinodactyly of the little finger. Lymphedema of the dorsum of the hands is common during early infancy and decreases in severity or disappears with advancing age. Patients with Turner's syndrome have only 45 chromosomes (Fig. 17-11), probably the result of meiotic nondisjunction resulting in the loss of one of the sex chromosomes. Buccal smears show absence of sex chromatin bodies.

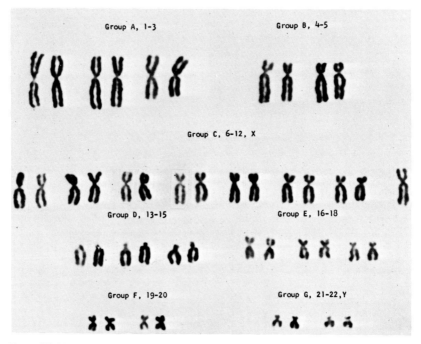

Fig. 17-11. Karyotype of patient with Turner's syndrome showing 45 chromosomes and a single X chromosome. (Courtesy of Dr. J. R. Seely)

Chromosomal abnormalities have also been described in the syndrome of congenital telangiectatic erythema and stunted growth (Bloom's syndrome), in congenital rubella, in Cockayne's syndrome (nanism, retinal degeneration, optic atrophy, cataract, deafness, skeletal defects, and mental retardation), and in Cornelia de Lange syndrome (psychomotor retardation, microcephaly, dwarfism, bushy eyebrows meeting in the midline, hirsutism, long eyelashes, a carplike mouth, a long and thin upper lip, low-set ears, and skeletal malformations, especially of the upper extremities).

In recent years a number of new syndromes have been described which by analogy are highly suggestive of being due to some sort of chromosomal aberration. However, studies of their karyotypes with present techniques have not revealed gross structural anomalies or abnormalities in the number of chromosomes.

REFERENCES

Edwards, J. H., et al.   A new trisomic syndrome. *Lancet* 1:787, 1960.

Falek, A., et al.   Familial de Lange syndrome with chromosome abnormalities. *Pediatrics* 37:92, 1966.

Federman, D. D.   Down's syndrome. *Clin. Pediat.* (Phila.) 4:331, 1965.

Hall, B.   Mongolism in newborn infants. *Clin. Pediat.* (Phila.) 5:4, 1966.

Insley, J.   Syndrome associated with a deficiency of part of the long arm of chromosome No. 18. *Arch. Dis. Child.* 42:140, 1967.

Lejeune, J., et al.   Étude des chromosomes somatiques de neuf enfants mongoliens. *C. R. Acad. Sci.* [D] (Paris) 248:1721, 1959.

Lejeune, J., et al.   Trois cas de délétion partielle du bras court du chromosome 5. *C. R. Acad. Sci.* [D] (Paris) 257:3098, 1963.

Lejeune, J., et al.   Partial deletion of short arm of chromosome 5: Differentiation of a new syndrome. *Sem. Hop. Paris* 40:1069, 1964.

Lejeune, J., et al.   Monosomie partielle pour un petit acrocentrique. *C. R. Acad. Sci.* [D] (Paris) 259:4187, 1964.

Lejeune, J., et al.   La délétion partielle du bras long du chromosome 18: Individualisation d'un nouvel état morbide. *Ann. Genet.* (Paris) 9:32, 1966.

Lemli, L., and Smith, D. W.   The XO syndrome: A study of the differentiated phenotype in 25 patients. *J. Pediat.* 63:577, 1963.

McArthur, R. G., and Edwards, J. H.   De Lange syndrome: Report of 20 cases. *Canad. Med. Ass. J.* 96:1185, 1967.

Patau, K., et al.   Multiple congenital anomaly caused by an extra chromosome. *Lancet* 1:790, 1960.

Penrose, L. S., and Smith, G. F.   *Down's Anomaly.* Boston: Little, Brown, 1966.

Reisman, L. E., et al.   Antimongolism: Studies in infant with partial monosomy of the 21 chromosome. *Lancet* 1:394, 1966.

Turner, H. H.   A syndrome of infantilism, congenital webbed neck, and cubitus valgus. *Endocrinology* 23:566, 1938.

Warkany, J., et al.   Congenital malformations in autosomal trisomy syndromes. *Amer. J. Dis. Child.* 112:502, 1966.

an easy labor and delivery. Not even babies born by cesarean section are exempt from intracranial pathology. Cesarean section is, to be sure, by no means equivalent to an easy birth. This method of delivery is used in many instances after rupture of the amniotic sac, when spontaneous delivery has already proved impossible. Frequently a cesarean section is done because of serious maternal complications, and even if surgery is performed before rupture of the membranes, the fetal head is often firmly fixed in the pelvis before the beginning of labor.

It is well known that the pressure which the baby's head withstands throughout the process of delivery is, indeed, formidable. It has been estimated that approximately 15 percent of newborn infants have some blood in the cerebrospinal fluid and that in about 20 to 25 percent, retinal hemorrhages are present; the bleeding probably results from small, inconsequential ruptures of cortical, subependymal, or retinal capillaries. Fortunately, nature has made the skull of the fetus readily adaptable to sudden changes in environmental pressure. In addition, at birth, the brain is smaller in relation to the cranial cavity than at any other time in extrauterine life. These two factors appear to be of importance in the ability of the fetal brain to stand high pressures as well as sudden changes. Nevertheless, it is surprising that such a high percentage of newborns who are able to go through such a traumatic experience suffers little, if any, permanent brain damage.

Cerebral Hypoxia and Edema

Cerebral hypoxia, brain edema, and intracerebral capillary bleeding are probably important etiologic factors in many patients with neonatal seizures.

Intracranial Bleeding

Intracranial hemorrhage probably occurs to some extent in most deliveries. In only some of these babies, however, is the bleeding of such magnitude as to constitute a real and immediate danger. Gross intracranial bleeding may occur in any of five main anatomic locations: extradural, subdural, subarachnoid, intracerebral, and intraventricular. This is, of course, an oversimplified classification and indicates only the main site of bleeding. In many neonates there is more than a single source of bleeding, and frequently the intracranial hemorrhage is but one of several disturbances complicating the clinical picture.

Extradural hemorrhage is extremely rare in the neonate.

Subdural hemorrhage is an important cause of seizures and death in the neonate and of psychomotor disabilities in infancy and childhood. Subdural hemorrhage occurs usually in large babies born to primiparas or elderly multiparas. It is ten times more frequent in breech than in vertex presentations and occurs twice as often in infants of primiparas as in infants of multiparas. Most acute subdural hematomas in neonates occur in association with difficult instrumental delivery. Subdural hematomas at this age are frequently bilateral. Important signs in these infants are: (1) a tense anterior fontanelle, (2) the presence of large and numerous retinal hemorrhages, and (3) progressive enlargement of the head and spreading of the cranial sutures. This suture separation can be clinically evaluated by palpation of the sagittal suture and measured more accurately by roentgenographic examination of the skull. Focal neurologic signs may or may not be present. The demonstration of abnormal areas of transillumination of the skull is of help in the diagnosis. In the neonate this diagnostic procedure may, however, give unreliable results, or the skull may actually be less translucent on the side of the hematoma than on the normal side. If the anterior fontanelle is excessively tense in the presence of one or more of the previously mentioned signs, subdural taps are indicated. They should be performed initially on both sides and then on alternate sides every other day until the subdural space has dried out.

CASE DESCRIPTION. A 12-day-old infant was admitted to the hospital after several major seizures. He had been the product of a normal pregnancy and a difficult breech delivery, during which he suffered a fracture of the right humerus. On the first day of life he had several left-sided seizures, for which phenobarbital was given. He then seemed well until the day of admission, when there were several episodes of apnea, cyanosis, and limpness. Examination showed a palpable callus in the midshaft of the right humerus, right brachial palsy, retinal hemorrhages bilaterally, and a tense anterior fontanelle. The electroencephalogram showed marked asymmetry with suppression of the alpha rhythm over the left hemisphere. Bilateral subdural taps yielded 15 ml. of old blood from the left subdural space. Several more taps were done on subsequent days until the subdural space had dried out. At the ages of 1 and 2 years he was found to be developing normally and the electroencephalograms were normal (Lagos and Sicket, 1969).

Subarachnoid hemorrhage usually follows complicated pregnancies with uncomplicated deliveries. The most important etiologic factor is probably anoxia, and the clinical picture is characterized by spells of apnea and by a poor color which often improves with crying. Generalized or focal seizures occur frequently with this type of intracranial hemorrhage.

Gross intracerebral hemorrhage is the least common of all the intracranial hemorrhages in the newborn and preferentially affects large full-term infants born after a prolonged labor or a difficult instrumental delivery.

Intraventricular hemorrhage is particularly common in premature infants born by spontaneous delivery. Traditionally, it has been accepted that the causative mechanism is a generalized venous congestion with damage to the cerebral blood vessels and subsequent rupture of the terminal veins or the transverse caudate veins or their tributaries. Anoxia seems to play an important role in this type of hemorrhage. Intraventricular bleeding is believed to be almost always fatal, death usually following a generalized convulsion.

METABOLIC DISTURBANCES

Hypoglycemia

Hypoglycemia may occur in infants of diabetic or prediabetic mothers and is frequently observed in low-birth-weight infants as well as in the smaller of twins. Convulsions may occur when the level of blood glucose is under 20 mg./100 ml. in the premature or low-birth-weight infant, under 30 mg./100 ml. from birth to 72 hours of age, and under 40 mg./100 ml. thereafter in the full-term infant. The CSF glucose is always decreased or absent in the presence of symptomatic hypoglycemia. Cerebral hemorrhage, infections, or congenital malformations of the CNS have also been associated with symptomatic neonatal hypoglycemia. If hypoglycemia persists beyond the neonatal period, a number of diseases have to be considered in the differential diagnosis, such as leucine-sensitive hypoglycemia, islet-cell adenoma of the pancreas, and hereditary defects of carbohydrate metabolism such as glycogen storage disease, glycogen synthetase deficiency, hereditary fructose intolerance, and galactosemia.

The intravenous administration of glucose for two or three days usually controls symptoms. Oral feedings should be given as soon as the condition of the baby permits.

Hypocalcemia

Hypocalcemia may occur during the first two and between the fifth and tenth days of life after oral feedings have been started. The second type is usually related to an excessive amount of phosphorus in the baby's formula. It is well known that cow's milk has a lower calcium: phosphorus ratio than human milk or any of the commercial formulas which simulate breast milk. Hypocalcemia is one of the many metabolic disturbances which may occur in infants of diabetic mothers. Low-birth-weight infants may also have low serum calcium values. Maternal hyperparathyroidism has recently been incriminated as another cause of neonatal seizures due to low serum calcium.

Hypocalcemia in the newborn is manifested by focal or generalized tonic-clonic seizures rather than by the typical signs of tetany. The intravenous administration of a calcium preparation is both diagnostic and therapeutic. Seizures rapidly subside following this maneuver. Initially a 10% solution of calcium gluconate can be given intravenously. The amount of calcium gluconate necessary to control seizures varies from 5 to 10 ml. The baby's heart rate should be monitored with a stethoscope or by electrocardiogram during intravenous administration of calcium. During the next 24 hours the infant can be given calcium chloride by mouth in a solution not exceeding 2% concentration. One gram of calcium for each 3 ounces of formula may be given every 8 hours. After two days, calcium therapy is continued with calcium gluconate or lactate in a dose of 3 to 4 gm. per day in two or three divided doses over a period of four weeks.

Pyridoxine Dependency

Pyridoxine dependency is a rare cause of convulsions in the neonatal period. It is, however, one which the clinician should always keep in mind in the absence of any clear-cut etiologic factor (obvious history of birth trauma, asphyxia, infection, etc.) and especially if the infant fails to respond to conventional anticonvulsant therapy. All convulsive activity ceases within a few minutes after the intravenous or intramuscular administration of 50–100 mg. of pyridoxine. Seizures recur if pyridoxine is not administered on a regular basis. A daily intake of 10–20 mg. of pyridoxine, which is several times higher than normal, is needed throughout infancy and childhood and probably during the entire life of the patient.

INBORN ERRORS OF METABOLISM

Maple Syrup Urine Disease

Maple syrup urine disease is the result of an inborn error of metabolism of the branched-chain amino acids, leucine, isoleucine, and valine. Symptoms begin shortly after birth with poor feeding, vomiting, hypertonicity, and generalized intractable convulsions. The diagnosis is confirmed in the laboratory by the demonstration of an elevation of the branched-chain amino acids or their keto-acids or by demonstrating the metabolic defect in the peripheral leukocytes. If the patient survives long enough, mental retardation and neurologic deficit become apparent. A diet containing reduced amounts of the branched-chain amino acids may prevent the neurologic complications of this disease.

INFECTIONS

Septicemia with or without meningitis is an important cause of seizures in the neonate. Meningitis and septicemia should be suspected in any newborn who is not "doing well" and in whom there is no obvious and significant cause for his difficulties. The usual signs of meningeal irritation are absent in the newborn, and the temperature may often be subnormal in the presence of severe infection or meningitis. Neonates with septicemia and/or meningitis are lethargic, difficult to arouse, and have poor sucking and Moro reflexes. Blood cultures and examination of the CSF should not be neglected in a neonate with the above-mentioned signs. Meningitis in this age group still carries a very high mortality rate and also a high incidence of neurologic sequelae in those infants who survive (hydrocephalus, spastic hemiplegia, and psychomotor retardation).

CEREBRAL MALFORMATIONS

Cerebral malformations, such as hydrocephalus and porencephaly, may occasionally give rise to seizures during the neonatal period. Transillumination of the skull and serial measurements of the head circumference are the most reliable indicators of these types of anomalies.

INFANTILE SPASMS

Infantile spasms may occasionally appear during the first month of life. It is very important that the physician be able to recognize this type of seizure since it is likely that early treatment with ACTH or steroids may render the prognosis less ominous by influencing the associated severe psychomotor retardation.

NARCOTIC WITHDRAWAL SYNDROME

Seizures in the neonate may occur in newborns whose mothers are drug addicts. The clinical picture is characterized by the onset within the first 24 hours of life of extreme irritability, tremors, a high-pitched cry, nausea, vomiting, diarrhea, yawning, sneezing, hyperpyrexia, and generalized convulsions followed by shock and death. A combination of paregoric and chlorpromazine is the treatment of choice in newborns with withdrawal symptoms due to maternal addiction. The dose of each drug should be adjusted to the needs of the individual infant. Paregoric is gradually withdrawn over two to six weeks and followed by the withdrawal of chlorpromazine within the next three to seven days. The mortality rate in these babies is very high if the condition is not recognized and treated in time. Convulsions have also been described as part of a withdrawal syndrome in newborn babies of alcoholic mothers.

DIAGNOSTIC THERAPEUTIC ROUTINE

The following is a diagnostic scheme which we have found useful in the evaluation of seizures in the neonate:

1. Detailed information of pregnancy, labor, and delivery.
2. Careful observation of the baby regarding state of alertness, position, type of cry, and color.
3. Brief but relevant general and neurologic examination, paying special attention to the degree of tension of the anterior fontanelle and to the optic fundi. Newborns have very small pupils and it is a tour de force to visualize the eyegrounds without proper dilation of the pupils with a short-acting mydriatic.
4. Roentgenographic examination of the skull, which may show abnormal spreading of the sutures.
5. An electroencephalogram, usually revealing a diffuse disturbance of cerebral activity with bilateral independent spike foci. In patients with unilateral subdural hematoma the EEG may show asymmetry or a slow-wave focus on the side of the lesion.
6. Determination of serum electrolytes, including calcium, magnesium, blood sugar, urinalysis, blood and urine cultures, CSF examination, and, in selected cases, 24-hour urine determination of amino acids.

If no specific metabolic abnormality is found, treatment should be initiated with phenobarbital 8 mg./kg. body weight daily by the intramuscular route or by mouth if the infant is able to swallow. Diphenylhydantoin is rarely, if ever, indicated in this age group. If seizures are difficult to control with phenobarbital, diazepam (Valium) intravenously or intramuscularly in a dose of 1 to 2 mg. can be used. A trial of pyridoxine (50 mg. IM or IV) should be given to infants who do not respond to conventional anticonvulsant therapy or when there is a family history of previous siblings with seizures due to pyridoxine dependency.

The daily examination of a newborn with seizures should include as a routine procedure the measurement of head circumference. This may be the only clue to the presence of a subdural hematoma or a congenital malformation of the central nervous system.

Questions that always come up regarding the treatment of seizures in the neonatal period are what type of anticonvulsant to use, how much, and for how long. I prefer phenobarbital and believe that the minimum dose for a full-term infant is 8 mg. three times a day. If seizures are under control on this dosage no adjustments need to be made as the infant gains in weight. If seizures are not controlled, a not-uncommon situation with seizures secondary to neonatal meningitis, a rule of thumb is to give as much additional anticonvulsant as is needed to stop them (See Appendix 3).

The immediate and long-term prognosis of seizures in the neonate is directly related to their etiology. Thus, a high mortality rate as well as a high incidence of neurologic sequelae is associated with severe intracranial bleeding, severe hypoxia, or meningitis. Single or multiple seizures, in otherwise normal infants, appear to carry a relatively benign prognosis. During the first few months of life it is often impossible to predict with any degree of accuracy whether neurologic sequelae will be present at a later age. Periodic examination during the first year of life will almost always clarify this point.

References

Burke, J. B.   The prognostic significance of neonatal convulsions. *Arch. Dis. Child.* 29:342, 1954.
Craig, W. S.   Convulsive movements occurring in the first 10 days of life. *Arch. Dis. Child.* 35:336, 1960.
Dancis, J., et al.   The diagnosis of maple syrup urine disease (branched-chain ketoaciduria) by the in vitro study of the peripheral leukocyte. *Pediatrics* 32:234, 1963.
Freeman, J. M.   Neonatal seizures: Diagnosis and management. *J. Pediat.* 77:701, 1970.
Gomez, M. R.   Prenatal and neonatal seizure disorders. *Postgrad. Med.* 46:71, 1969.
Lagos, J. C., and Siekert, R. G.   Intracranial hemorrhage in infancy and childhood. *Clin. Pediat.* (Phila.) 8:90, 1969.
McInerny, T. K., and Schubert, W. K.   Prognosis of neonatal seizures. *Amer. J. Dis. Child.* 117:261, 1969.
Mims, L. C., and Riley, H. D., Jr.   The narcotic withdrawal syndrome in the newborn infant. *Olka. State Med. J.* 62:411, 1969.
Mizrahi, A., et al.   Neonatal hypocalcemia: Its causes and treatment. *New Eng. J. Med.* 278:1163, 1968.

19

Seizures in Infancy
and Childhood

SEIZURES AND MENTAL RETARDATION are the two most common neurologic problems encountered in pediatrics. The incidence of seizures in children under the age of 5 years has been estimated by different authors to vary from 6.7 to 8 percent. These figures, which include patients who have had one or more febrile seizures, are many times higher than the incidence of 0.2 to 0.5 percent reported in adult populations. Although the pathophysiology of febrile as well as nonfebrile seizures is still poorly understood, the magnitude of the problem and the fact that approximately 75 to 80 percent of seizures in children can be controlled on anticonvulsant therapy makes it imperative that an attempt be made to uncover treatable causes such as hypoglycemia, hypocalcemia, subdural hematoma, or lead poisoning, or in the case of a child with a chronic idiopathic or secondary convulsive disorder that the physician be able to categorize accurately his type of seizure in order to institute the appropriate treatment.

Idiopathic epilepsy is rare in the first few years of life, but increases sharply after the age of 4. In early childhood seizures are almost always secondary to some structural abnormality of the brain or to some metabolic disturbance. Symptomatic epilepsy may be secondary to a large number of diverse etiologies (see list on p. 294) ranging from birth injury to degenerative diseases of the central nervous system.

Irrespective of etiologic mechanisms, seizures can be classified from a clinical standpoint into major motor, psychomotor, petit mal, myoclonic, akinetic, and convulsive equivalents.

MAJOR MOTOR SEIZURES

Major motor seizures may be generalized or focal. Probably the great majority of generalized seizures have a focal onset. This type of convulsive activity is characterized by sudden loss of consciousness, with or without a preceding aura; followed by a tonic phase during which the

Symptomatic Epilepsy

Cerebral Trauma or Anoxia
Birth trauma
Postnatal head trauma
Subdural hematoma
Postnatal anoxia of any cause

Central Nervous System Infections
Meningitis (bacterial, viral, or fungal)
Viral encephalitis
Subacute sclerosing panencephalitis
Brain abscess

Metabolic Abnormalities
Inborn errors of amino acid metabolism (phenylketonuria, maple syrup urine disease, etc.)
Inborn errors of carbohydrate metabolism
  Galactosemia
  Hereditary fructose intolerance
  Glycogen synthetase deficiency
Inborn errors of lipid metabolism
  Tay-Sachs disease
  Sulfatide lipidosis
  Gaucher's disease (infantile form)
  Niemann-Pick's disease
Inborn errors of porphyrin metabolism
  Acute intermittent porphyria
Hypoglycemia
Hypocalcemia
Hypomagnesemia
Water intoxication and hypertonic dehydration

Developmental and Hereditary Defects of the Central Nervous System
Porencephaly
Arteriovenous malformations
Hydrocephalus
Megalencephaly
Neurocutaneous syndromes
Tuberous sclerosis
Sturge-Weber syndrome
Neurofibromatosis

Leukodystrophies
Krabbe's disease

Demyelinating Diseases
Schilder's disease

Degenerative Diseases of the Nervous System
Alper's disease
Spongy degeneration of the white matter (Canavan's disease)
Familial myoclonus epilepsy
Huntington's chorea

Cerebrovascular Accidents
Acute infantile hemiplegia
Subarachnoid hemorrhage or intracranial hematomas secondary to rupture of small angiomatous malformations or ruptured berry aneurysms

Neoplasias
Brain tumor
Meningeal and cerebral leukemia

Miscellaneous
Febrile seizures
Paroxysmal choreoathetosis
Subacute necrotizing encephalomyelitis
Hypertensive encephalopathy
Liver encephalopathy
Acute renal failure or late stages of renal diseases
Intoxications: lead, arsenic, thallium, parathion, mushroom poisoning, alcohol, penicillin given intravenously in very high dosages, phenothiazines, carbon monoxide, iodine, salicylates, digitalis, aniline dyes, and camphor.

entire body assumes a position of hyperextension. A clonic phase during which the four extremities jerk intermittently usually follows the tonic phase. Biting of the tongue and urinary or fecal incontinence may or may not occur. The attacks last as a rule from 2 to 10 minutes and are generally followed by a period of deep sleep. Occasionally a major motor seizure is manifested by sudden loss of consciousness and total limpness (axial seizures) lasting from 1 to 5 minutes. As in the more common major motor attack this atonic type may be associated with urinary or fecal incontinence and is as a rule followed by a period of confusion or sleep. The duration of the attack as well as the lack of premonitory signs permits differentiation of this variety of major motor attacks from fainting spells or syncopal attacks. The frequency of major motor seizures varies from one patient to another. They may occur at any age and are commonly associated with organic brain disease.

The electroencephalogram in patients with generalized seizures may show spike discharges in the temporal or temporal-central regions, atypical spike and wave discharges, slow spike and waves (1–2 per second), polyspikes and waves, and 6-per-second spike and waves (Fig. 19-1). The drugs of choice in the treatment of major motor seizures are phenobarbital and diphenylhydantoin (Dilantin).

Focal motor seizures are attacks initiated by local changes in specific areas of the cerebral cortex and may or may not be associated with loss of consciousness. They are clinically manifested by motor phenomena, usually beginning on one side of the face and subsequently spreading to the ipsilateral arm and leg. Occasionally the attack consists of jerking of one arm or one leg for brief periods of time. Sensory disturbances

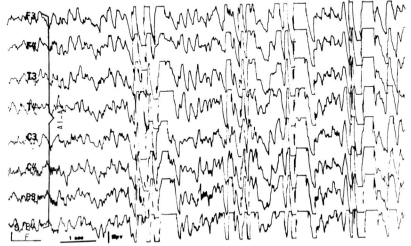

Fig. 19-1.   Electroencephalogram of 6-year-old boy with a history of major motor seizures showing brief bursts of generalized spike and wave activity interrupting an otherwise normal background.

zures are of short duration (1 or 2 seconds) and consist of sudden flexion of the neck, trunk, and arms and flexion or extension of the legs (Fig. 19-5). A cry may follow the jerk, and loss of consciousness, if at all present, is only momentary. A less common form of infantile spasms is that in which the infant hyperextends his entire body and cries for 15

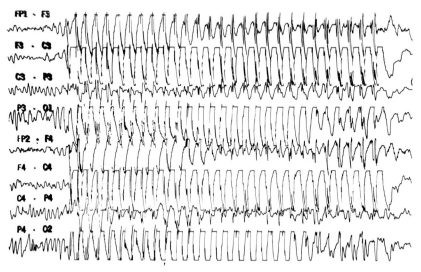

Fig. 19-4. Electroencephalogram in patient with petit mal showing bilateral and synchronous 3-per-second spike and wave complexes.

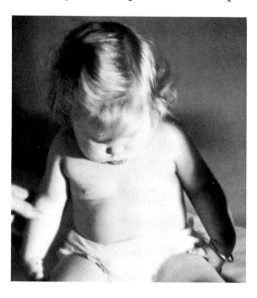

Fig. 19-5. 10-month-old infant with infantile spasms during a seizure manifested by sudden flexion of the head of about 1-second duration. No postictal manifestations.

to 30 seconds. During the attack there is no apparent loss of consciousness and the seizure is not followed by postictal manifestations. Infantile spasms often occur in clusters of 15 to 30 seizures over a 5-to-10-minute period. An affected infant may have anywhere from a few to 100 or 200 seizures daily.

Infantile spasms appear to be the response of an immature brain to a great variety of focal or widespread cerebral abnormalities. The diffuse nature of the brain response is well exemplified by the electroencephalogram, which in about 75 percent of cases shows a total disruption of normal rhythms (hypsarrhythmia) with a chaotic complex of high-voltage spikes, polyspikes, and slow waves (Fig. 19-6A,B). As the child grows, the clinical and EEG patterns are modified and new ones arise; infantile spasms rarely persist after the age of 3 years, at which time other types of seizure activity may become apparent. Similarly the electroencephalogram tends to improve with advancing age, and the hypsarrhythmia is replaced by more mature electrical patterns or other cerebral dysrhythmias. Even though infantile spasms have been recognized as a distinct form of seizure activity for more than 100 years, very little insight into their pathogenesis or therapy has been gained since their description by Dr. W. J. West in 1841. Infantile spasms, like other forms of seizure activity, are a symptom and not a disease. Listed below are the most common causes of infantile spasms.

INFANTILE SPASMS

Idiopathic (40 percent)
Phenylketonuria
Subdural hematoma
Hydrocephalus
Sturge-Weber syndrome
Following DPT vaccination
Tuberous sclerosis
Birth injury and neonatal anoxia
Developmental defects of the central nervous system
Postinfectious encephalopathy
Hypoglycemia
Maple syrup urine disease
Pyridoxine dependency
Postencephalitis

In approximately 40 percent of patients with infantile spasms an etiologic diagnosis cannot be made. This high percentage decreases considerably when neuropathological examination is carried out. At autopsy many of these patients show gross pathologic abnormalities such as polymicrogyria, macrogyria, brain atrophy, or unilateral magalencephaly (Fig. 19-6C).

The treatment of infantile spasms remains highly unsatisfactory. The seizures and the electroencephalographic abnormalities improve or cease altogether in about 75 percent of patients treated with daily doses

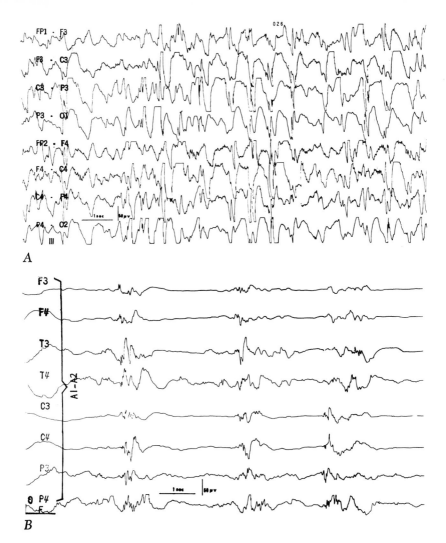

A

B

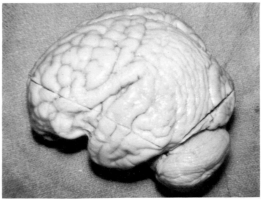

C

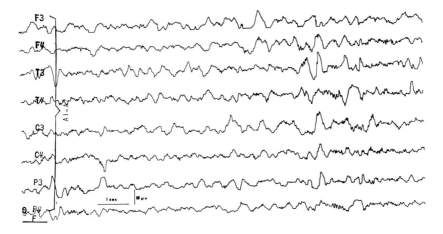

Fig. 19-7. Marked improvement in the electroencephalogram shown in Fig. 19-6 after 15 days of treatment with ACTH. Hypsarrhythmia pattern is no longer recognizable.

of ACTH or prednisone (Fig. 19-7). However, in only about 5 percent of patients is there improvement or a return to a normal psychomotor development. Mental deterioration progresses rapidly over a 2-to-3-month period and then remains more or less stationary. Similar good results in the control of seizures and improvement of electroencephalographic abnormalities have been obtained with a Librium analogue (LA-1), which is no longer available for clinical use in this country. However, as with ACTH the efficacy of this drug is entirely symptomatic and has no influence on the underlying pathologic process. Prompt therapy of treatable conditions such as episodes of hypoglycemia, phenylketonuria, hydrocephalus, pyridoxine dependency, and subdural hematoma will, in most instances, stop seizures and prevent further injury to an already damaged brain. A return to complete normality could hardly be expected in cases where the brain has suffered irreversible damage at such a critical stage of development.

MYOCLONIC SEIZURES OF CHILDHOOD

This type of seizure has its onset between 2 and 6 years of age. The attacks are characterized by head nodding, flexion of the arms, or a sud-

Fig. 19-6. *A,* electroencephalogram in 3-month-old infant with infantile spasms. Hypsarrhythmia pattern consisting of a chaotic mixture of high-voltage slow waves, spikes, and polyspikes. *B,* during sleep, pattern is intermittent with periods of flattening separating abnormal electrical discharges. *C,* brain of patient with infantile spasms, showing polymicrogyria.

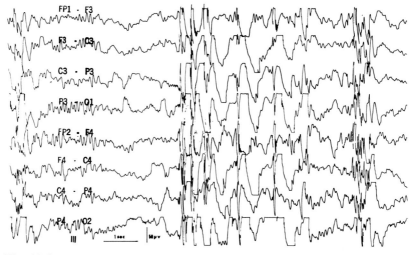

Fig. 19-8. Electroencephalogram in 6-year-old boy with myoclonic seizures showing bursts of diffuse spike, polyspikes, and spike and wave discharges.

den flexion of the entire body followed by a fall. Occasionally the muscle contraction produces extension of part or the entire body instead of the more common type of flexion attack. Myoclonic seizures may occur many times daily; they occur with greater frequency when the child is falling asleep or awakening. In rare instances the myoclonic jerk is limited to one side of the body. The attack in these cases is often confused with focal motor seizures. In some patients myoclonic seizures are manifested by sudden and momentary loss of awareness lasting a few seconds and accompanied by repetitive fluttering of the eyelids without loss of postural tone. This form of myoclonic jerks closely resembles petit mal. Myoclonic seizures are abrupt in onset, terminate in 1 to 3 seconds, and are not followed by postictal depression or sleep. The electroencephalogram may show 2-per-second spike and waves, polyspikes, and polyspike and waves complexes (Fig. 19-8). Patients with myoclonic seizures often suffer also from major motor attacks. As a group they are less bright than patients with petit mal or idiopathic generalized seizures. Myoclonic seizures are often refractory to treatment. Diazepam (Valium) is the only anticonvulsant with a fairly consistent beneficial effect. Other drugs such as phenobarbital, Zarontin, Dilantin, and Mysoline are less effective.

AKINETIC SEIZURES

Akinetic seizures are manifested clinically by sudden loss of postural tone followed by a fall. The attack lasts as a general rule from 1 to 3 seconds. If there is any loss of consciousness, it is only momentary. The child recovers promptly and there are no postictal manifestations. The electroencephalogram may show changes similar to those seen in myoclonic seizures.

Akinetic and generalized seizures often occur in the same patient. Diazepam (Valium) and phenobarbital are the most effective drugs in the treatment of akinetic seizures.

CONVULSIVE EQUIVALENTS

Cyclic vomiting; episodes of recurrent attacks of headaches, nausea, or abdominal pain; or other symptoms referable to dysfunction of the autonomic nervous system may occur as a manifestation of transient abnormal cerebral activity. A diagnosis of convulsive equivalent is one of exclusion. A family history of epilepsy, the sudden onset and termination of the attack, the presence of electroencephalographic abnormalities, and the response to anticonvulsant therapy (Dilantin or phenobarbital) are helpful in establishing a diagnosis of this type of seizure activity.

FEBRILE SEIZURES

A febrile seizure has been defined as a convulsion associated with any fever of extracranial origin, a convulsion precipitated by fever in a patient who has a potential convulsive disorder, and a generalized or focal seizure of less than 20 minutes in association with extracranial infection in a child less than 5 years old in whom a normal electroencephalogram is obtained one week after temperature has returned to normal. Approximately 2 to 4 percent of children under 5 years will experience one or more febrile seizures. As a rule the precipitating illness is an upper respiratory infection, tonsillitis, or otitis media. They do not occur often in the usual childhood exanthems, except for roseola. Most febrile seizures occur in children between 6 months and 3 years of age. Generalized clonic seizures are most common, although tonic or focal seizures may occur.

The efficacy of prophylactic anticonvulsant therapy in the prevention of febrile seizures is still a matter of controversy. Some workers feel that a child with febrile seizures of short duration and in whom a normal electroencephalogram is obtained not earlier than five to seven days after recovery from the convulsion and who does not show permanent neurologic signs or evidence of a structural cerebral lesion should receive intermittent therapy (antipyretics and phenobarbital) during febrile illnesses. Others feel that all children with febrile seizures should be treated with continuous prophylactic anticonvulsant therapy, the rationale being that in our present state of knowledge it is difficult if not impossible to differentiate between simple febrile seizures from an epileptic attack precipitated by fever, and that statistically approximately 20 percent of children with febrile seizures will subsequently develop nonfebrile seizures.

COMMENT

Since the success in the treatment of a patient with seizures depends primarily on a proper diagnosis as to the type of convulsive activity, it is necessary to emphasize that to elicit an accurate and complete history of the attacks is of paramount importance. This will enable the examiner to categorize accurately the type of seizure in the great majority of instances and institute the appropriate therapy. In our experience a large percentage of young children referred with a diagnosis of petit mal suffer from myoclonic or psychomotor seizures. It is necessary to reemphasize that true petit mal rarely occurs before the age of 4 and probably never before the age of 3 years.

The diagnostic investigation of a child seen during or immediately following a first generalized seizure should include a complete general and neurologic examination in order to determine whether the seizure is the first episode of a chronic convulsive disorder or it is secondary to metabolic disturbances, extracranial or intracranial infections, intoxications (lead poisoning, drugs), the first manifestation of a subdural hematoma or some other kind of intracranial bleeding, or a symptom of pathology elsewhere in the body (acute glomerulonephritis). Pertinent laboratory investigations include a complete blood count, urinalysis, serum electrolytes, blood glucose, calcium, and blood urea nitrogen. Skull x-rays may reveal unsuspected evidence of head trauma, intracerebral calcification, or signs of increased intracranial pressure. The electroencephalogram may demonstrate abnormal electrical discharges or a persistent slow-wave focus in cases of a supratentorial space-occupying lesion (brain tumor, subdural hematoma, brain abscess). A number of children are admitted to a hospital following their first convulsion. In most instances a spinal tap is performed, especially if the child has fever. If no apparent reason for the fever is encountered, examination of the cerebrospinal fluid should be done in all patients to rule out bacterial meningitis or other intracranial infections. If a child is seen weeks or months after one or more generalized seizures the diagnostic investigation is usually less extensive. If the history and neurologic examination do not suggest a structural abnormality of the brain (hydrocephalus, porencephaly, etc.), a degenerative disease, or some other ongoing process (subdural hematoma), laboratory tests should include determination of fasting blood sugar, serum calcium, urinalysis, skull x-rays, and an electroencephalogram.

A specific abnormality amenable to therapy (hypoglycemia, hypocalcemia, pyridoxine dependency, intoxications, brain tumor, subdural hematoma) is found only in a very small percentage of children with seizures. The rest should receive continuous anticonvulsant therapy as soon as a diagnosis is made. Therapy should be started with the drug which is most likely to control seizure activity. Initially, a moderate-sized dosage should be given and increments made until seizures are under control or toxic effects develop. The proper dosage is that which controls seizures without producing side effects, such as somnolence, drowsiness, or ataxia, which interfere with the patient's well-being. If the first drug does not completely control seizures at high dosages or produces adverse reactions, a second or third drug can be added and again increased until control of seizure is obtained or toxic effects develop. If a child is seizure-free for a fairly prolonged period, a gradual and spontaneous tapering off takes place as he gains in weight. Anticonvulsant therapy should be continued for at least three years after the last attack. It may then be gradually discontinued over a 9- to 12-month period depending on the dosage and the number of anticonvulsants. If a large amount of anticonvulsant was needed to gain control of seizures, it may be necessary to prolong this period for more than one year.

As long as a patient's seizures have not stopped, he should be reevaluated at frequent intervals since during this period increments in the dosage of one medication or the addition of new ones will have to be made. Once the patient is asymptomatic he may be reexamined every three or six months. If for any reason a complete neurologic evaluation cannot be performed during these visits, the physical examination of a child with seizures should always include examination of the optic fundi and the visual fields by gross confrontation, auscultation of the skull for bruits, and testing of plantar responses (Babinski sign). It is our impression that almost any other neurologic sign or symptom is in most instances more or less obvious and is invariably volunteered by the patient or the parents. Laboratory tests during the follow-up examinations should include a complete blood count, urinalysis or liver function tests if the patient is taking a drug which may have adverse effects on the bone marrow, the kidneys, or the liver. Skull x-rays and an electroencephalogram are recommended at yearly intervals.

In order of preference we use the following drugs for seizures:

Major motor: phenobarbital, Dilantin, Mysoline
Psychomotor: phenobarbital, Mysoline, Dilantin
Petit mal: Zarontin, Tridione, Paradione, Diamox
Myoclonic: Valium, phenobarbital
Akinetic: Valium, phenobarbital
Convulsive equivalents: Dilantin, phenobarbital.

See Appendix 2 for a more detailed description of drugs used in the treatment of seizures in children.

REFERENCES

Carter, S., and Gold, A. Convulsions in children. *New Eng. J. Med.* 278: 315, 1968.
Gibbs, F. A., and Gibbs, E. L. Age factor in epilepsy: A summary and synthesis. *New Eng. J. Med.* 269:1230, 1963.
Greer, M. Managing a child's first convulsion. *Postgrad. Med.* 46:109, 1969.
Hammill, J. F., and Carter, S. Febrile convulsions. *New Eng. J. Med.* 274:563, 1966.
Keith, H. M. *Convulsive Disorders in Children with Reference to Treatment with Ketogenic Diet.* Boston: Little, Brown, 1963.
Lagos, J. C. Febrile seizures: To treat or not to treat. *Postgrad. Med.* 47:189, 1970.
Livingston, S. *The Diagnosis and Treatment of Convulsive Disorders in Children.* Springfield, Ill.: Thomas, 1954.
Livingston, S. *Drug Therapy for Epilepsy.* Springfield, Ill.: Thomas, 1966.
Millichap, J. G. *Febrile Convulsions.* New York: Macmillan, 1968.
Millichap, J. G., et al. Cyclic vomiting as a form of epilepsy in children. *Pediatrics* 15:705, 1955.
Snyder, C. H. Myoclonic epilepsy in children: Short-term comparative study of two benzodiazepine derivatives in treatment. *South. Med. J.* 61:17, 1968.
Swaiman, K. F. Petit mal seizures. *Postgrad. Med.* 46:93, 1969.
Weinberg, W. A., and Harwell, J. L. Diazepam (Valium) in myoclonic seizures. *Amer. J. Dis. Child.* 109:123, 1965.
Wright, F. S. Myoclonic seizures in infancy and childhood. *Postgrad. Med.* 46:100, 1969.

Appendix 1

Neonatal Reflexes and Developmental Milestones

NEONATAL REFLEXES

The neurologic examination of the newborn includes for the most part the elicitation of reflexes and reactions. Reflexes are obligatory responses, in contrast to reactions which are nonobligatory and are often modified by different physiologic states.

Cephalic Reflexes

1. *Corneal reflex*, pupillary reactions to light, and closure of the eyes in response to a strong light (blinking reflex) are present since birth.
2. *Ciliary reflex:* Unilateral or bilateral closure of the eyes when eyelashes are touched.
3. *Nasopalpebral reflex:* Tapping the root of the nose causes homolateral or bilateral blinking.
4. *McCarthy reflex:* Similar response to nasopalpebral reflex when the supraorbital region is tapped.
5. *Rooting reflex:* Stimulation of the corners of the mouth causes the baby to lower the ipsilateral corner of the mouth and to move the head toward the examiner's finger if this is kept in contact with the cheek. Stimulation of the upper and lower lips produces an upward or downward elevation of the lips. If the finger is slightly moved from this position the baby hyperextends or flexes his head.
6. *Sucking reflex:* If a finger is placed in the baby's mouth, it evokes rhythmic sucking and swallowing movements of variable duration.

Neck Reflexes

Moro reflex: This consists of abduction of the arms and extension of the forearms and fingers followed by a return to the normal position of flexion (embrace) when the head of the baby is abruptly moved in relation to the spine. It can be elicited by several maneuvers such as lifting the head of the baby to a 45-degree angle and letting it drop over the mattress, or by hitting the infant's pillow with both hands as originally described by Moro.

Loud noises seldom cause a Moro reflex. Infants may respond to loud noises with a startle reaction (flexion movement) which is the opposite of the Moro reflex.

Tonic neck reflex: This reflex consists of extension of the arm and leg on one side of the body and flexion of the opposite extremities when the head is moved to one side (fencing position). This reflex can only be elicited if both shoulders are kept in contact with the examining table; it is difficult to elicit in the neonate. An obligatory tonic neck reflex is always pathologic.

Trunk Incurvation Reflex (Galant's Reflex)

Stimulation of the back between the ribs and the iliac crest produces incurvation of the trunk toward the stimulated side. This is a very primitive and constant reflex.

Upper Extremities

Palmar grasp: Stimulation of the ulnar side of the palm produces flexion of the fingers. This reaction is not synonymous with the pathologic grasp of adults with lesions of the central nervous system. It is also called the *tonic reaction of the finger flexors.* The *biceps reflex* and *supinator reflex* are present at birth. Because of the marked predominance of the flexor muscles of the arms the *triceps jerk* can only rarely be elicited.

Lower Extremities

The *plantar grasp* or *tonic reaction of the toe flexors* consists of flexion of the toes as a response to pressure by the examiner's fingers on the sole of the foot between the first and second toe.

The *crossed extension reflex* consists of flexion followed by adduction and then extension of one leg when the extended opposite leg is stimulated at the sole. Of all the muscle stretch reflexes of the lower extremities, only the *knee jerk* can be elicited in the newborn.

Plantar responses are extensor in this age group and persist in most infants until they begin to walk.

Righting and Stepping Reactions

When the baby is held in ventral suspension there is spontaneous righting of the head. If he is held in the upright position with both feet touching the table there is righting of the lower extremities. If he is held with his back against the front of the examiner and pressure is applied on the soles or the foot is moved up and down at the ankle, there is first righting of the trunk and then of the head. If the baby is held by the examiner's hands with both feet on the table and his body tilted forward, stepping movements can be elicited.

REFERENCES

André-Thomas, Chesni, Y., and Saint-Anne Dargassies, S. *The Neurological Examination of the Infant.* Little Club Clinics in Developmental Medicine No. 1, Mac Keith, R. C., Polani, P. E., and Clayton-Jones, E. (Eds.). London: The Spastics Society, 1960.

Peiper, A. *Cerebral Function in Infancy and Childhood*. New York: Consultants Bureau Enterprises, Inc., 1963.

DEVELOPMENTAL MILESTONES

One Month

Posture of flexion predominates in the supine and the prone as well as the vertical position. The infant is able to hold chin up on prone position and to rotate head from side to side. In ventral suspension the infant's head hangs down. Hands are closed. There is a marked head lag when the infant is pulled to the sitting position. By the end of the first month baby regards mother and is able to fix eyes on objects or people. Undifferentiated cry (first manifestation of language) in response to any unpleasant experience.

Two Months

In ventral suspension the head is maintained at same level as body. In the prone position infant is able to lift head to an angle of 45 degrees from the mattress. Less head lag when baby is pulled by hands to sitting position. Hands frequently open. Infant smiles and listens to voices. Differentiated cry according to stimulus (hunger, pain, etc.).

Three Months

In prone position baby lifts head and chest from table, bearing weight on arms. Holds head up with minimal wobbling. Rolls over from supine position. Grasps rattle. There is lateral arm activity with hands clasped at midline. Maintains hands open most of the time. Baby anticipates feeding with increased motor activity. Inspects fingers. Smiles spontaneously and laughs. Begins to babble.

Four Months

No head lag when baby is pulled by hands to sitting, and no wobbling of head in the upright position. Bears some weight on legs. Rolls over from prone position. Reaches for objects; beginning of thumb apposition. There is finger manipulation of one hand with the other. Baby laughs aloud and exhibits anticipatory response of welcome to mother's presence. Babbling.

Six Months

Sits with support. Able to take two cubes. Transfers a cube from hand to hand. Holds objects with a primitive grasp using radial palm. Reaches for objects unilaterally and persistently. Strong emotional attachment to mother already established. Cries if left alone with strangers. Begins to repeat self-made sounds (lallation).

Seven Months

Sits without support. Pulls up to stand from a sitting position if held by hands. Holds objects with palm and thumb. Plays peek-a-boo.

Nine Months

Begins to crawl. Has become increasingly aware and curious about his environment. Will follow disappearing visual stimulus. Seeks attention. Plays pat-a-cake. Pokes at objects with index finger. Able to hold object between finger and thumb. Begins to repeat sounds made by other persons (echolalia).

Ten to Twelve Months

Walks with assistance or holding on to furniture. Plays with two objects in combination; attempts to take third cube while holding two cubes. Interested in pictures in book. First meaningful word by 12 months. Holds objects between tip of thumb and index finger (pincer grasp). Walks without help with a broad-based gait by end of twelfth month.

Fourteen Months

Walks backward. Climbs stairs on all four extremities. Makes a tower of two cubes.

Eighteen to Twenty Months

Climbs on furniture. Can kick and throw ball. Walks up and down stairs with help. Builds tower of four cubes. Vocabulary of about 12 to 15 words. Feeds self and spills little.

Two Years

Can jump in place. Builds tower of four or more cubes. Helps to undress himself. Open doors. Attempts to fold paper into book form; turns pages in a book singly. By the end of the second year vocabulary reaches 25 or more words, and child begins to make two-word sentences. Able to understand a larger number of words.

Three Years

Walks downstairs alone. Builds tower of nine blocks. Unbuttons accessible buttons. Able to ride tricycle. Can copy circle. Answers in four-word sentences.

Four Years

Can copy a square. Walks downstairs alternating feet. Can hop more than 10 steps, and tiptoe 10 feet. Answers in five-word sentences.

Five Years

May learn to skip. Able to balance on toes and to stand for long periods on one foot. Can copy a triangle. Answers in six-word sentences.

Six Years

Learns to tie shoelaces. Can ride a bicycle without training wheels. Can trace a diamond. Answers in seven-word sentences.

REFERENCES

Falkner, F. (Ed.). *Human Development*. Philadelphia: Saunders, 1966.
Illingworth, R. S. *The Development of the Infant and Young Child*. Edinburgh: Livingstone, 1960.

Appendix 2
Drugs Most Commonly Used in Pediatric Neurology

AT PRESENT, no specific drug therapy is available for a number of diseases affecting the nervous system in infancy and childhood. Most of these conditions are either congenital or hereditary disorders or are developmental anomalies of the central nervous system. Here, reference is made primarily to drugs used in the treatment of seizures and acute bacterial meningitis. Seizures are a very common problem in the practice of pediatrics, and the vast majority of them can be adequately controlled with anticonvulsant drugs. It is necessary to reemphasize that success in the control of any type of seizure depends on an accurate categorization of its type and the selection of the drug most likely to be effective for that particular type of seizure. Therapeutic failures are often related to one or both of these factors and/or to the administration of insufficient amounts of anticonvulsant drugs.

Early diagnosis and isolation of the causative organism causing acute bacterial meningitis and the selection of the antibiotic to which the organism is most sensitive are, needless to say, crucial determinants in its morbidity and mortality.

DRUGS USED IN TREATMENT OF HYPERACTIVITY

The following drugs are useful in the treatment of hyperactive children. The best results are obtained with central nervous system stimulants such as Dexedrine or Ritalin.
1. Amphetamines (Dexedrine): 5–20 mg. daily in two divided doses given early in the morning and afternoon.
2. Methylphenidate (Ritalin): 5–40 mg. daily in two divided doses given early in the morning and afternoon.
3. Chlordiazepoxide (Librium): 5–30 mg. daily in divided doses.
4. Chlorpromazine (Thorazine): 10–50 mg. daily in divided doses.
5. Thioridazine (Mellaril): 10 mg. two or three times daily for preschool children and 25 mg. two or three times daily for school-age children.

DRUGS USED IN THE TREATMENT OF SEIZURES IN CHILDHOOD

Drug	Type of Seizure	Dosage in Daily Divided Doses	Preparation	Toxic Effects

Phenobarbital	Major motor
	  Generalized
	  Focal
	Psychomotor
	Myoclonic
	Akinetic
	Convulsive equivalents
		3–6 mg./kg.	16, 32, 64, and 100 mg. tablets; elixir, 16 mg. per 4 cc. (tsp.)	Drowsiness
				Hyperactivity
				Skin rashes (rare)
				Stevens-Johnson syndrome (rare)

Diphenylhydantoin (Dilantin)	Major motor
	  Generalized
	  Focal
	Psychomotor
	Convulsive equivalents
		4–8 mg./kg.	30 and 100 mg. capsules; 50-mg. chewable tablets; suspension, 30 and 125 mg. per 5 cc.	Gum hypertrophy
				Ataxia
				Nystagmus
				Skin rashes
				Granulocytopenia
				Thrombocytopenia
				Leukopenia
				Hirsutism
				Lymphadenopathy
				Stevens-Johnson syndrome

Primidone (Mysoline)	Psychomotor Major motor Myoclonic	10–25 mg./kg.	50 and 250 mg. tablets; suspension, 250 mg. per 5 cc.	Drowsiness Ataxia Skin rashes Leukopenia Megaloblastic anemia
Ethosuximide (Zarontin)	Petit mal	20–40 mg./kg.	250 mg. capsules	Leukopenia

Drug	Indications	Dosage	Preparations	Side Effects
Trimethadione (Tridione)	Petit mal	20–40 mg./kg.	300 mg. capsules; 150 mg. tablets; solution, 150 mg. per 4 cc.	Pancytopenia Thrombocytopenia Agranulocytosis Skin rashes Nephrosis Blood dyscrasias Skin rashes Aplastic anemia Stevens-Johnson syndrome
Paramethadione (Paradione)	Petit mal	20–40 mg./kg.	150 and 300 mg. capsules; solution, 300 mg. per cc.	Drowsiness Other side effects similar to Tridione (less frequent and less severe)
Acetazolamide (Diamox)	Petit mal	15–30 mg./kg.	125 and 250 mg. tablets	Renal crystalluria Agranulocytosis Thrombocytopenia
Diazepam (Valium)	Status epilepticus Myoclonic Akinetic	0.5–2 mg./kg.; start with small doses (e.g., 2 mg. three times a day) and increase at weekly intervals as needed and tolerated. Status epilepticus (see Appendix 3)	2, 5, and 10 mg. tablets	Drowsiness Incoordination (common) Hypotension (rare) Nausea (rare) Skin rash (rare) Neutropenia (rare)
Mephobarbital (Mebaral)	Major motor Generalized	4–12 mg./kg.	32, 50, 100, and 200 mg. tablets	Same as phenobarbital but occur with less frequency and severity

REFERENCES

Burks, H. F.   Effects of amphetamine therapy on hyperkinetic children. *Arch. Gen. Psychiat.* 11:604, 1964.
Millichap, J. G., and Fowler, G. W.   Treatment of "minimal brain dysfunction" syndromes. *Pediat. Clin. N. Amer.* 14:767, 1967.

DRUGS USED IN TREATMENT OF ACUTE BACTERIAL MENINGITIS

Unknown etiology (first 2 months: ampicillin or penicillin and kanamycin)
    Ampicillin: 100 to 300 mg./kg./day depending on age IM or IV in 4 doses.
    Penicillin G: 100,000 U/kg./day IM or IV in 2 doses during first week of life and afterward 500,000 U/kg./day IV in 4 to 6 doses.
    Kanamycin: 15 mg./kg./day IM in 2 doses.
Unknown etiology (after 2 months)
    Ampicillin: 300 to 400 mg./kg./day IM or IV in 4 doses.
Escherichia coli (gentamicin, kanamycin, or cephalothin)
    Gentamicin: 3 to 5 mg./kg./day IM in 2 doses to premature infants during the first week of life and 3 doses at any other age.
    Kanamycin: 15 mg./kg./day IM in 3 doses.
    Cephalothin: 120 mg./kg./day IM or IV in 4 to 6 doses.
Haemophilus influenzae (ampicillin or chloramphenicol)
    Ampicillin (drug of choice): 300 to 400 mg./kg./day IM or IV in 4 doses.
    Chloramphenicol (use only if patient is allergic to penicillin): 50 to 100 mg./kg./day IV in 3 to 4 doses. Give 25 to 50 mg./kg./day if jaundice or renal impairment is present. Premature and full-term newborn (up to 2 weeks): 25 mg./kg./day.
Pneumococcus (penicillin or ampicillin)
    Sodium or potassium penicillin G: 5 to 10 million units per day IM or IV. Newborn infant: same dosage as for meningitis of unknown etiology. When large amounts of sodium or potassium penicillin G are given IV consider amount of sodium and potassium present: 1 million units of potassium penicillin G contains 65.8 mg. of potassium (1.68 mEq.) and 1 million units of sodium penicillin G contains 38.7 mg. of sodium (1.68 mEq.).
    Ampicillin: same dosage as that for *H. influenzae*.
Meningococcus (penicillin or ampicillin: same dosage as that for pneumococcus).
Staphylococcus (methicillin, oxacillin, or cephalothin)
    Methicillin: 200 to 400 mg./kg./day IM or IV in 4 to 6 doses.
    Oxacillin: 100 to 150 mg./kg./day IM in 4 doses or IV in 4 to 6 doses in infants and young children; 4 to 6 gm./day in 6 doses for older children.
    Cephalothin: same dosage as that for *E. coli*.
    In severe cases not responding to above medications recommended drug is vancomycin: 40 mg./kg./day IV in 4 doses.
Streptococcus
    Penicillin and Kanamycin initially. Subsequent therapy depends on sensitivity and grouping.

Pseudomonas aeruginosa (gentamicin, carbenicillin, polymyxin B, or colistin)
Gentamicin: same dosage as that for *E. coli.*
Carbenicillin: 300 to 400 mg./kg./day IM or IV in 6 doses.
Polymyxin B: 2.5 mg./kg./day IV in 2 to 3 doses or IM in 4 to 6 doses
up to 200 mg./24 hours. If there is renal impairment give 1.5
mg./kg./day IV or IM. Polymyxin B can also be used intrathecally, in
addition to systemic therapy, in a dosage of 2 mg./day for 3 to 4 days
followed by 2.5 mg. every other day in children under the age of 2 years
or in a dosage of 5 mg./day for 3 to 4 days, followed by 5 mg. every
other day in children older than 2 years.
Colistin: 5 mg./kg./day IM in 2 to 4 doses (not for intrathecal use).

Penicillin may cause allergic and occasionally serious anaphylactic reactions. All other drugs used in the treatment of bacterial meningitis are
potentially toxic to the kidney, liver, acoustic nerve, or bone marrow.
For a detailed description of contraindications to their use and precautions to be taken during therapy, see latest edition of the readily available *Physician's Desk Reference* or the *American Hospital Formulary.*

REFERENCES

Mathies, A. W., Jr., and Wehrle, P. F.   Management of bacterial meningitis
in children. *Pediat. Clin. N. Amer.* 15:185, 1968.
Report of the Committee on Infectious Diseases, American Academy of
Pediatrics (ed. by F. H. Top), 1970.

DRUGS USED IN TREATMENT OF MIGRAINE

Since as early as 1940, a number of investigators have reported that a
significant percentage of children and adults with migraine experience improvement or complete relief of symptoms when treated with Dilantin. We
have also been impressed by the beneficial effect of Dilantin in children suffering from migraine. In general, if the child is going to improve on this
form of therapy, he will do so on a smaller amount of Dilantin than is
needed to control major motor or other types of seizures. It is possible that
some of these children with periodic episodes of headaches and who respond favorably to this drug suffer from convulsive-equivalent attacks rather
than vascular headaches.

The use of ergotamine tartrate, a useful drug in the treatment of migraine
in adults, is less effective in children. A possible explanation for this difference may be that treatment is not given early enough during an attack due
to the lack of premonitory symptoms or because these symptoms go unrecog-
nized in young children. Methysergide (Sansert), a drug used in the prevention of attacks in adults, may cause serious complications such as retroperitoneal fibrosis or phlebothrombosis; its use is not recommended in
children. A combination of acetylsalicylic acid (60 mg. per year of age up to
600 mg.) and amobarbital (16 mg. for a young child and 32 mg. for a school-
age child) orally, or in suppositories when attacks are associated with vomiting, is effective at the time of the attack.

REFERENCES

Burke, C. E., and Peters, G. A.   Migraine in childhood. *Amer. J. Dis. Child.* 92:330, 1956.
Gellis, S. S., and Kagan, B. M. (Eds.).   *Current Pediatric Therapy.* Philadelphia: Saunders, 1970.   .

DRUGS USED IN TREATMENT OF MENINGEAL LEUKEMIA

Since the advent of effective antileukemic therapy, meningeal leukemia occurs in as many as 50 percent of children with acute leukemia. Currently methotrexate and cytosine arabinoside are effective drugs in the treatment of meningeal leukemia. Radiation therapy is less effective than chemotherapy.

1. Methotrexate: 12 mg./sq.M. intrathecally every 5 days until cerebrospinal fluid cell count (WBC) falls to normal levels. The prophylactic administration of methotrexate at 6–8-week intervals produces more prolonged remissions. Side effects of this form of therapy are severe headache, vomiting, and/or fever. The simultaneous administration of hydrocortisone intrathecally (15 mg./sq.M. up to 15 mg.) appears to reduce the incidence of side effects produced by methotrexate.

2. The intrathecal administration of cytosine arabinoside produces less toxic effects but is also less effective than methotrexate therapy. The proper dosage of this drug has not been definitely established. The efficacy of a combined intrathecal therapy using methotraxate, cytosine arabinoside and hydrocortisone is being evaluated at the present time.

3. Radiation therapy to entire neuraxis. At present recommended dose is 2000 R; this appears to produce more prolonged remissions than the formerly used dose of 1200 R.

REFERENCES

Evans, A. E., and Craig, M.   Central nervous system involvement in children with acute leukemia. A study of 921 patients. *Cancer* 17:256, 1964.
Halikowski, B., et al. Cytosine arabinoside administered intrathecally in cerebromeningeal leukemia. *Acta Paediat. Scand.* 59:164, 1970.

Appendix 3

Treatment of Some Medical Emergencies

SEVERE HEAD TRAUMA

Emergency Management

1. Maintenance of an adequate oxygen supply to the brain. A comatose patient usually has difficulty breathing and he may need a mouthpiece airway, tracheal intubation, or tracheotomy, aspiration of secretions, and use of oxygen.
2. Maintenance of an adequate cerebral perfusion. If the patient is in shock this can be accomplished by the parenteral administration of vasoconstrictors (Aramine, Isuprel, Levophed or Neo-Synephrine) and the administration of blood or plasma.
3. Reduction of cerebral metabolism and cerebral edema: Hypothermia and dehydrated agents such as intravenous (IV) urea, mannitol, or intramuscular (IM) or IV steroids (Decadron).

   Check vital signs every 15 minutes during acute stage. Neurologic examination or subsequent clinical course may provide indications for specific diagnostic studies to rule out an expanding intracranial lesion (extradural, subdural, or intracerebral hematoma).

STATUS EPILEPTICUS

1. *Valium:* 1 to 2 mg. IM or IV for infants and 2.5 to 10 mg. for children given slowly over a period of 2 minutes. Same dose can be repeated in 20 to 30 minutes.
2. *Sodium phenobarbital (Luminal):* 5 to 6 mg./kg. IM or IV given slowly over a period of 5 to 10 minutes. Too rapid administration may cause laryngospasm or shock; a larger amount may produce respiratory arrest. Initial dose followed by a maintenance dosage of 5 to 6 mg. per day in three divided doses.
3. *Paraldehyde:* IM in a dose of 1 cc. per year of age not exceeding 5 cc. or 0.3 to 0.6 cc./kg. per rectum mixed in equal amount of olive oil in an amount of up to 10 cc.
4. *Inhalation anesthesia:* A general anesthetic may in some instances be needed to stop status epilepticus.

Livingston recommends the administration of Valium followed immediately by the subcutaneous injection of phenobarbital in a dose of 65 mg. per year of age in a total dose not exceeding 325 mg. The IV or IM administration of Valium will stop status epilepticus in the great majority of patients. It is difficult to set a rigid scheme for the treatment of status epilepticus, since success varies from one patient to the other and most importantly according to etiology. Since the natural course of events in this medical emergency is either death or cessation of seizures, a rule of thumb is to give as much anticonvulsant medication and as frequently as needed to stop seizure activity provided that the necessary precautions be taken and that the physician be prepared to handle on the spot adverse reactions to the administration of large amounts of anticonvulsants. Whenever drugs such as phenobarbital or Valium, which are known to depress respiration, are used in large amounts, the physician should have on hand the equipment necessary to intubate the patient and provide artificial respiration.

REFERENCES

Livingston, S.   Seizure Disorders. In Gellis, S. S., and Kagan, B. M. (Eds.), *Current Pediatric Therapy*. Philadelphia: Saunders, 1970.
McMorris, S., and McWilliam, P. K. A.   Status epilepticus in infants and young children treated with parenteral diazepam. *Arch. Dis. Child.* 44:604, 1969.

CEREBRAL EDEMA

1. Hypothermia of 32.2° to 33.3°C (90° to 92°F). This decreases cerebral edema as well as oxygen consumption of the brain. Shivering can be prevented by the use of chlorpromazine in a dosage of 2 mg./kg. per day in three or four divided doses.
2. Urea* (30% solution) IV in 10% invert sugar in a dosage of 1 gm./kg. given over a 20 to 30 minute period. Same dose can be repeated in 8 hours if needed.
3. Mannitol (20% solution) IV in distilled water in a dosage of 1.5 gm./kg. given over a period of 20 to 30 minutes.
4. Decadron (Dexamethasone) 5 mg. IM or IV stat. Same dose can be repeated once, followed by a maintenance dose of 2 mg. every 6 hours for 3 to 4 days and tapered by 7 to 10 days.

REFERENCES

Matson, D. D.   Treatment of cerebral swelling. *New Eng. J. Med.* 272:626, 1965.
Rabe, E. F.   Cerebral Edema. In Gellis, S. S., and Kagan, B. M. (Eds.), *Current Pediatric Therapy*. Philadelphia: Saunders, 1970.
Shenkin, H. A., and Bouzarth, W. F.   Clinical methods of reducing intracranial pressure. *New Eng. J. Med.* 282:1465, 1970.

* Contraindicated in severely dehydrated patients, in patients with severe renal insufficiency or in those with intracranial hematoma prior to the evacuation of the clot.

LEAD ENCEPHALOPATHY

1. BAL (Dimercaprol) 2.5 mg./kg. IM every 4 hours for 2–3 days.
2. Calcium disodium versenate 75 mg./kg. daily IV or IM for 5–7 days. A second course can be given two weeks later if blood levels remain above 80 μg./100 ml.
3. Treatment of cerebral edema with Decadron 3–4 mg. every 6 hours for 2 days. Dehydrating agents (urea, mannitol) may be used if there is severe brain edema. In life-threatening situations surgical decompression may be necessary.
4. Give only maintenance amount of fluids (40–60 ml./kg. per 24 hours) even if patient is dehydrated.
5. For treatment of seizures paraldehyde rectally (0.3–0.6 cc./kg. up to 10 cc.), chloral hydrate rectally (0.05 gm./kg. not exceeding 1 gm. per day), or an inhalation anesthetic (ether) may be used. Phenobarbital is not effective in the control of seizures of lead encephalopathy, and large amounts of it may precipitate respiratory arrest.

REFERENCES

Coffin, R., et al.   Treatment of lead encephalopathy in children. *J. Pediat.* 69:198, 1966.
Greenhard, J.   Lead poisoning in childhood: Signs, symptoms, current therapy, clinical expressions. *Clin. Pediat.* (Phila.) 5:269, 1966.

Appendix 4

Evaluation of Child in Coma of Unknown Etiology

THE EVALUATION of a child with sudden impairment or loss of consciousness is frequently a difficult diagnostic problem. In many instances, and due to the seriousness of the situation, supportive and symptomatic treatment has to be instituted even before the physician can begin to speculate upon the many diagnostic possibilities. If this is the case, it is mandatory that one or more people provide the initial emergency care and that another person obtain the history from parents or relatives. They should be questioned not only about the present or preceding illnesses or symptoms but also about the probabilities of drug ingestion. Direct questioning regarding all medicines kept at home as well as the possibility of ingestion of toxic household products is necessary. It should be remembered that a history of pica is almost always elicited in patients with lead intoxication.

The general physical examination of a patient in coma includes a search for external evidence of trauma, bitten tongue, hemorrhage or cerebrospinal fluid leakage from the nose or ears, evidence of congenital or acquired heart disease, hepatomegaly, presence of cranial bruits, and examination of the peripheral pulses, including palpation and auscultation of the carotid arteries. Vital signs should be checked at frequent intervals. Deep and labored breathing, a high blood pressure, and a slow pulse usually indicate increased intracranial pressure. The neurologic examination should note the size and equality of the pupils and their reaction to light, the corneal reflex, and the doll's-eye phenomenon; the absence of the latter, as a rule, indicates severe brain stem dysfunction. Examination of the eyegrounds may reveal papilledema, fat emboli, angiomatous malformations, or retinal hemorrhages. There may be stiffness of the neck or other signs of meningeal irritation (meningitis, subarachnoid bleeding). Muscle tone, muscle stretch reflexes, and plantar responses should be noted. A hemiplegia is suggested by the lack of spontaneous movement of an extremity or lack of withdrawal following a painful stimulus. This can best be accomplished without injury to the child by a firm squeeze of the fingernails or toenails.

Laboratory tests should include a complete blood count, and urinalysis (glucose, acetone, diacetic acid, and albumin), electrolytes, blood urea nitrogen, blood glucose and calcium, serum salicylate level, qualitative screening for coproporphyrins in the urine, and if there is liver enlargement, serum levels of SGOT (for Reye's syndrome). Skull x-rays may show a fracture and on rare occasions suprasellar or posterior fossa calcification in a patient with a craniopharyngioma or posterior fossa tumor and acutely decompensated obstructive hydrocephalus. X-rays of long bones and a flat plate of the abdomen are indicated if lead poisoning is suspected. If signs of meningeal irritation are present a lumbar puncture should be done even in patients with increased intracranial pressure (for this the use of a small needle and the withdrawal of small amounts of cerebrospinal fluid are recommended). If the history and physical examination do not suggest a diagnosis of meningitis or subarachnoid bleeding in a patient who is comatose and has signs and symptoms of increased intracranial pressure, a lumbar puncture is of little diagnostic help and may prove fatal as a result of herniation of the uncus or cerebellar tonsils and pressure on the brain stem. Intracranial space-occupying lesions (tumor, abscess, etc.) other than extradural, subdural, or spontaneous intracerebral bleeding seldom have an acute onset. In most instances a history of recurrent headache, vomiting, limping, limb incoordination or gait ataxia, cranial nerve palsies, etc., can be obtained.

The electroencephalogram may be of help by demonstrating focal slowing in a patient with a supratentorial space-occupying lesion. Brain scanning may show an area of increased uptake of radioisotope in patients with intracranial bleeding or tumors or abscesses of the cerebral hemispheres. The echoencephalogram may demonstrate displacement of midline structures away from the side of the lesion in supratentorial space-occupying lesions of any nature. Contrast studies (ventriculogram and/or carotid angiograms) are indicated in any patient with progressive deepening coma and a history or clinical findings consistent with an expanding intracranial lesion.

The emergency treatment of a child who is in coma and has signs of increased intracranial pressure is similar to that of severe head trauma (see Appendix 3).

Appendix 5
Blood, Urine, and Cerebrospinal Fluid Values

NORMAL BLOOD VALUES

Determination	*Per 100 ml. or otherwise as given*
Bromides, as NaBr	1–1.5 mg.
Calcium	4.8–5.8 mEq./L.
Carboxyhemoglobin	Up to 5% of total Hb.
Ceruloplasmin	23–43 mg.
Cholinesterase (plasma, Michel method)	0.5–1.3 pH units
Cholinesterase, RBC	0.5–1.0 pH units
Copper	75–145 μg.
Creatine phosphokinase	Males, 71; females 55 units/L. (values vary with different methods)
Glucose, fasting	65–90 mg.
Iron	75–175 μg.
Lead	Less than 60 μg.
Magnesium	1.8–2.7 mg.
PBI	4–8 μg.
Phenylalanine	0.7–2.8 mg.
Transaminase	
SGOT	4–40 units (higher in infants)
SGPT	1–45 units (values vary with different methods)
Uric acid	2–6 mg.

NORMAL URINE VALUES

Arsenic	Less than 100 μg./L.
Copper	15–40 μg./24 hr.
Coproporphyrin	Up to 160 μg./24 hr.
Delta-aminolevulinic acid	1.3–7.0 mg./24 hr.
Lead	Less than 40 μg./L.

Mercury	Less than 10 μg./L.
Mucopolysaccharide	5 mg./gm. of creatinine
Myoglobin	Less than 4 mg./L.
Uric acid	250–750 mg./24 hr.
Urobilinogen	Less than 4 mg./24 hr.
Uroporphyrin	Less than 27 μg./24 hr.
Vanilmandelic acid (VMA)	Less than 5.0 mg./24 hr.

CEREBROSPINAL FLUID

Pressure: Less than 200 mm. of water.

Protein: 15–45 mg./100 ml.; full-term newborn, up to 100 mg./100 ml.; prematures, up to 200 mg./100 ml. (values inversely related to degree of prematurity).

Glucose: Two-thirds of blood glucose (drawn at same time).

Cells (only lymphocytes): Up to 10 cells/cu. mm. under 1 year, up to 8 cells/cu. mm. between 1 and 5 years, and up to 5 cells/cu. mm. after 5 years.

Chlorides: 120–132 mEq./L. or 690–760 mg./100 ml. as NaCl (values somewhat lower during first year of life).

Gamma globulin: 6–13 percent of total protein.

Queckenstedt test: In recumbent position pressure less than 200 mm. of water. Following bilateral jugular compression time for return to normal up to 10 seconds.

Glossary of Eponymic Terms

Alper's disease	Progressive cerebral poliodystrophy
Apert's syndrome	Acrocephalosyndactyly
Arnold-Chiari malformation	Congenital anomaly consisting of downward displacement of brain stem, and parts of cerebellum into spinal canal
Bell's Palsy	Peripheral facial nerve palsy
Bassen-Kornzweig syndrome	A-beta-lipoproteinemia
Batten's disease	Juvenile amaurotic family idiocy
Bloch-Sulzberger syndrome	Incontinentia pigmenti
Canavan's disease	Spongy degeneration of the white matter
Charcot-Marie-Tooth disease	Peroneal muscular atrophy
Cornelia de Lange syndrome	Mental retardation, microcephaly, dwarfism, bushy eyebrows meeting in midline, etc.
Crouzon's disease	Craniofacial dysostosis
Dandy-Walker syndrome	Obstructive hydrocephalus due to congenital atresia of foramina of Luschka and Magendie
Dejerine-Sottas disease	Hypertrophic interstitial neuritis
Devic's disease	Neuromyelitis optica
Down's syndrome	Trisomy 21, mongolism

Duane syndrome	Congenital fibrosis of one or both lateral recti muscles
Eaton-Lambert syndrome	Myasthenic syndrome
Ellis-van Creveld syndrome	Chondroectodermal dysplasia
Feuerstein-Mims syndrome	Linear nevus sebaceus, seizures, mental retardation
Forbes' disease	Amylo-1, 6-glucosidase deficiency
Friedreich's ataxia	Familial spinocerebellar degeneration
Gaucher's disease	Glucocerebroside lipidosis
Gilles de la Tourette's syndrome	Movement disorder, inarticulate vocalizations, echolalia
Gradenigo syndrome	Abducens paralysis, swelling and pain in face, deafness
Guillain-Barré syndrome	Polyradiculoneuropathy
Hallerman-Streiff syndrome	Mandibulo-oculofacial dyscephaly with hypotrichosis
Hallervorden-Spatz disease	Pigmentary degeneration of globus pallidus
Hartnup disease	Recurrent episodes of cerebellar ataxia and pellagra-like skin lesions
Heller's infantile dementia	Progressive dementia
Hers' disease	Liver glycogen phosphorylase deficiency
Hunter's syndrome	Mucopolysaccharidosis II
Huntington's chorea	Familial chorea, dementia, suicidal tendencies
Hurler's syndrome	Mucopolysaccharidosis I
Hutchinson-Gilford syndrome	Progeria (premature aging)
Jervell-Lange-Nielsen syndrome	Deafness, prolonged Q-T interval in ECG with Stokes-Adams attacks, sudden death
Klinefelter's syndrome	Testicular atrophy and azoospermia (karyotype has one or more extra X chromosomes)

Klippel-Feil anomaly	Congenital fusion of cervical vertebrae
Krabbe's disease	Globoid-cell leukodystrophy
Kugelberg-Welander disease	Juvenile spinal muscular dystrophy
Laurence-Moon-Biedl syndrome	Retinitis pigmentosa, mental retardation, hypogenitalism, obesity, polydactyly
Lesch-Nyhan syndrome	Choreoathetosis, self-mutilation, hyperuricemia
Letterer-Siwe disease, Hand-Schüller-Christian disease and eosinophilic granuloma	Histiocytosis X
Louis-Bar syndrome	Ataxia-telangiectasia
Lowe's syndrome	Oculocerebrorenal syndrome
Marfan's syndrome	Arachnodactyly
Marinesco-Sjören syndrome	Hereditary spinocerebellar ataxia, nystagmus, congenital cataracts, and severe mental retardation
Melkersson's syndrome	Facial nerve paralysis, edema of face
Möbius syndrome	Congenital facial diplegia and other congenital anomalies
Niemann-Pick disease	Sphingomyelin lipidosis
Paget's disease	Chronic disturbance in bone metabolism (osteitis deformans)
Pelizaeus-Merzbacher disease	Chronic infantile cerebral sclerosis
Pendred's disease	Congenital deafness, goiter
Pierre Robin syndrome	Micrognathia and glossoptosis with or without cleft palate
Pompe's disease	Glycogen storage disease II
Prader-Willi syndrome	Hypotonia, mental retardation, obesity
Pyle's disease	Familial metaphyseal dysplasia
Ramsay Hunt syndrome	Geniculate herpes neuropathy
Refsum's disease	Heredopathia atactica polyneuritiformis